LOVE IN ANCIENT ROME

By the same author

Ethics of the Great Religions
Pioneers of Social Change
Encyclopaedia of Religion & Religions
Slayers of Superstition
Finding Out About the Etruscans
Mohammed
Ancient India

E. ROYSTON PIKE

LOVE IN ANCIENT ROME

FREDERICK MULLER LIMITED
LONDON

First published in Great Britain 1965 by
Frederick Muller Limited
Printed and bound by C. Tinling & Co. Ltd.,
Liverpool, London and Prescot

CONTENTS

Chapter   *Page*

      Foreword   9

SACRED AND PROFANE

   I Married Love   17

  II Come to the Wedding!   36

 III The Cult of the Courtesan   53

THE LOVES OF THE POETS

 IV Catullus and Lesbia   73

  V "Dear Delia"   88

 VI Horace's Sweethearts   97

VII Golden Cynthia   105

THE LOVE-HATE OF THE SATIRISTS

VIII What Martial Wrote about Women   123

 IX Juvenal's Gallery of Roman Dames   129

"IMPERIAL WHORES"

  X Fantastic Messalina   145

 XI Queens of Nero's Court   155

RELIGION AND SEX

XII The Virgins of Vesta   171

XIII The Worship of Priapus   182

THE BUSINESS OF SEX

XIV	The Roman Prostitute	195
XV	Who's Who of Strumpets	205
XVI	Cicero for the Defence	212
XVII	The Traffic in "Frail Beauty"	217

SEX IN THEORY AND PRACTICE

XVIII	The Roman Kiss	227
XIX	Corinna's Sin	234
XX	The "Odious Vice"	243
XXI	Lucretius Looks at Sex	250
XXII	The Mysteries of Venus	260
XXIII	The Legacy of Roman Love	270
	Table of Dates	275
	Index	277

ILLUSTRATIONS

The Roman Graces   *facing page* 64
Mysteries of Venus   65
The Bridal Bed   65

Charm of Roman Girlhood   80
Dignified Roman Matron   81

Woman, Wine, and Song   160
Bacchanalian Orgy   160
Woman Tempted by Cupid   161
Inside Pompeii's Lupanar   161

The Nymph Surprised   176
Vestal Virgin   177
Empress Messalina   177
Empress Agrippina and the boy Nero   177

FOREWORD

OF RECENT YEARS A more appreciative understanding of the Roman achievement has appeared. For long there was a tendency to see the Romans as efficient but plodding soldiers and administrators, who extended urban forms but added nothing creative to their inheritance from the Greeks. True, neither the Romans nor anyone else could hope to repeat the dawn-freshness and originality of Greek culture in its great days; but the Romans did much more than carry on that culture in uninspired ways. They made many great new contributions in the fields of law, engineering, architecture, and the arts in general. They impressed their own peculiar character, with its tenacious sense of tradition and continuity, on almost all their borrowings. The Roman stage was a genuinely new one, not just an expansion and dilution of Greek bases.

The Roman character found its expression in all the spheres of life, and so we may as validly speak of Roman Love as of Roman Engineering. We can distinguish a set of new attitudes to the relations between the sexes, which is a specific Roman contribution. As the old patriarchal forms of the Roman family broke down, there indeed resulted many dislocations and conflicts, which the satirists seized on as revealing a general collapse of morality. But that was only one part of the picture. Elements of the old *gravitas* or moral seriousness continued; and at the same time there emerged a new sort of give-and-take between men and women. The new freedoms were many-sided. Despite various legal disabilities on women that never quite disappeared, and despite the way in which the law stressed property-relations, a degree of effective equality appeared which had no parallel in the Greek world. Many more changes were yet to come, with the triumph of Christianity and the growth of the medieval systems, but the Roman developments left their indelible mark. Without them, the later phases, including that of our own world, could never have come about as they did.

The most exciting and vivid period, from which much love-poetry of a new kind came, was that of the great convulsion of change, when the Republic broke down and imperial society was born. During this crisis, of the last century B.C. and the first century A.D., men were deeply aware of old boundaries broken down and all sorts of new possibilities, good and bad, swarming across the scene. Since this was the main period of literary evidence for the behaviour of men and women in the pangs and ardours of love, Mr Royston Pike has naturally concentrated on it in his lively and informative study, well suited for the general reader. There it is that we see both the hectic breakdown of old sanctions and their steady reaffirmation in terms of the new situation. From one angle the new freedoms seem best expressed in terms of the loose or adulterous relations that the poets described; but family-life was substantially unbroken. Indeed a fresh vitality was infused in it; a securer respect for women was brought about.

Mr Pike tells the remarkable tale of marital devotion that has come down to us in the *Laudatio Turiae*; and since he is rightly concerned for the most part with the defiant and delighted ethic or etiquette of adultery set out by the poets, I should like here to cite a few more examples from the epitaphs. From the Rome of the Gracchi we get a charming picture of the happy wife: "Friend, I have not much to say, stop and read it. This tomb, which is not fair, is for a fair woman. Her parents gave her the name Claudia. With her heart she loved her husband. She bore two sons, one of whom she left on earth, the other below it. She was pleasant to talk with and she walked with grace. She kept the house and worked in wool. That is all. You may go."

That was composed in Republican days; but if you jump over some five centuries, we find the same note still in the account given by a consular of the late fourth century A.D. on the tomb of his wife Paulina. He recounts how closely associated she was with him in all his duties, religious and secular.

> Praise her, I beg. Children remain to me,
> born from my only wife, faced like their father.
> Flourishing in their strength, the lads are three,
> and there's one maid, who blossoms tenderly.

The claim that the children resemble the father, as a proof of wifely fidelity, is not uncommon.

Anicia of Aquileia says, "I pleased a good man who raised me from the lowest ranks to the highest social honours." A husband of Byzacena is made to declare: "I strove with you, wife, in piety and virtue, frugality and love, but O, I died." A man of Rome laments, "We lived together so little a time, and while we should have lived, an evil hand has parted us." He prays for a vision of his wife and hopes to rejoin her soon. Another Roman sums up: "This it is to have loved." Sometimes prosaic detail goes hand in hand with intense emotion. "To my dearest wife, with whom I lived 2 years, 6 months, 3 days, 10 hours; till the day of my death I utter my gratitude among men and gods."

The amount of truth in epitaphs is notoriously hard to define; but what is certain is that the gravestones state the common ideal. And this is an ideal that gives considerable importance to the place of women in the household. They are regarded, not as subservient and dependent, but as free partners, the happiness and the success of the family derive in large part from their qualities. Unless this were so, the widowers would not have bothered to set out even untrue accounts on the stones.

For the details of daily intercourse we are mainly dependent on the poets. But occasionally we meet verses that are not meant primarily as literary exercises or for the public view. Thus, a girl Sulpicia was related to the patron of Tibullus, Messalla, and six little poems of hers have come down to us. They must have been passed round among the group, but they have a warm and simple spontaneity about them. The first runs thus:

> Gossip, at last a love has come to me.
> Veils and not naked candours I detest.
> Venus, won over by my Muses' plea,
> led him and laid him here upon my breast.
> Her promise is fulfilled. Let whisperers frown,
> who never had a lover of their own.
> I'll write him notes, but scorn to seal them down
> or keep my faithful thoughts for him alone.
> I love my fault. No masks shall mar my face.
> Worthy of one another, we embrace.

Next, "My birthday's near, I hate it." She doesn't want to go to the country with her uncle for its celebration. But after all she finds she can stay. She hails "this day which comes by merest whim of happiness." Then a proud poem of six lines records her discovery of the lover's unfaithfulness. The key-line has a mounting rhythm of dignified scorn: her lover prefers "the slut to Servius' girl, Sulpicia, me." After that she falls ill of fever, and wonders if the lad is affected; she doesn't want health if he is callous. Finally comes a poem of delicate sensibility:

May you, my life, forget the tender truth
that's fed, these last few days, your love with flame,
if there's a single folly of my youth
which makes me shrink with such repentant shame
as that I left you yesternight alone,
afraid that all my passion might be shown.

Roman Love was certainly a great phase in the development
of love in all its bodily and spiritual richness.

JACK LINDSAY

SACRED AND PROFANE

I

Married Love

OF THE MANY GRAND old stories that have come down to us from Ancient Rome there is none better known than that of the Rape of the Sabines. It has caught the imagination of writers and artists from generation to generation, and even though a good deal of cold water has been thrown upon it by modern critics there is no fear of its being expelled from the history books altogether. What if it *were* invented to explain some relic of "marriage by capture" that had survived from primitive times? It makes a good story, and not all good stories are bound to be untrue.

For vividness and human interest Plutarch's narrative still holds the field. The Rome that had just been founded by Romulus was, we are given to understand, a men's town, a colony of lusty young bachelors, since those who had been drawn thither by the promise of free land and no questions asked were very seldom accompanied by their women friends, and the men's reputations were not such as to make them desirable matches among the families of the neighbourhood. Since brides were slow in putting in an appearance, they must be fetched. Romulus proclaimed a feast, and invited his Sabine neighbours to join in its celebration. This they did, and at the given moment the young Romans made a dash for the Sabine girls, hoisted them on their shoulders, and started to carry them off. The maidens shrieked and scratched and struggled, and cried out to their fathers and brothers to hurry up to come to their rescue. But the Sabine men were too taken aback to do anything, and the girls were successfully abducted and dumped down in the huts of mud and straw that were henceforth to be their homes. Some say that but thirty were taken, reports Plutarch; but one of his informants had given the figure of 527, and another capped this with 687. All unmarried girls, be it noted—all save one, Hersilia by name, and the Romans apologized for having included her in their bag. It was just a mistake, they averred, the sort of thing that might happen to anybody in the heat of such a moment. They did not offer to send her back, however, but they promised to make sure that she should have the best husband going, even Romulus himself.

"Rape" and "Romans" is a pleasing alliteration, but we should not suppose that the Romans made a habit of this sort of thing. They were not particularly bellicose lovers. They were not given to predatory promiscuity. From the very beginning of their story they seem to have had a high regard for marriage as an institution: when they raided the Sabines they were after wives, not female slaves or even concubines. And there is something else to be noted, something that is of vast importance although it has been but seldom remarked upon. When the captured women were distributed, it was on the basis of one girl per man. Not even Romulus himself was allotted more than one of the female prizes. From this it may be gathered that the early Romans, like all their descendants in the Republic and the Empire—and like their cousins the Greeks, but unlike their other Aryan relatives in India and Persia, unlike the Old Testament Hebrews and the Egyptians and many another ancient people—had arrived at monogamy as the normal rule.

How and why and when this came about is difficult to discover, but there is not the slightest doubt about the fact. At no period of Roman history known to us were there any traces of polygamy, or even of concubinage in which the girl was a secondary wife. The Roman woman was her husband's only wife, and in this as in so many other things the Romans set the pattern. Our western society is monogamist today because the Romans were monogamist all those many centuries ago.

There is something else to be deduced from the Sabine story. The Romans, it seems clear, turned out to be excellent husbands, so much so that the captive women seem to have become very soon reconciled to their lot. Following upon the raid, the Sabines went to war with the Romans to compel them to return their captives. At first the Sabines had the better of it, then the Romans rallied and drove the Sabines back. The fight was about to be resumed when suddenly (to quote from the "Dryden" translation of Plutarch's "life" of Romulus) the daughters of the Sabines, who had been carried off, came running in great confusion, some on this side, some on that, with miserable cries and lamentations, like creatures possessed, in the midst of the army and among the dead bodies, to come at their husbands and fathers, some with their young babes in their arms, others their hair loose about their ears, but all calling, now upon the Sabines, now upon the Romans, in the most tender and endearing words.

What had they done, they demanded (like the sensible girls that they obviously were) that they should be treated in this fashion? "You did not come to vindicate our honour," they told their fathers and brothers and countrymen, "while we were virgins, against our assailants, but do come now to force away wives from their husbands and mothers from their children. Which shall we call the worst, their love-making, or your compassion?"

Perhaps they were moved by the women's tears, or they saw the force of the argument, or they may have been just plain tired. Whatever the truth of the matter, Romans and Sabines agreed to come to terms and for the future the two peoples lived together as one. To consolidate their victory, the Sabine virgins who were now Roman wives insisted that they might stay with their husbands, but were to be exempt from all drudgery and labour and "servile offices to their husbands" save spinning. Nor were they content with this. When Rome came to be peopled by members of both races "many honourable privileges were conferred upon the women", among them that men should "give them the way wherever they met them, speak no ill word in their presence, and not to appear naked before them . . ."

According to the time-honoured legend, this was the way, then, in which the Sabine virgins became the first Roman matrons. The word is Latin, and it came to mean something that was essentially and distinctively Roman. We can be sure of nothing in Roman history before 390 B.C., the year in which the invading Gauls took Rome and sacked it, and in the conflagration all the national records were destroyed. Once again we have to resort to legend to fill the gap, and out of the mists we see emerging the noble figures of such women as Lucretia who on the morning after her rape by Prince Sextus called upon her husband and her father to avenge her and then stabbed herself; and the wife of Coriolanus, who when he turned renegade out of spite, brought the blush of shame to his cheeks and induced in him a tardy attempt at reparation.

Whatever the truth that may lie in these ancient tales, they are valuable in that they show the sort of woman that the Romans held in highest esteem and hoped that their wives and daughters would take as models. There is a feminine grandeur about them, a matronly dignity, a noble graciousness, a pride in their spotless chastity, and a dauntless patriotism.

True, in the eyes of the law the wife was in a position of marked inferiority to her husband. She was his slave according to the lawbooks, and he might exercise over her the ultimate power of life or death. She could own no property of her own. She was not a person but a thing. There was always a man in her life who might control all her actions, for even when she had outlived the custody of her father and of her husband, she came under the jurisdiction of her eldest son or, failing him, of a guardian. This was the legal position, but in practice the married woman of the developing Roman Republic was well on the way to becoming "the equal and voluntary companion of her lord" that she had become in Imperial times. As early as the third century B.C. we find that stern old moralist Cato the Elder bitterly complaining that "men usually rule over women, and we Romans rule over all men, but *our* women rule over *us*".

One incident in particular aroused the old man's disgust. When the war with Hannibal was at its height the state had been so pressed for funds that it had been decreed that no woman should wear any garment of more than one colour (since dyes cost money), nor own more than a half-ounce of gold, nor drive through the streets in a horsed carriage except when going to church. The Roman matrons had put up with these restrictions while the war was on, but with the coming of peace they demanded their removal. Not content with urging their case in the privacy of their homes, some abandoned ladies even ventured to lobby the senators and solicit their votes! Cato made a long and bitter speech against the abolition of the Oppian Law, as it was styled, and concluded with the warning that "as soon as the law shall cease to limit the expenditure of a wife, the husband will be powerless to set bounds to their extravagance".

But he lost the day. One of the tribunes as soon as Cato had sat down rose to champion the women's cause. "Who rushed into the forum in the days of Romulus," he demanded, "and stopped the fight with the Sabines? Who went out and turned back the army of Coriolanus? Who brought their gold and jewels when the Gauls demanded an enormous ransom for the city? Who poured their riches into a depleted treasury during the war with the Carthaginians just over? Who, but the Roman matrons? We don't refuse to give ear to the petitions of our slaves, but we are expected to be deaf to the entreaties of our wives! Shall we men wear purple, and deny it to our wives and mothers? Jewels and ornaments and dainty dresses are a woman's world; and although of course we have the power to keep them from our women, we would be cruel and unjust to do so. The greater the power, the greater the moderation with which it should be exercised." These arguments went home, and Cato had the mortification of seeing the Oppian Law repealed.

The process of women's emancipation, in practice if not in legal form, went on apace, and the position of the Roman matron became the wonder, and the envy, of women everywhere. About a century after Cato a Roman writer named Cornelius Nepos included in a volume of "illustrious lives" a passage comparing the position of Roman women with those of contemporary Greece. "Many things that are considered improper and unfitting among the Greeks," he wrote, "are allowed by *our* customs. Is there by chance any Roman who is ashamed to take his wife out to dinner away from home? Does it happen that the mistress of a Roman house does not enter the anterooms frequented by strangers and show herself among the visitors? Things aren't like this in Greece. *There* a woman accepts invitations only among families to which she is related, and she remains withdrawn in that inner part of the house which is called the gynaeceum [Greek, women's quarters], where only the nearest relatives are admitted."

Nepos was not overstressing the comparison. Athens bulks so largely in the history of civilization that we tend to forget that she was a slave-state, in which a small number of free citizens lorded it over a vast number of slaves who supported them and their culture by their hard and ill-paid labours. All the women—half the population—were slaves, most of them in law and the rest by convention. The respectable married woman hardly ever went out, not even to attend a public performance of one of the great dramas that are among the masterpieces of the world's literature. She was not expected to take an interest in anything outside the four walls of her home; indeed, intelligence in a wife was suspect. She could never share her husband's interests, and he did not want her even to make the attempt. Nor did he expect to find in her a lover. Passionate love between husband and wife was looked upon as not altogether proper or nice. The Athenian gentlemen when he felt the need for that sort of thing knew where to look for it—in the arms of one of the *hetairai* or courtesan class, the only educated and cultured and the least oppressed of Greek women.

As we shall see, there were plenty of courtesans in ancient Rome, but they never occupied the same place as their sisters in Athens, largely because there was nothing to prevent a Roman lady from making herself a companion to her husband in most, if not all, of his interests and pursuits. Why this should have been so is hard to discover, and to ascribe it to the influence of the Etruscans, as has been sometimes done, is only to push the question a little farther back.

The Etruscans were a mysterious people who are known to us mainly through their graves, since their language is still waiting decipherment, and even so, Etruscan inscriptions are few. They seem to have reached Italy, probably from Asia Minor, between 1000 and 700 B.C., intermarried with people of the Iron Age culture known as the Villanovans (because remains of one of their great settlements have been found at the village of Villanova, near Bologna), and eventually settled in that part of Italy that was called Etruria after them and has since been known as Tuscany. For centuries there was rivalry and often a state of war between Romans and Etruscans, but by the middle of the third century B.C. the Etruscan cities had been absorbed in the Roman state. But Etruscan influence on Roman culture was most marked and permanent. In nothing was this influence more marked than in the treatment of women.

This was first pointed out for English readers by the travel-
ler George Dennis whose *Cities and Cemeteries of Etruria* was
published in 1848. In Etruria, he wrote, "woman was
honoured and respected; she took her place at the board by
her husband's side, which she was never permitted to do in
Athens; she was educated and accomplished; her children
assumed her name as well as their father's; and her grave
was honoured with even more splendour than that of her
lord".

When the Greeks learnt about the tomb paintings and
sculptured urns on which Etruscan women were shown
reclining beside their men-folk at the festive board they were
deeply shocked, and jumped to the conclusion that the ladies
must have been no better than courtesans. Their suspicions
seemed to be confirmed by what one of their writers, a man
named Theopompus, who flourished about 350 B.C., said
about the Etruscan ladies. They were extremely attractive;
they took great care of their bodies, and often performed
gymnastic exercises to keep themselves fit—and this, moreover, in the presence of the men and as naked as the men
were; at the banquets in which they reclined so indecorously
they proposed toasts, and they had the reputation of being
heavy drinkers; their morals were also very loose, so that it
was quite customary to see them openly making love to their
partners on the same couch. Worse still, perhaps, they even
shaved the superfluous hair off their bodies! And, shameless
hussies that they were, when this was being done they sat
right in the window of the beauty-parlour so that the passers-
by could see all that was going on!

The Romans were not so easily shocked as the Greeks,
however, and they knew their Etruscan neighbours too well to
credit all the nasty tales that were told about them. What they
thought good among the Etruscan customs they were not
slow to adopt, although they did insist that when their ladies
joined them at dinner they should not recline as the Etruscans

did, since that might prove too provocative, but *sit* on chairs.

All in all, then, the position of women in ancient Rome was far superior to that of the Athenian or Spartan. And surely it may be claimed that the Roman system was justified by its fruits, since some of the noblest women of antiquity were Roman matrons. Mention has been made already of Lucretia and of Coriolanus's wife; and no less worthy of a place on the roll of honour was Cornelia, the mother of the early Roman democratic leaders, Tiberius and Caius Gracchus. Daughter of Scipio Africanus, the conqueror of Hannibal, she was married very young to Tiberius Gracchus, a man considerably older than herself, by whom she became the mother of twelve children. Plutarch relates a story told of her husband that one day he found in his bed-chamber two snakes, and on consulting the soothsayers concerning the prodigy was advised to kill one of the snakes and let the other go—adding, that if the male serpent were killed, Tiberius himself would shortly die, but if the female then it would be Cornelia's fate. "And therefore Tiberius, who extremely loved his wife, and thought besides that it was much more his part who was an old man to die, than it was hers who was still but a young woman, killed the male serpent, and let the female escape; and soon after himself died."

Whereupon Cornelia, "taking upon herself all the care of the household and the education of her children, approved herself so discreet a matron, so affectionate a mother, and so constant and noble-spirited a widow, that Tiberius seemed to all men to have done nothing unreasonable in choosing to die for such a woman".

There is another famous story told of this Cornelia, that when a lady came one day to visit her and made a great show of her jewellery, and asked to be shown hers, Cornelia took her into the nursery where her two boys were sleeping and said, "These are *my* jewels".

Even when she was yet alive, the Roman people erected a

monument in her honour, and inscribed it with the words,
"The Mother of the Gracchi".

Another Cornelia was married to Julius Caesar, who loved
her dearly; and yet another, their daughter, was the last wife
of Pompey, Caesar's great rival, and was held in high regard
for her virtues.

Living in the same age of savage rivalries and civil wars
was Portia, a daughter of Cato the Philosopher and wife of
Brutus, the fanatical republican who took the lead in the
assassination of Julius Caesar. When the plot was thickening,
Brutus would have kept all knowledge of it from his young
wife, but she deeply resented this exclusion. "You've ungently
stole from my bed, Brutus," Shakespeare makes her say in an
unforgettable scene in *Julius Caesar*:

> You have some sick offence within your mind,
> Which, by the right and virtue of my place,
> I ought to know of; and upon my knees
> I charm you, by my once commended beauty,
> By all your vows of love, and that great vow
> Which did incorporate and make us one,
> That you unfold to me, yourself, your half,
> Why you are heavy . . . Tell me, Brutus,
> Is it excepted I should know no secrets
> That appertain to you? Am I yourself
> But, as it were, in sort or limitation;
> To keep with you at meals, comfort your bed,
> And talk to you sometimes? Dwell I but in the suburbs
> Of your good pleasure? If it be no more,
> Portia is Brutus's harlot, not his wife.

> *Brutus.* You are my true and honourable wife;
> As dear to me as are the ruddy drops
> That visit my sad heart . . .

Noble in her life, Portia matched it with what Romans would
have considered was the nobility of her end. When Brutus

had been slain at Philippi, the devoted woman, rather than survive him, committed suicide by thrusting burning charcoal down her throat and so suffocating herself.

By the time the Republic was superseded by the grandeur and concentrated power of the Empire, Roman women, of the upper classes at least, had become very largely emancipated. As Dean Inge wrote in his *Society in Rome under the Caesars*, "marriage for the Roman woman meant a transition from rigid seclusion to almost unbounded liberty. She appeared, as a matter of course, at her husband's table, whether he had company or not; she could go where she liked, either to the temples of Isis and Serapis or to the arena and amphitheatre; she had her own troop of slaves, over whom she ruled without interference; she could frequent the public baths; in short, no restraint was put upon her except such as her own modesty might dictate". And L. T. Hobhouse asserts in his *Morals in Evolution* that "the Roman matron of the Empire was more fully her own mistress than the married woman of any earlier civilization, with the possible exception of a certain period in Egyptian history, and, it must be added, than the wife of any later civilization down to our own generation".

This tremendous revolution in human arrangements had its bad side. There was, we are told, a great loosening of morals, the marriage laws became a laughing stock, divorce (of a wife by her husband only, be it noted—which had once been so rare that for five hundred years from the foundation of the city no instance was recorded) became an everyday thing, and the emancipated woman showed herself a danger to herself and often to others as well.

Under Augustus, the first emperor, the situation became so bad that he attempted to improve the morals of his people by legislation. What with the growth of luxury and immorality there had grown up a disinclination to marriage, in the upper classes at least; celibacy was the order of the day, with the alarming consequence that the number of Roman citizens showed signs of a decline. At first Augustus tried to break the stubbornness of the bachelor males by laying various penalties, such as inability to receive legacies, on those who did not marry, while similar disabilities were imposed on those who had married but were childless. These provisions were not very effective, and nearly thirty years later Augustus tried again, but this time he established a system of rewards. The father of three legitimate children at Rome was relieved of some of the burden of taxation, was not required to perform the often onerous duties of a guardian, and was given preference when he put up for a magistracy. These privileges were known compendiously as the *jus trium liberorum* ("right of three children"), and in the rest of Italy they were extended to the fathers of four children, and in the provinces to those of five. Augustus also endeavoured to put down adultery by making it a public offence and not merely a private one as heretofore. These enactments aroused intense hostility, and made the emperor highly unpopular. What effect they had is impossible to judge; we are told that population did increase towards the end of Augustus's reign, but this may well have been owing to economic causes.

There can be no question that the moral tone of the period was very low, and yet it was in this same period that there occurred some of the most striking and unforgettable instances of conjugal heroism and devotion.

One of those who most richly deserve mention is the "dame named Mallonia", as Philemon Holland calls her in his translation (made in 1606) of Suetonius, the Roman biographer of the first twelve Caesars. She was one of the highborn ladies who attracted the infamous attentions of Tiberius, the stepson and successor of Augustus on the throne. "When she was by force brought unto his bed, and most resolutely refused" to have anything to do with him, "and evermore as she pleaded in her own defence, he asked her still, whether she repented her not yet of her obstinacy? which he followed so long, until at length she left the court, made haste home to her house, and there ran herself through with a sword, after she had openly and aloud reproached the shag-haired and rammish old churl with his filthy and beastly mouth".

A few years later Arria, the wife of Caecina Paetus, who had taken part in an unsuccessful rising against the Emperor Claudius, and, carried prisoner to Rome, resolved to anticipate his fate by suicide, "taught her husband how to die". Taking the dagger in her hand she first stabbed herself, then passed the reeking blade to him, uttering at the same time the remark that Martial has recorded: *"Paete, non dolet "*—" My Paetus, it doesn't hurt."

Not less noble than Arria's famous deed, wrote Pliny the Younger in one of his "Letters", was the act of a woman of Como, and the only reason why it was not so widely celebrated was because she was of a lower social position. The husband of this woman was afflicted by an ulcer, "in those parts which modesty conceals". She insisted on being shown it, and at once realized that it was bound to be fatal. So she advised him to put an end to his existence, and declared that she who had been his companion in life should accompany him in death. She tied her body to his, and they plunged together into the lake.

Among Nero's many victims was Seneca, the philosopher-statesman who had not always lived up to the high ideals he expressed in his writings. Accused of plotting against his master, he was told to take his own life. When the message of death was brought, Paulina declared her resolution of dying with her husband, and they severed the veins of their arms. Seneca at length died, but Paulina's wounds were bound up by her attendants by order of the soldiers (since Nero had no cause of hatred against her) and she was thus compelled to live. For the rest of her life, however, her countenance was marked by what the Romans respected as a sacred pallor.

It was Modestinus, one of the most eminent of the imperial jurists, who defined Roman Marriage as "a lifelong fellowship of a man and a woman in all things, human and divine". That this ideal was often carried into practice is evidenced by the numerous inscriptions that have been preserved, in which tribute is paid to husband or wife by the surviving partner of a union that has lasted for many years. The instances of conjugal devotion given above are all taken from the upper classes of society, but the inscriptions make it clear that the same qualities were present in the lower ranks as well. Quite often one finds the abbreviations S.V.Q., which stands for *sine ulla querela*, "without a quarrel". In the British Museum one may see a monument to a Roman butcher who had his shop on the Quirinal hill; in the centre is a sculpture of the worthy man and his wife, and on either side the inscription gives the husband's eulogy of his wife's chastity, modesty and devotion, and the wife's tribute to a man who had been everything that a husband ought to be all the years of their life together.

The most famous of these conjugal memorials is the so-called *Laudation Turiae,* a long inscription on marble in which a husband records his departed wife's many virtues and the story of their unbroken love affair. It is generally thought that the inscription was prepared by one Q. Lucretius Vespillo, who served in Pompey's army during the Civil Wars, and after numerous adventures was made a consul by Augustus in 19 B.C. The wife's name was Turia, and the inscription is in the form of a laudation, or funeral encomium, in which the husband addresses his deceased wife as though she were still living.

The story contained in the inscription opens when the pair were about to be married, probably in 49 B.C. But the civil war between Pompey and Julius Caesar must have interfered with their plans, and furthermore Turia's parents were suddenly murdered at their country house—very likely, as Mommsen suggests, by their own slaves. Immediately afterwards Lucretius had to leave for the front, and Turia was left alone, to do what she could to bring her parents' murderers to account. Aided only by a married sister, she did at length succeed in tracking them down, and they met with the punishment they deserved.

While Lucretius was away across the sea in Epirus, the girl kept him supplied with money, provisions, and even slaves. But in Italy Caesar was everywhere triumphant, and Turia seems to have been threatened by a band of roving soldiery. Through her own courage, and also the clemency of a certain great one, who was almost certainly Caesar himself, she managed to escape. A year later she was again in terrible danger, when she had to defend her house against an armed band of robbers.

At length the war was over, and Lucretius returned home and made his submission to Caesar. Probably it was now that the long-delayed marriage was consummated. But then Caesar was assassinated, and in the next year (43 B.C.) the Triumvirs set about the extermination of their political opponents. Lucretius's name appeared on one of the fatal lists. It seems that he was away in the country at the time but Turia heard of it and sent a message to him, imploring him not to join in the revolt that was mooted but to return to Rome at once, to their own house, in which she was preparing a hiding-place. He took her advice, and hurried back to Rome, accompanied only by two faithful slaves who risked their lives on his behalf. Arrived in the house, he was concealed by Turia between the roof and the ceiling of one of the bedrooms.

After a time he sued for pardon, and Octavian (later the Emperor Augustus) conceded it. But when Turia went to Rome to obtain confirmation of the grant from Lepidus, Octavian's colleague, he—rough fellow that he was—ordered her to be thrust out of the room. Before long, however, Octavian returned to Italy, and Lepidus's harsh treatment of

Turia was one of the charges against him that led to his fall from grace.

This was the last of the couple's perilous escapes, and now a long period of wedded bliss lay ahead. Only one thing was wanting to complete their happiness, a child; and when Turia at last had to conclude that she was to remain barren she made a proposal which might not have seemed so astonishing to a family-loving Roman as it does to us. This was that her husband should divorce her and take another wife in her place, in the hope that the latter would be successful in providing him with a son and heir. She promised that in this event she would mother the child as though it were her own, and she would be to Lucretius as a sister, sharing all things with him and refraining from claiming the return of that part of their property which she had brought as her marriage portion.

This was the noble woman's proposition, and Lucretius rejected it out of hand. "I must confess," he declares in the encomium, as though she were actually alive and present to hear him, "that I was so angry that my senses almost left me. To think that you should deem it possible that we should ever be separated by anything but death! What was my desire for children compared with my loyalty to you? Why should I exchange a happy present for a doubtful future? But enough of this: I will say no more. You stayed with me, and the one sorrow that lay in store for me was that I was destined to survive you."

Then the inscription concludes with a description of the dead woman. "You were a faithful wife to me, all the forty-one years that we were together. You were ever kind and gracious, sociable and friendly. When my old mother was living with us you looked after her just as tenderly as though she were your own. You never dressed to show off. You performed the religious rites of your family and the State, and never went in for those foreign cults or that disgusting magic. You managed your household in the most admirable fashion.

There are ever so many other excellent qualities that I might mention, but those that I have referred to were most especially yours."

Something similar is the story of Julius Sabinus and his wife Epponina, but in their case there was no happy ending. Sabinus was a Roman Gaul, wealthy and ambitious, who claimed descent from Julius Caesar, who (so he maintained) had had an affair with his grandmother when he was pro-consul in Gaul. Following upon the death of Nero in A.D. 68 the empire was in a turmoil, and three emperors followed one another in the space of a single year. Some of the Gauls took the opportunity to revolt against Roman rule, among them Sabinus. The rising was easily suppressed, and most of the ringleaders were taken and executed. Sabinus might have escaped across the Rhine, but he would not abandon his young wife. So with the connivance of two faithful freedmen he was hidden in a secret cavern beneath his country house, which was then set on fire and it was given out that he had perished in the flames.

Epponina was not at first in the secret, but she was so inconsolable that Sabinus insisted that she should be told. She hurried down at once to the cave, and repeated her visit each night for seven months, by which time she was pregnant. She was at her wits' end to keep her condition secret, especially when she accompanied her women friends to the public baths. But before her condition became too obvious she was able to secure a certain ointment that had the property of reducing swelling, and this she applied liberally to her whole person. When her time came she was delivered (without the aid, of course, of any female helper) of twin boys, whom she pro-ceeded to nurse in darkness and secrecy.

Since Sabinus's name was till on the "wanted" list, husband and wife maintained their strange existence for nine years, the one upstairs moving as a gentle widow among her servants and the other down below, kept alive by her ministrations.

c

Then suspicion was aroused, a watch was kept on her movements, and Sabinus was discovered and arrested. Taken away to Rome he was condemned to death by the Emperor Vespasian. Epponina fell on her knees before him, together with her children, and begged for mercy. "I brought them into the world in a sort of tomb," she told him, "and it is almost true to say that they never saw the light of day until now. Be moved by our tears, Sire, our sighs, our misfortunes!" But the stern old man was inexorable: Sabinus was a soldier who had deserted his post, and the punishment for desertion was death. The sentence was carried out, and it may be that his devoted wife was allowed to die with him as she had wished.

This would be too sad a note on which to leave this exploration of Married Love, so here is a letter which Pliny the Younger addressed to the aunt of the young girl he had recently taken as his second wife, his first wife having died some time before. The lady had had charge of her niece's education and upbringing. The young bride's name was Calpurnia.

"It is because you are yourself a model of family affections," he writes, "because you loved, as well as he loved you, that most excellent and affectionate brother of yours and still love his daughter, showing to her the affection not only of an aunt but of her dead father, I am sure you will feel the greatest joy in knowing that she is proving herself worthy of her father, worthy of you, worthy of her grandfather. Her intelligence is very great, very great also her frugality; in loving me she shows how good a heart she has. And she has now a fondness for letters which springs from her affection for me. She keeps my books by her, loves to read them, even learns them by heart. How anxious she is when she sees that I am going to speak (in the law-courts), and how delighted when I have spoken! She takes care to have messengers to let her know how far I have convinced, how often moved my audience to applaud, and what has been the result of the trial.

"If ever I give a reading of my writings, she sits close by, separated from the audience by a curtain, and drinks in my praises with greediest ears. She sings my verses, and sets them to the harp; and it is not any professor who teaches her, but love, who is the best of masters. These things make me feel a most certain hope that there will be a perpetual and ever-growing harmony between us."

II

Come to the Wedding!

FROM VERY EARLY TIMES there were three kinds of marriage practised in the Roman Republic. The first (*confarreatio*) was characterized by a solemn ritual of a sacramental nature, and may be compared with our wedding in church. The second (*coemptio*) was contracted by a legal form, and the nearest equivalent is our marriage in a register office; while as for the third (*usus*), this was marked by no religious or legal ceremony but resembled the Scottish form whereby a marriage is completed by the mutual consent of the parties.

The word *confarreatio* comes from the Latin *far,* the name for an old Italian grain used to make a sacred cake that was offered to the god Jupiter Farreus. This cake was partaken of by the bride and bridegroom, seated side by side on a bench or on two chairs across which was stretched the skin of an animal sacrificed just before the ceremony began. This probably means that the deity was believed to reside in the cake, and that in eating it the communicants not only entered into communion with each other but also with him.

This was done in the presence of the Pontifex Maximus, the chief priest of the old Roman religion; the Flamen Dialis, the priest of the supreme god Jupiter; and ten other witnesses. The fact that this kind of marriage required the presence of the most prominent dignitaries of the ecclesiastical establishment is an indication of its comparative rarity: translated into present-day terms it could be performed only in the presence of the Pope of Rome, or the Archbishop of Canterbury. In fact it was reserved for marriages in the highest and most exclusive circles of Roman society, the upper ranks of the Patrician class. It was the highest and most respectable form of marriage, and only those who had been married in this way were eligible to hold certain of the most responsible posts in the Roman establishment. It was a State ceremony of the most solemn kind, bringing into existence a *justum matrimonium* beyond any possibility of challenge.

Coemptio was a much simpler matter. It seems to have been a survival of the primitive practice of marriage by purchase, since it was characterized by what may be termed a fictitious sale of the woman to the man. The two parties met before a magistrate or lawyer and the husband handed to the father of the bride a coin—a penny perhaps—by way of her purchase-price. The father manumitted or released his daughter from his *manus* ("hand") and transferred her to the manus of her husband. This form of marriage was in vogue among the middle and lower classes of the community, the plebeians or plebs.

Even simpler was *usus*. It was the acquisition of the wife by prescription, through her cohabitation with the husband for one year without having been absent from his house three continuous nights. Until the year was "up" the woman retained full control of her person and the man had no rights of property in her—in other words, the transfer of the manus was postponed, the wife still being theoretically under the control of her father or guardian who may be supposed to have exercised far less control over her actions than a husband would do. Furthermore, she remained in possession of any property that she might own; although against this was the disadvantage that she had no claim for maintenance against her partner. Even so, this form of marriage was very popular with women who by absenting themselves from the marriage-bed for three nights might defeat the man's prescriptive right to their person.

One thing to be noted about these forms of marriage is that

the ceremony, such as it was, did not make the marriage. In Roman eyes marriage was the state of living together as husband and wife, with mutual consent and compatibility, displaying conjugal affection, and when children came matching parental love with filial respect and reverence. Consummation was imperative.

Long before the last century of the Republic, all three forms of marriage had fallen into disuse, or were used only occasionally for particular purposes. In course of time it had been found that it was more convenient for a woman to remain after her marriage in the "hand" of her father, or if her father were dead, of a man appointed to be her guardian, rather than pass into that of her husband, since in this case all her property became the husband's abolutely. This abandonment of marriage *cum manu* did not affect the validity of the union in the slightest: it was just as valid for all purposes, public and private, as if it had been celebrated with all the pomp and ceremonial of the confarreatio. It meant simply that certain legal consequences of the marriage were dropped, and with them just those parts of the ceremony which had those consequences. And from the woman's point of view—especially in the eyes of the "free woman" who became increasingly numerous and influential as the years passed—it had most obvious advantages. Whereas before there had always been a man in every woman's life—father, husband, guardian, son— now she was becoming her own mistress.

Another thing to be appreciated is that Roman marriages were not usually unions of love to begin with, although love often followed their consummation. Falling in love was a delightful experience, a personal matter, something that you couldn't help doing and wouldn't if you could; but marriage —that was something very different. It was the most serious undertaking a man could put his hand to. The family came into it, for its primary object was the raising of children. The State came into it, for it was the Roman's duty and privilege to bear sons who should play their part in preserving and promoting the greatness of Roman rule. And Religion came into it also, for in the Roman conception of things the home did not comprise only the human members but a variety of divine members, spirits of one kind and another, including those of dead-and-gone ancestors. Before a new member in the person of a bride could be introduced into a family, therefore, those in charge of the matter had to be assured that she would be *persona grata* not only to the human members of the family she was about to join but the divine members also.

For these reasons the field of marriage was much restricted, at least in earlier times. Not everybody could marry, legally, anybody. Romans of the patrician class might marry only into their class; and if they insisted on uniting themselves with plebeian women the resulting offspring were illegitimate. Romans might not marry foreigners, or even Italians who came from cities with which Rome had not agreed the right of *conubium*, or intermarriage. A freeborn Roman lady might not marry a slave; and it is difficult to believe that a Roman gentleman would ever want to, since all the slave girls in his establishment were at his disposal as concubines or temporary mistresses. These restrictions had their roots in the Roman citizenship laws. Citizens were freeborn members of the community, and they enjoyed a number of privileges, such as the right to vote at the assemblies and the remission of taxation; it was in the interest of the State, therefore, to see that their number did not get out of control. Then there were also eugenic considerations. The Romans took great pains to ensure that their blood stream was not polluted by alien mixtures.

Roman marriages, then, were arranged, as marriages are arranged to this day in those countries which have inherited the Roman ways of doing things. The father had the bigger say, but the mother was usually consulted, and almost always in the case of a daughter. The youth's father fixed up an appointment with the father of the girl he had in mind for his son, and talked the matter over. If the families were well off, the question of a dowry would be sure to be raised—a sum of money, perhaps, or something in kind, such as furniture or even an apartment—that the girl might contribute to the setting up of the new home, and which, in the event of the marriage breaking up, she might take back with her to her father's house.

An actual illustration of Roman matchmakers at work is given in the Letters of Pliny the Younger. A friend of his named Junius Mauricus had consulted him about choosing a husband for his niece. Pliny was immensely gratified at being asked, and wasted no time in looking for someone who would fill the bill. He had just the right man already in view, he told his friend. He came from a part of Italy that they both knew well and had the reputation of producing excellent sons. He belonged to a good middle-class family, and was well educated, good looking and well behaved, sincere, studious, and of the most becoming modesty.

All these things were worth mentioning, wrote Pliny, since they might be looked upon as "the proper tribute to virgin innocence". But there were yet other advantages of the proposed match. The young man had already made a start on an official career, so Mauricus would not have to worry himself about giving him a push up the official ladder. Then his father was wealthy. "I feel it should not be necessary to mention this fact, but there is no denying that the manners of our age and the laws of Rome put a premium on a man's possessions. Indeed, in choosing a husband for a girl it is well to consider whether the man in mind is likely to be able to support a numerous progeny. Perhaps you will think that affection has led me to draw a too favourable picture of the young man, but I will stake my reputation on its accuracy. In fact you will find that everything surpasses what I have represented. I do indeed love Minicius, and he deserves it. And for this very reason I have tried not to be too lavish in my encomiums."

Betrothals were effected sometimes when the parties were still in the cradle, but usually they were postponed until the boy at least was about seven, at which age he was considered to be capable of understanding what was proposed on his behalf. The engagement was made in the presence of relations and friends. It was sealed with a kiss, and the boy gave his fiancée a ring, generally of iron as were most Roman rings, which she slipped on the third finger of the left hand—the one on which the engagement-ring is still worn—because the ancients believed that a specially delicate nerve ran from this finger direct to the heart, the seat of the affections. This pretty little ceremony was called a *sponsalia*.

The ordinary age for marriage was twelve or thirteen for girls and up to eighteen for males, but many young men did not assume the responsibilities of matrimony until they were in their late twenties or early thirties. It was not expected that in such cases the man should come to the marriage-bed a virgin, but the unstained purity of the bride was insisted upon.

In ancient Rome as with us May was considered to be an unlucky month for weddings. This was because it was the month when the festival of the Lemuria was celebrated—the period in which the spirits of the dead were assumed to be at large and only too ready to engage in malevolent practices against the living. The days in February when sacrifices were offered in honour or in propitiation of the spirits of the dead were similarly avoided. There were days in August, October, and November which were unpropitious, and also the days of certain great national disasters. The best time for getting married was held to be in the second half of June, when the fields and orchards were displaying that fruitfulness which it was hoped would attend the union of man and woman.

Now we may suppose that the wedding-morn has dawned. The first thing the young bride does on getting out of bed is to make a formal surrender of her dolls and other childhood toys, laying them on the shelf on which stand the images in the family shrine, as a sacrifice to the spiritual beings who have watched over her since she was born. Then, standing reverently before the shrine, she offers up a prayer to the Goddess of Virginity to guard and guide her in what is to come. Perhaps she spares a glance for the *toga praetexta* (toga with a border), the dress of girlhood which has now been laid aside for ever. There is no looking-glass in the chamber, but she has to make do with a small mirror of polished bronze. And now the ritual of the coiffure is begun.

Up to now she has always worn her hair not parted but gathered in a bun or pigtail; now it is parted into six tresses by a comb shaped like a spear. (Why spear-shaped? Because, so Plutarch explains, the first marriages that were celebrated in the Roman state, those of the Sabine virgins with Romulus's hefty young bachelors, were "brought about in a warlike fashion".) The hair is fastened by woollen bands on the top of the head, and then imprisoned in a crimson net.

Now the bride puts on her wedding-costume, the principal item of which is the *tunica recta* (plain tunic), a garment of white flannel or muslin that is secured round the waist, just below the breasts, by a girdle which is tied in a special way— the "knot of Hercules" it is called, and it possesses a suggestive significance since only the bridegroom may untie it. Over this is placed a cloak or *palla* of saffron colour, matching the sandals into which the bride slips her feet. Then she is crowned with a bridal veil of flaming orange—the *flammeum*—made of some light, transparent stuff and arranged so as to veil with becoming modesty the upper part of the face. Finally, a bridal wreath made of verbena, marjoram, myrtle, or orange-blossom is laid on the top of all.

Meanwhile the omens have been taken at the family shrine or at the village sanctuary. The augurs or soothsayers have carefully observed the flight of birds passing overhead, or

they have peered anxiously into the entrails of an animal—
generally a pig but sometimes an ewe or more rarely an ox—
that has been slain as a sacrifice. Did the birds come from an
unlucky region of the heavens? Were there any ominous
indications in the entrails? If the signs are generally favourable,
the wedding is gone on with; if otherwise, it would be
decided to postpone the celebration to a more propitious
day.

Now the bridegroom makes his appearance, dressed in a
new toga and garlanded with flowers, and accompanied by his
relations and a band of young friends. He makes his way into
the atrium, the central hall or chamber, of the bride's home,
where the wedding parties and guests have assembled and his
bride is waiting. Standing side by side in front of the company,
bride and bridegroom hold hands and exchange the ancient
formula that is the equivalent of our "in sickness and in health
. . . until death do us part".

Quando tu Gaius, ego Gaia.

"So long as you are Gaius, I am Gaia." This is explained by
Plutarch in his *Roman Questions* as meaning that a kind of
agreement has been made to share everything and manage all
in common; in other words, "Where you are lord and master,
I am lady and mistress". The names Gaius and Gaia, he
explains further, "are common and used merely for illustration".

This pledging of mutual belonging, in the presence of witnesses, was the kernel of the Roman marriage rite.

The little ceremony was followed by the wedding-breakfast,
at which bride and bridegroom sat or reclined on the *triclinium*
(couch running round three sides of the room) side by side.
The meal lasted several hours, and it was generally evening
when it came to an end and the guests assembled round the
door to "see them go away". As a rule, there seems to have

been nothing in the nature of a wedding-coach but a procession was formed on foot.

The bride, making a great show of weeping reluctance, was firmly detached from her mother's arms and placed beside her husband, with three little boys (sons of parents still alive—otherwise it would have been thought unlucky) in attendance; one of the boys walked at the bride's left hand and another on her right, while the third went ahead with a torch that had just been lit at the fire that was kept burning (in accordance with the old Roman custom) on the hearth in the home she was about to leave. The bride carried in her hand three coins, one to be offered to the god of the crossroads and one to the god of the house she was going to, and one as a kind of symbolic dowry for her husband.

So they moved off, with flute-players and torch-bearers in front, and the marriage party coming along behind, singing and laughing and (some of them) making bawdy jokes. The scene is well described in one of Catullus's poems—the Epithalamium (nuptial song) celebrating the marriage of Manlius and Julia, two young friends of his; the verses that follow are taken from the metrical translation by the Hon. George Lamb, a younger brother of Lord Melbourne, the famous Prime Minister of the young Queen Victoria.

Around thy brow the chaplet bind,
Of fragrant marjoram entwined;
And bring the veil with crimson dyed,
The refuge of the blushing bride.
Come, joyous, while thy feet of snow
With yellow sandals brightly glow!

Unbar the door, the gates unfold!
The bashful virgin comes.—Behold,
How red the nuptial torches glare,
How bright they shake their splendid hair!
Come, gentle bride!—The waning day
Rebukes thy lingering, cold delay.

We will not blame thy bashful fears,
Reluctant step, and gushing tears,
That chide the swift approach of night
To give thy bridegroom all his right.
Yet come, sweet bride!—The waning day
Rebukes thy lingering, cold delay.

* * *

Raise, boys, the beaming torches high!
She comes—but veil'd from every eye;
The deeper dyes her blushes hide;
With songs, with paeans, greet the bride!
Hail, Hymen! god of faithful pairs!
Hail, Hymen! Who hast heard our prayers!

Hymen was in Greek mythology the god of marriage, and
in art he is generally represented as a very handsome youth,
garlanded with flowers, usually roses and marjoram, and holding in one hand the flaming bridal torch and in the other a
purple veil. The Romans thought that any wedding at which
he was not present would be ill-fated, and it was for this
reason that they invoked him in the song sung by the companions of the bride as she passed from her father's house to
that of the bridegroom.

As they went along, the bridegroom scattered walnuts
about him, which were scrambled for by the onlookers. These
were the ancestors of our rice and confetti, and they had the
same hopeful significance of a union that should prove richly
fertile. When they arrived at the husband's home, the bride
was handed oil and fat with which she smeared the doorposts
and then she tied a woollen fillet round each. The threshold
would have been covered with a white cloth and decorated
with greenery, and in order to avoid the risk of stumbling
(which would have been a very bad omen indeed) the bride
was carried over it in her husband's arms; or, as Catullus has
it: "Let not the threshold be with thy golden slipper prest,
but swiftly spring with lightness o'er and swiftly pass the

polish'd door." Then the husband as soon as they were indoors offered his bride gifts of fire and water, symbols of her
new position as the mistress, and with the torch that the boy
had brought lit the fire laid ready on the hearth. Then they
passed into the atrium, where there may have stood a small
couch called the *lectus genialis*, "bed of the Genius", which was
intended not for the bridal pair but for their spirit doubles,
the *Genius* of the man and the *Juno* of the woman.

The bridal bed stood in the bride-chamber, a room set
apart specially for the occasion. Standing beside it would be
several matrons, led by a senior matron known as the *pronuba*,
who was in charge of the proceedings. All these ladies were
married, with their husbands living. These now proceeded to
give the bride some instruction in what was shortly to be
expected of her.

> Purple-robed boy, whose pleasing care
> Has been to lead the lingering fair,
> Release her arm. By others led
> She now ascends the bridal bed.
> Hail, Hymen! etc.
>
> Ye chaster matrons, who have known
> One honour'd husband's love alone,
> Of truth in years long virtuous tried,
> 'Tis yours to place the lovely bride.
> Hail, Hymen! etc.

Next the pronuba and her assistants undressed the bride
save for her bridal gown, attended to her coiffure, and touched
up her face with the paints and lotions that were available.
Then, if we may take one of Plutarch's *Roman Questions*
literally, the husband made his approach in the dark, with the
lights all extinguished. "Why does the groom approach the
bride for the first time in the dark, without any light? Is it
out of respect for her, he for his part not considering her to
be his until he has possessed her carnally? Or is it perhaps to

accustom him to act after a modest fashion even in relations with his own wife? Or may it be in order that the husband when he sees his bride for the first time in a state of nakedness shall not be 'put off' by any bodily blemish or unpleasantness? (In this case we may compare it with that law of Solon, the Athenian lawgiver, which bids the bride eat a quince before entering the nuptial chamber, in order that the first intimate greeting may not be uninviting or unpleasing.) Or, finally, is the arrangement intended to serve as a reminder that even the lawful pleasures of sex have something shamefaced about them and are best performed in the dark, and that unlawful ones must be avoided altogether?"

But we are not to suppose that such unpleasant or ungallant reflections as these are passing through the mind of the young husband, "on the Tyrian couch reclining, for the summons pining".

> Now haste, young bridegroom, swiftly haste;
> The bride is in the chamber placed:
> Inspiring blushes warmly streak
> The fairness of her snowy cheek.
> So mix'd with poppies' crimson glow
> The white parthenium's flow'rets blow.
>
> Nor is thy form, by Heaven above!
> Unworthy such a fair one's love,
> Venus in rival charms array'd,
> The manly youth and tender maid.
> Haste, bridegroom, haste! One western ray,
> Still faintly lingering, chides delay.
>
> Needs not to chide: thou swift hast sped,
> Propitious Venus bless thy bed!
> For sanction'd passion, solemn rites,
> On thee bestow thy wish'd delight:
> Not lust perverted, shame supprest,
> The pure desires that warm thy breast.

Now the moment of consummation has come. The Romans

thought of this as being effected by the man's indwelling spirit, the *Genius*, and the corresponding *Juno* of the woman. The male spirit enabled the husband to exercise his generating power, and the female spirit made it possible for the wife to conceive. But in the popular mythology a number of other spirit beings, gods and goddesses, were believed to play a vital part. Who and what these were is shown in a chapter of St. Augustine's *De Civitate Dei* ("The City of God"), the book that the great Christian "Father of the Church" wrote in the last years of his life, early in the fifth century A.D. The passages that follow are taken from the translation from the Latin made by John Healey in 1610.

It is in the chapter on "the offices of each peculiar god" that we find listed and described the pagan deities supposed to be involved in the marriage relation. St. Augustine wrote out of full knowledge since he was born a pagan and had been one until manhood, and it may be that he still thought of the pagan gods and goddesses as having real existence, although not as divinities but as demons. The first he mentions is "Liber, that lets loose the masculine sperm in men at carnal copulation, and one Libera for the women, whom they hold Venus (for women, they say, do let forth sperm also), and therefore they dedicate a man's privy member to Liber, and a woman's to Libera; besides wine and the women assigned unto Liber as the provokers of lust".

When men and women are wed together, god Jugatinus has to function, and when the bride is led home it is in charge of god Domiducus. "Now who must protect her at home? god Domitius. Aye, but who must make her stay with her husband? Why, that can goddess Manturna do. Oh, why proceed we further! Spare, spare man's chaster ears: let carnal effect and shamefaced secrecy give end to the rest! What does all that crew of gods in the bridal chamber upon the departure of the *paranymphi*, the feast-masters? They are there, not to make the woman more shamefaced by their being present but, because she is weak and timorous, to help her to lose her virginity with less difficulty. For there is goddess Virginensis, god Subigus, goddess Prema, goddess Pertunda, and Venus, and Priapus. If the man stood in need of help in this business, why were not one of them sufficient to help him? Would not Venus' power serve, who they said was so called because virginity could not be lost without her help? If there be any shame in man that is not in the gods, when the married couple shall think that so many gods of both sexes do stand by at their carnal conjunction, and have their hands in this business, will not he be less forward and she more reluctant? If Virginensis be there to loose the virgin girdle, Subigus to subject her under the man, and Prema to press her down from moving after the act, what shall Pertunda [Latin, *pertundo*, make a hole through, perforate] have to do but blush and get her out of doors, and leave the husband to do his business. For it were very dishonest for any one to fulfil her name upon the bride but he . . .

"But why talk I of this, when Priapus (that unreasonable male) is there, upon whose huge and beastly member the new bride was commanded (after a most honest, old, and religious order observed by the matrons) to get up and sit!"

St. Augustine wrote as a Christian convert and we may suspect that his account of the bridal scene is coloured by malice. In particular his statement concerning the artificial rupture of the hymen by the image of Priapus (whether to remove the physical impediment to coition, or out of some primitive notion of eliminating the danger to the husband inherent in the first act of sexual intercourse) is as far-fetched as it is repulsive.

After he had removed his bride's wedding-dress the husband proceeded to untie the knot in the girdle she had worn as a virgin. This custom was common to Greeks and Romans, and "to untie the zone" (Latin, *zona*, girdle or belt) came to mean the loss of virginity. The editor of the version of

Catullus we are using thought it worthy of mention that the same significance attached to the band or snood with which Scottish maidens bound up their hair, "and in Scotland formerly the lassie who had 'lost her snood' without permission of the kirk was in danger of the cutty-stool", i.e. the special seat in Scottish churches where offenders against chastity had to sit during divine service and receive a public rebuke from the minister.

> Now close the doors, ye maiden friends:
> Our sports, our rite, our service ends.
> With you let virtue still reside
> O bridegroom brave, and gentle bride!
> And youth its lusty hours employ
> In constant love and ardent joy.

The morrow would find the bride already a *materfamilias*, taking her seat in the atrium among her maids, or in the more private apartments that lay behind it. Plutarch says that it was customary for the husband to provide an entertainment, when the bride sat beside him at table on the same couch in the presence of the guests, "leaned upon him with a great show of familiarity, and in her talk seemed to glory to such an extent in having thrown off her maiden modesty that it became a proverb in Rome, when a woman talked indecently, to say that 'she talks like a bride' ". To continue with Catullus,

> Soon may we see a baby rest
> Upon its lovely mother's breast;
> Which, feebly playful, stretching out
> Its little arms to those about,
> With lips apart a tiny space,
> Is laughing in its father's face.

When the woman was in childbed, St. Augustine informs us, a fresh set of divinities were supposed to come into action. "She must have three gods to look after her deliverance, lest

Sylvanus come in the night and torment her: in signification whereof, three men must go about the house at night and first strike the thresholds with an hatchet, then with a pestle, and then sweep them out with besoms, that by these signs of worship they may keep Sylvanus out. From these three acts, three gods got names: Intercidona, from the hatchet's cutting, *intercisio*; Pilumnus, from *pilum*, the pestle or mortar; Deverra, from *verro*, to sweep. And these kept Sylvanus from the woman in bed. Thus were they fain to have three good against one bad, or all of them had been too little."

By the Roman Laws of the Twelve Tables (450 B.C.) the extreme period of utero-gestation was declared to be 300 days, or ten months; it may be noted that the French code follows this as the extreme limit of pregnancy, but in Britain it is usually taken as between 270 and 280 days.

Such in outline was the wedding of a Roman man and woman belonging to the middle and upper classes of society. Practically nothing is known of the marriage customs of the lower orders. In families where the ancient gods were still honoured, there may have been a formal presentation of the bride to the guardian spirits of her new home, symbolized by the images in the little shrine that was the centre of family worship, and this would be followed by the formal plighting of troth in the presence of witnesses. Then the company might partake of a wedding-breakfast either in the house of the girl's parents or in some convenient tavern.

There was no religious ceremony of a special kind, but in the better-governed cities there may have been a registration of the marriage at the municipal offices. It may be remarked that there was no special form of Christian marriage service until about the sixth century, and it was not until Christianity had been in being for a thousand years that it was generally held that a valid marriage should be celebrated by a priest in church.

If we compare the weddings of the present with those

described by Catullus and other writers of the Roman world, we cannot fail to note that they have many things in common. The betrothal or engagement, the giving of a ring, to be placed on the third finger of the left hand, the avoidance of May as "unlucky", the bride's wedding-dress, the plighting of troth in the presence of witnesses, the mutual consent of the man and the woman to be joined as husband and wife, the bridal bouquet, the orange blossom, the wedding cake, the reception, the wedding-breakfast, the "going away", the nuts (instead of confetti or rice), the arrival at the new home—all these things have come down to us from Ancient Rome.

III

The Cult of the Courtesan

WHEN THE GODDESS WHO was born of the foam of the sea stepped ashore with dripping limbs and windblown hair, it was not on the coast of Italy but on the sandy beach of one of the Greek islands. She soon made the crossing, however, and the Romans made her welcome. They changed her name from Aphrodite to Venus, which up to then had been the name of a Latin goddess of the spring; they built temples in her honour, and worshipped her as the Goddess of Beauty and of Love.

Like the Greeks, the Romans distinguished between the Venus who presided over the higher, purer, sacred form of Love, and she who was the goddess of sensual lust, the form of Love that was profane (Latin, *profanus*, outside the temple; not holy). The Roman matrons worshipped her under the first guise, but her worshippers under the second were women of a very different class. So now we place over against the portrait of the *materfamilias*, the woman of spotless virtue and un-challengeable reputation, that of a woman who, while also Roman to the fingertips, is gay and charming and loosely accommodating in her behaviour. For her Sex is not a con-jugal chore but an amorous adventure reaching a climax of sensual gratification. And so far from contenting herself with one man, she is ready to grant her favours to such men as please her.

All the same, we should be wrong in thinking of her as a prostitute, if by this term we mean what it means in English law, "a woman who offers her body commonly for lewdness in return for payment". True, she offers her body, and is not averse from lewdness, but she does not do it always and only for payment. Usually affection enters into the relationship; she can pick and choose her lovers and may deny if she feels so inclined. It is not economic necessity that drives her on so much as delight in men's company.

This woman is not, then, to be described as a *meretrix*, or by any of the other names which (as we shall learn in a later chapter) the Romans applied to their purveyors of extra-marital sex. The word that may be most appropriately given to her is Courtesan, although this is not a word that the Romans actually used—it comes from the Italian, meaning originally "a woman of the court", and came into use at the time of the Renaissance to denote the often licentious ladies of the courts of the Pope and the other Italian princes. The word that Ovid uses—and he spoke out of a rich and intimate knowledge of the species—is *puella*, "girl".

It is from Ovid's writings that we know most of what we do know about the Roman patterns of love. His full name was Publius Ovidius Naso, and he was born at Sulmo, in the Abruzzi mountain country, in 43 B.C. and died in A.D. 18 at Tomi, a port on the Black Sea to which he had been banished by the Emperor Augustus for something that has never been certainly ascertained. He was educated at Rome and read for the bar, but his taste for poetry asserted itself. Since he came of a middle-class family he was never short of money, and he was also given from time to time some official posts. He travelled widely, and was thrice married; his first two marriages were of short duration, but his third wife remained devoted and loyal to him during his exile, in which she was apparently unable to join him.

Ovid's first literary production seems to have been a tragedy, of which only a couple of lines survive. Then came his *Heroides*, imaginary love letters from ladies of legendary times to their lords, and not long after appeared the *Amores*, the first of that kind of publication that he made particularly his own. Love in all its aspects (save perhaps the love of the sober matron and the well-brought-up young maiden) was his chosen theme; and although Catullus, Tibullus, and Propertius, not to mention one or two more, had preceded him along that path he soon outstripped them all. His *Medicamine Faciei*—a practical little poem on the art of painting the face as an aid to beauty—seems to have been a preliminary to what proved to be his true masterwork, the *Ars Amatoria*, "Art of Love". This appeared about 1 B.C. and was followed by a subsidiary book entitled *Remedia Amoris*, which is concerned with remedies that may be adopted against the inconvenient passions that the previous volume may have aroused.

Of these books the *Ars Amatoria* is the most important, and it may be claimed for it that it is the most famous book on Love ever written. Published nearly two thousand years ago, it has worn well. A number of editions have been printed, and fresh versions continue to appear. It has been savaged by critics, emasculated by editors, denounced as the most licentious, or the most immoral, book ever written. Not surprisingly, such charges have but added to its popularity. The little work is full of humour and charm, the style is easy, and the subject is one that has deeply interested men and women from the beginning of time and is likely to interest the generations that have still to enter upon this world's stage. It was very popular among the Romans, and quotations from it have been deciphered on the walls of Pompeii. In the wreck of the Middle Ages it somehow managed to survive, in stray manuscripts hidden away in a monastery closet or passed from hand to hand as a treasured if somewhat surreptitious heirloom—such may have been the copy that the Wife of Bath's fifth husband had in his tiny collection of books. In modern times it has become more generally appreciated, partly because its bawdiness is no longer a bar to its

circulation, but also because of Ovid's strikingly modern
approach to the problems of love. In its pages he writes of
love as something that is, and ought to be, an altogether
pleasurable experience; there is nothing in the least to be
ashamed of, he makes clear, in the act of sex by itself, although
the case may be very different when selfish lust, violence,
power uncontrolled, and exploitation enter into it. Furthermore, Ovid states quite clearly that sexual pleasure in its
highest expression is one which the woman shares equally
with her male partner. These are modern attitudes, but they
are not modern discoveries. They were known to Ovid, and
doubtless to others, in the classical world of more than two
thousand years ago, but it is only within the last half-century
or so that they have been rediscovered and incorporated in
the accepted body of Sexology.

Not that Ovid is likely to have written his books, the *Ars
Amatoria* and the *Amores* in particular, with any didactic or
scientific purpose in mind. He was a professional author, and
he had his eye on the returns, in cash and circulation and
reputation. His poetry brought him popularity in the rather
idle, somewhat dissipated, fashionable circles of the metropolis. The great civil wars were over. The *Pax Romana* was
being established throughout the world of the Mediterranean.
Politics were going out of fashion, since the Emperor was
now the source and instrument of power. Business was
thriving, and the city was filled with get-rich-quick *parvenus*,
who had money to spend and sought pleasurable ways
of spending it. Ovid came along with the suggestion
that the pursuit of Love was the most pleasurable pastime
going.

The *Art of Love* consists of three books. The first advises
a lover where he is most likely to find a mistress, a *puella*,
to his taste, and then, what is the best way of going about
winning her. In the second book he is told how to retain the
affections of the *puella* he has won. Then in the third book

it is the woman's turn: she is advised how to capture her man, and how to keep him.

Who were these lively ladies of easy virtue? If we were to put the question to Ovid he would start off by stating quite definitely who they were *not*. When the Emperor Augustus reproved him for writing verses in which the joys of extra-marital love were related, the poet rejoined (probably with his tongue some little way in cheek) that he was not writing for the *matrona*, the mother with a young family, or for the *virgo*, the unmarried girl of good birth and breeding. Nor was he concerned with the professional strumpet. The women he had most in mind were those who had become emancipated from the rules and regulations that had once given a husband the power of life and death over his wife, the women who were resolved to lead their own lives, who took the fullest advantage of the liberalization of the marriage laws and the loosening of social customs and conventions.

Many of these women were *libertinae*, that is, they were "freedwomen", who had either been born into slavery and had managed to obtain their freedom or were the daughters or granddaughters of men who had been slaves and had become emancipated. These were, in a sense, "new women", and they were quite capable of looking after themselves. They knew the "facts of life". They knew the dangers of the love-game as well as its pleasures. Intrigues with them were surely allowable, since they did not endanger the domestic hearth nor the public weal. With no recognized social position and excluded from good society by their ignoble origin, they often possessed personal attractions and education that led to their company being much sought after, especially by bohemian men of letters. They were part of the spice of life.

But the *libertinae* were only a part of a much larger whole, and indeed the courtesan class seem to have drawn its recruits from almost every social grade.

Some of the *puellae* were married. The Lesbia of Catullus
was a Consul's wife, and Tibullus's Delia was very probably
married to a soldier. The women drawn by Juvenal's poisonous pen are mostly wives, and so also are many of Martial's
victims. Some were divorcees, since by Ovid's time divorce
had taken a firm hold of Roman life and was quite common; a
man might divorce his wife (but a wife could not divorce her
husband) for almost any reason, however trivial, but her
family usually insisted that she should be given a substantial
alimony, since they did not wish to have the responsibility
and expense of maintaining her. Some were widows in the
prime of life, who had enjoyed being married and missed its
pleasures; a sprightly young, or youngish, widow, who was
experienced and knew what was expected of her, was not too
demanding, and was quick to show her appreciation of favours
rendered, made a highly satisfactory mistress. Yet others
were unmarried women of a good position in life, who were
possessed of a private income and valued their independence.
Why should they put their heads in a marital noose? Provided
they did not make themselves too notorious or objectionable
to the neighbours they might go with whom they pleased.
Finally, there were women who were entirely dependent on
their men friends for support. Here we are getting very close
to the prostitute proper, but these women were perhaps
comparable to the call-girls who operate on the fringe of
modern society. Of such was Propertius's Cynthia; she has
been called a high-class whore, but she was not promiscuous,
she was reasonably well behaved and circumspect, and she
chose her lovers with care and kept them for years at a
time.

So much for the *puellae* of Ovid's muse, the women and
girls who were fair game in more senses than one. Now
for the ways in which they might be caught and brought
down, which, as already stated, is the subject of the first
part of the *Ars Amatoria*. Here are the opening lines, in

John Dryden's translation into English verse, made in 1709:

> In Cupid's School, who'er wou'd take Degree,
> Must learn his Rudiments, by reading me.
>
> You, who in Cupid's Rolls inscribe your Name,
> First seek an Object worthy of your Flame;
> Then strive with Art, your Lady's Mind to gain:
> And last, provide your Love may long remain.
>
> On these three Precepts all my Work shall move:
> These are the Rules and Principles of Love.

The poet makes it clear that he is writing primarily for the beginner, the novice in the lists of love, the youth or young man who has not yet married or even been affianced at his parents' behest.

> Before your Youth with Marriage is opprest,
> Make choice of one who suits your Humour best;
> And such a Damsel drops not from the Sky;
> She must be sought for with a curious Eye.

Where is the best place to begin your search? Where, but in Rome, the city which holds as many *puellae* as are the stars of heaven or the birds that twitter in the boughs or the fishes that swim in the sea? Here there is someone to everybody's taste. Does a young maiden attract you, a girl on the threshold of womanhood, one whose charms are still in the bud? You should have no difficulty in finding such an "unstained maiden". Or does your fancy lie in the direction of a full-blown rose? A thousand such will be there for your viewing, and your only difficulty will be to choose one from among so many luscious beauties. Or perhaps you have your mind set on a more mature charmer, a woman of a certain age who is experienced in the arts of love? Believe me, you will find that these are even more numerous, and again your difficulty will be to decide, which.

And now, the poet goes on, let me mention one or two places where you are most likely to bag a beauty. The Portico of Pompey, near to the theatre of the same name, is an excellent place, since women like to walk and linger among its palm trees and fountains. Livia's Porch is another good place, since there is generally a crowd of people looking at the paintings that adorn its walls. Don't make the mistake of avoiding the Temple of Isis: "many a maid does she make what she herself was to the god." Nor should you avoid the law-courts in the Forum. You would be surprised to learn how often the lawyer is cheated by Love, and he who has shown himself so glib a speaker is lost for words in his own cause! And how Venus laughs from her shrine hard by! But there is one place that is better than any other:

> Above all, the Play-House is the Place . . .
> There take thy Stand, and sharply looking out,
> Soon mayst thou find a Mistress in the Rout,
> For length of time, or for a single Bout.

> To see, and to be seen, in Heaps they run;
> Some to undo, and some to be undone.

Like so many ants the women flock to the theatre, or as bees that flit from blossom to blossom in the fragrant pastures. Here modesty is left behind; the place is absolutely fatal to chastity. And so it has always been, since that day when Romulus led his young men to the Rape of the Sabine girls in the pristine theatre of the city that he had so recently founded. Hardly less advantageous a place for the amatory stakes is the circus or arena, where the public games and gladiatorial displays and great processions are put on. To continue with Dryden's translation:

Nor shun the Chariots, and the Courser' Race;
The Circus is no inconvenient Place.
No need is there of talking in the Hand;
Nor Nods, nor Sighs, which Lovers understand.
But boldly next the fair your Seat provide;
Close as you can to hers; and Side by Side;
Pleas'd or unpleas'd, no matter; crowding fit.

Then find Occasion to begin Discourse;
Enquire whose Chariot this, and whose that Horse?
To whatsoever Side she is inclin'd,
Suit all your Inclination to her Mind.
Like what she likes, from thence your Court begin;
And whom she favours, with that he may win ...

If Dust be on her Lap, or Graine of Sand,
Brush both away with your officious Hand.
If none be there, yet brush that nothing thence.
And still to touch her lap make some Pretence.
Touch anything of hers; and if her Train
Sweep on the Ground, let it not sweep in vain;
But gently take it up, and wipe it clean:
And while you wipe it, with observing Eyes,
Who knows but you may see her naked thighs!

Observe who sits behind her; and beware,
Lest his incroaching Knee should press the Fair.
Light Service takes light Minds; For some can tell
Of Favours won, by laying Cushions well:
By Fanning Faces, some their Fortune meet;
And some by laying Footstools for their Feet.

Banquets, too, may give opportunities for the love-chase, "when something besides wine draws you there". Wine gives men courage and fills them with amorous thoughts, but at the same time it impairs their judgment. Furthermore, just as no one in his senses would choose jewels or a dress by artificial light, so it is well to remember that in the light of the "treacherous lamp" every woman *looks* beautiful.

Then there are innumerable places and occasions when women in large numbers get together, and one and all should provide opportunities for good hunting. Surely there is no need to mention Baiae, the famous seaside resort on the Bay of Naples. It is famed for its health-giving sulphur springs, but a man may leave the place saying to himself, "those waters were not so healthy after all!"

But enough of the places in which to seek and find the Fair; supposing now you have made your selection, and have a mistress in mind, how should you go about to win her and make her yours?

First of all, be assured of this: all women *can* be caught, and most of them *want* to be caught. They will fall into your net, if you fling it aright. A woman can no more resist a lover than birds can resist singing in the springtime, or grasshoppers from chirping on summer evenings, or dogs from baying when chasing the hare across the fields. Even those women who make a show of appearing cruel may prove kind in the end. And just as stolen love is pleasant to a man, so it is likewise with a woman. The difference between them is chiefly this, that while a man finds it hard to dissemble, the woman conceals her desires better. But how many of the crimes we read about in history and legend had their origin in women's lust? It is keener than men's, it has in it more of the element of madness, of ungovernable passion. Let us be quite sure of this, then, that every woman may be won. Do not hesitate to make your approaches to the woman who pleases you: she can but say no if she feels that way! And even though she turns your proposal down, you may be sure that she will feel flattered at its having been made.

In the remainder of this first part of his little manual Ovid gives worldly-wise instruction in the way a love affair should be managed. It is sometimes worth while, he says, to make up to the maid—but the lover should be careful not to get too deeply involved with the girl, for fear her mistress may come to hear of it and feel jealous, or the girl herself may not want to give him up! When you call upon your lady, give her some small gift as a token of your regard—but be careful not to call on her birthday, or she will have a long list ready of all the presents she would like to have, and it won't be the slightest use to say that you have left your purse at home. Be lavish with your compliments. To quote another passage from Dryden:

> Tell her, her Face is Fair, her Eyes are Sweet;
> Her Taper Fingers praise, and her little Feet.
> Such praises ev'n the Chast are pleas'd to hear;
> Both Maids and Matrons hold their Beauty dear.
>
> Beg her, with Tears, thy warm Desires to grant,
> For Tears will pierce a Heart of Adamant.
> If Tears will not be squeez'd, then rub your Eye,
> Or 'noint the Lids, and seem at least to cry.

Nor should the lover hesitate to use a little force. Some women expect it to be offered, and will feel offended or even insulted if they are not compelled to grant what they are willing to give. A woman taken by sudden assault may count the audacity as a compliment to her charms and attractiveness.

> Kiss if you can: Resistance if she make,
> And will not give you Kisses, let her take.
> "Fie, fie, you naughty man!" are words of course;
> She struggles, but to be subdu'd by Force.
>
> Kiss only soft, I charge you, and beware,
> With too hard Bristles, not to brush the Fair.
> He who has gain'd a Kiss, and gains no more,
> Deserves to lose the Bliss he got before!

All this may sound very reprehensible, but nowhere does Ovid offer a word of encouragement to the cold-hearted schemer, the selfish seducer, the man who makes a boast of his betrayals of maiden innocence. There are no traps to be laid for inexperienced girls. In this love-game of his the partners are supposed to be equally matched and to know all the tricks of the play, the way of each move and every response.

Various indeed are the hearts of women, and a thousand different means must be devised to capture them. Some fish are caught with spears, and some with hooks, and some are dragged up in nets; similarly, different methods must be adopted when women are the catch. Should you seem to be learned to the woman who is simple and uneducated she will immediately feel at a disadvantage, and a wanton approach is only too likely to offend the prude and fill her with mistrust. It is because of such mistakes that a woman who may have been too timid to entrust herself to a lover whose method of wooing was not to her taste, will accept the advances of a man who is in every other way inferior.

This brings us to the end of the first part of the *Art of Love*, and the second part opens with a shout of triumph. "Hurrah! hurrah! I've won her, the girl's mine!" Excellent, the poet comments, but this isn't enough: you must learn how to keep her. And this is much more difficult than it would appear. The *puella*, it is clear, knows her own worth, and she is not slow to remind her lover that since there is no legal tie between them she must be continuously wooed if their relationship is to endure. It is in these pages that we learn something of the daily life of the *puellae*, their pleasure-loving existence, their demands for constant attention, their moods and manners, their greediness for presents, their tantrums and ecstasies, and much else that entered into the composition of these delightful and/or tormenting creatures.

Don't let the young man fancy himself, is the poet's first piece of advice. Beauty is a frail thing enough, and the fresh bloom will soon fade from the young man's cheeks. Seemingly

The Roman Graces: a wall painting from Pompeii
(National Museum at Naples)

Left, the Mysteries of Venus. One of twenty-nine frescoes from the Villa of the Mysteries at Pompeii, this scene of a woman undergoing a ritual flagellation is charged with erotic significance. *Below*, the Bridal Bed. From the fresco known as the Aldobrandini Marriage, this scene shows Hymen at the foot of the nuptial couch and a goddess about to disrobe the bride (Vatican Library, Rome)

he is aware of the shadow of the oncoming years, and has it in mind to present his mistress with a love-potion. The poet's reaction to this is contemptuous. The man who relies on magic arts is a fool, he declares bluntly. Such herbs as Medea gave to Jason, in the ancient legend of the Argonauts, won't keep love alive, he declares; and if Circe's spells had been really effective Odysseus would not have been able to sail away. Philtres given to girls are of not the slightest use, or they may make them mad, since what power they may possess has an influence over the mind. Just as useless is resort to the *hippomanes*, which Pliny the Elder in his work on natural history asserts was a growth upon the forehead of a foal that was bitten off by the mare immediately after giving birth, and which was supposed to have the power of a love-potion. Don't have anything to do with such things, Ovid urges: if you want to be loved, then you must be lovable.

Above all things, keep a civil tongue in your head. When you are with your mistress, don't nag. Don't complain. Don't point out her faults. Wives may rebuke their husbands and husbands their wives, but never forget that it is not by the law's behest that you and your mistress have come into one bed. The only bond between you is love.

Don't be stingy with your praises. If she has a new parting in her hair, admire it. If she has used the curling-irons, declare that her curls are lovely. When she dances, admire the way she moves her arms; and if she sings praise her voice and complain when she brings her song to an end. If she is wearing a Tyrian dress, say how well it suits her; if it is in the Coan style, make bold to say that it is absolutely fetching. Is her raiment cloth of gold? Then let it be as real gold in your sight. Or if she's in her woollens, praise them too. Should she pose before you in nothing but her chemise, protest that she sets you on fire, and then timidly murmur, "But, my dear, please take care not to catch cold!"

E

"Nor ask her age"—to quote another few lines from Dryden,

> consult no Register,
> Under whose reign she's born, or what's the year!
> If fading Youth chequers her hair with white,
> Experience makes her perfect in Delight;
> In her Embrace sublimer Joys are found,
> A Fruitful Soil, and cultivated Ground!

Give her presents—not necessarily costly ones (think of your old age!) but small gifts chosen with care. A basket of choice fruits is often acceptable, especially if you say that they come from your own orchards—although in fact you have bought them at the stall just round the corner. A singing-bird in a cage, or a dove, will show your affection in the most charming fashion. And if you are something of a poet, send her some of the verses you have composed in her honour.

Hold her parasol when she goes for a stroll, and clear the way for her through the throng. When indoors, hasten to place the footstool, bring her slippers or take them off her dainty feet, and though you may be freezing yourself warm her hands in yours. Offer to hold the mirror for her when her arms get tired. When she wants someone to take a message, jump up at once. No matter if it is blazing hot or the snow is falling, leave everything you are doing and hasten to obey her every whim. If she laughs, laugh with her. If she weeps, weep too. If she falls ill, be assiduous in your attendance at her bedside. But on the other hand, don't make yourself a nuisance or a bore.

All this is very exacting, but there is no necessity for a lover to keep away from every other charmer! What if his mistress does learn of his infidelities? What if she does scream and rage, scratch his face and half-drowns him in her tears? The angry mood will soon pass. Put your arms round her white shoulders, is the poet's advice; take her to your bosom. Kiss her tears away, and at the same time, "give her the joys of Venus". Then there will be peace at last, and everything will be as before, even better perhaps!

Having armed the man for the fight, Ovid addresses in the third part of the *Art of Love* the female contestant, in order that man and woman may "go into battle on equal terms".

Since the courtesan's chief interest was male admiration, she had to study how to make herself attractive. Good looks were of course a great advantage, but "Beauty is Heaven's gift, and how few can boast of it!" But there was no reason for the plain girl to despair. If she were clever enough, she could learn to make the most of her good features and disguise or hide those that were not so good. Here Ovid was in his element.

Don't load your ears with pearls or precious stones, he advises the *puella* who is his disciple; don't sew too much tinsel into the folds of your dress. It is elegance that counts, not show. Don't appear in public with your hair all over the place; if you cannot decide which coiffure suits you best, look in the glass and try the various modes. An oval face looks best with the hair unparted, but if your face is round you should wear your hair in a knot on the top of your head, so that your ears show. Some women look well with their hair falling over their shoulders, some should wear it braided or done up with a tortoise-shell comb. Hair that *looks* neglected may have a charm of its own; often you get the impression that it hasn't been combed since yesterday—and how wrong you are! (What's that? Your hair is falling out, thin in places, going grey? Then buy a wig.)

If you are fair, with a snow-white skin, you would do well to wear dark colours; but if you are dark-complexioned, white robes are what you should go in for. It should not be necessary to remind you to brush your teeth every morning and to wash your hands, but you should also get rid of that superfluous hair on your legs and under your arms. Don't put on your powder anyhow, but apply it gently and sparingly; touch up your eyebrows with a little soot, and a little powdered ash round the eyes is often effective. A tiny patch, skilfully stuck on, will hide that pimple or mole or other blemish on your face.

But a woman at her toilet should be careful not to leave the door of her chamber ajar. There are some things that it is not good for a man to know, especially a man on whom it is important to make a good impression. When you go to the theatre, you admire the painted scenery—but you don't expected to see the painters and gilders at work. A woman's make-up should be a private process, and the beholder should be shown only the finished picture.

But what if the materials for the picture are not all that they might be? The poet is once again ready with his most excellent advice. Here is what he has to say about the remedying of female defects, as put into English by the famous early eighteenth-century playwright William Congreve:

Faults in your Person, of your Face, correct;
And few are seen that have not some Defect!
The Nymph too short, her Seat should seldom quit
Lest, when she stands, she may be thought to sit.
And when extended on her Couch she lyes,
Let Length of Petticoats conceal her Size.

The Lean, of thick-wrought stuff her Cloathes should chuse
And fuller made, than what the Plumper use.

A Leg too lank, tight Garters still must wear;
Nor should an ill-shap'd foot be ever bare.
Round shoulders, bolster'd, will appear the least;
And lacing strait, confines too full a breast.
Whose fingers are too Fat, and Nails too coarse,
Should always shun too much Gesture in discourse . . .

From matters of dress, the instructor in the Art of Feminine

Attraction turns to deportment. The pupil must learn to laugh properly: she should not open her mouth too wide, especially if she has teeth that are black or missing, and she should not make a noise like a she-ass braying. Let her keep her lips over the top of her teeth, and practise a pleasant trill or tinkle. And a lisp can be very charming, as also amusing little slips of the tongue, a word pronounced wrong.

To make a real success of her career, the *puella* should be a *culta puella*, even a *docta puella*, a woman of culture and education. Ovid insists on a really high level of accomplishments. She should be tasteful and elegant, always scrupulously neat and clean in her person, displaying a nice fastidiousness in all things. She should know how to walk gracefully, moving with a seductive swaying of her figure and not striding along like a country miss. Her clothes should be light and airy, and the upper arm and shoulder should be left bare—but only if the skin is a snowy white. ("Whenever I see a shoulder exposed like this," confesses the poet, "I always want to kiss it!") Then she should learn how to sit down at the dinner-table and recline on her couch and rise up again; she should learn how to dance, representing by gesture and attitude the characters of the old-time legends; she should learn to sing, since "song is a persuasive thing, and many a woman has proved that a good voice can be a better enticer than a pretty face"; she should also learn to play on the harp—a well-shaped hand shows to advantage when sweeping the strings —and she may well find it useful to learn how to throw the dice and play marbles and other games that men take such an interest in.

Then if she be intelligent and reasonably well read, she should not hesitate to show off her learning. Let her have books on her dressing-table, and be able to quote from them when their names come up in conversation—Menander's comedies, the Greek poets, and something of wild Catullus or tender Tibullus. And perhaps—who knows?—the day will come when someone will ask her to read aloud something from Master Ovid—one of his Letters of Famous Heroines, for instance, or perhaps from one of those three little books of his that have the word LOVE on their cover!

THE LOVES OF THE POETS

IV

Catullus and Lesbia

"WHEN I FIRST SET eyes on you I couldn't speak. My voice failed me, my tongue stuck in my mouth. There was a humming in my ears, my eyes were dimmed and I couldn't see straight, and a kind of flame ran up and down my limbs. And now, it's as good as being a god in heaven just to sit opposite you, to feast my eyes on your beauty and to hear the merry tinkle of your laugh. As good, did I say? At the risk of blasphemy I'll say it is better, ever so much better!"

This is how the young Roman poet Catullus described the opening stages of his passionately tempestuous love affair with the most beautiful, most sought after, and most rewarding of the society ladies. Swiftly it moved on to its climax, for the woman in the case was no modest violet but a flaming peony. There was nothing in the least coy or reluctant about her. She was bold and brazen, as luscious as fruit ripe for the picking (perhaps a little overripe). She was not the sort of woman to waste time over the preliminaries. There was an imperiousness in her desires that few men could resist, or resist for long.

Certainly not Catullus. Within a very few weeks of their first encounter—or it may have been only a matter of days— we find him imploring his mistress to "live and love" and let people say what they liked. After all, what could crabbed old men know of love? Give me a thousand kisses, he demands of her; then a hundred, another thousand and another hundred, then more hundreds, more thousands until they've lost count.

A few more weeks, and the poet is declaring that "he loves —and is in hell!" His passion burns as fiercely as ever, but hers is beginning to flicker and fail. There is a noticeable coolness in her welcome, the door of her house is sometimes shut in his face, there's another man who is much more sure of a smile.

The situation becomes more and more strained between the still eager man and the less than eager woman. At length he is compelled to acknowledge the existence of a state of affairs that his friends have seen coming for a long time. "Poor Catullus!" he addresses himself in a mood of self-pity; "it really is time that you stopped acting the fool, and wrote off what is obviously gone for good."

Easier said than done, of course, but the curtain comes down at last with a dreadful bang. "This woman I've loved as surely man never loved a woman before—what is she at bottom? I'll tell you. She's just a tart, a common street-walker!"

A sad little tale, but there is nothing new about it of course. What makes it worth remembering is its telling, for Catullus was one of the earliest, if not the first, of the poets who have transmuted the raw material of human love into something that is of deathless value and validity. Only those versed in the intricacies of the Latin language may be capable of appreciating Catullus as a poet, but the way in which he explores the relation of the sexes has aroused an understanding echo in the hearts and minds of generations of readers, most of whom have read him only in translation.

Gaius Valerius Catullus, as his full name was, was born at Verona, in northern Italy, in the eighties of the last century B.C. It may have been in 87 B.C. or a little later. We do not know, nor do we know when he died, although it was almost certainly when he was still in his early thirties. His father was a man of some wealth and station in life, judging from the fact that Julius Caesar used to stay overnight in his house on his way to and from his province of Gaul. Since the population of the district was largely Celtic in origin, there may have been a Celtic strain in the Catullan ancestry, which would go some way to account for the poet's temperament and genius. Even as a boy, as he tells us himself, "when my primrose youth was in its pleasant spring, I played at making rhymes". Nothing is discoverable of his education, and indeed all that is told of him is derived, with greater or less probability, from his poems. We may imagine him as a lively young spark in the Verona that, fifteen hundred years later, was the scene of the romantic love of Romeo and Juliet. And like Romeo, who before he was bewitched by the black eyes of the precocious teenager, had been enamoured of Rosaline's "bright eyes, high forehead and scarlet lip, fine foot, straight leg, and quivering thigh", the young Catullus had had his easy conquests among the local girls.

One of his lady-loves was named Ipsithilla; she was his "darling, his charmer", and he urged her to let him visit her one day at noon, when she had made no arrangements to go out during the afternoon. "If you will consent, send me a message at once," he implores her at the conclusion of his poetical little note. Another was Aufilena, and she it seems was not so accommodating. "You are no true mistress," he complains, "for you promised and now you back out. You are not one of those kind mistresses who are always well spoken of, because they never fail to carry out their part of the bargain. You take, and don't give, and that's a scurvy trick. To give what you promised would be excellent, and not to promise anything would be a sign of chastity. But to take all you can get and then cheat a man of his due shows you to be just plain greedy—no better in fact than one of those girls who offer to sell everything they've got!" Then there was another girl about whom he had thought seriously, but he could not get her to give a firm answer to his wooing.

"The girl I love," he writes—but here is how Sir Philip Sidney renders it:

"Unto nobody," my woman saith, "she had rather a wife be
Than to myself; not though Jove grew a suitor of hers."
These be her words, but a woman's words to a love that is eager,
In wind or water's streame do require to be writ.

As a youth with a well-to-do father Catullus doubtless received an allowance, and like most youths in similar circumstances he sometimes found his purse to be empty before the next month's instalment was due. So we find him writing to one of his young friends—a man this time—promising that he shall have a good dinner at his place in a few days' time, provided *he* brings with him all that is necessary—not forgetting a pretty girl. "If, I say, you bring all these with you, my charming friend, you *shall* have a good dinner. But as for me, the purse of your Catullus is full of nothing but cobwebs."

The youth became a man, and Catullus was still playing around among the light and easy loves of a provincial city when there swept into his life the woman whom he was to immortalize, in love and hate and final disillusionment. He calls her Lesbia in his poems, but there are good reasons for believing that she was the woman who in the histories of Rome is generally referred to as the "infamous Clodia".

Whatever else she was, she was a true-blue aristocrat. She was by birth a Claudian, a member of a family which over the years had given many a great name to the Roman story—men who combined arrogance and domineering assertiveness with a patriotism of the most fervent and unyielding character. She had a brother, Publius Clodius Pulcher, who made an unenviable name for himself as a gangster politician and who will appear later on in our story; and she was married as a young girl to Quintus Metellus Celer, who also came of one of the noblest and most highly regarded of the great Roman families. He, too, had a political career, in which there was nothing disreputable and much that was to his credit. In the last year of his life he was elected Consul, the highest post a Roman might attain.

Unfortunately he was generally so occupied with politics that he had little time for his wife—and she was not the sort of woman to sit down quietly at home while her husband was gadding about in the Forum and army headquarters. Clodia probably thought him stiff and stupid and a bit of a bore. He was often away, and when he was at home he had nothing to talk about but such dull things as elections and party jobs and political matters. Most people who met him must have come away with the impression that he was an excellent specimen of the fine old Roman gentleman, but he was quite incapable of keeping one of the "new women" of Roman society in order. In earlier times he might have kept her under lock and key when she showed signs of wanting to stray, and in earlier times still he might have knocked her about. Yet he was no fool, for if he had been he could not have served the State with such distinction.

Clodia, for her part, was handsome and proud, used to having her own way, a lover of luxurious living, and never happy unless she had a string of young men in attendance. Among these Catullus came to be numbered, perhaps when he was on a visit to Rome but more likely when she accompanied her husband to Verona in the spring of 62 B.C., on his appointment to the governorship of the province. Catullus was then in his early twenties, and she was at the interesting age of thirty or thereabouts. He must have found her the most beautiful, the most dangerously fascinating woman he had ever met. He does not give any clear description of her in the poems that her beauty inspired, but from various allusions we may gather that she possessed a dainty foot and tapering hand, small straight nose and flashing dark eyes. Those eyes were her most distinctive feature. The distinguished orator and statesman Cicero, who knew her well (too well, so his wife suspected) refers to her as "ox-eyed", which does not sound very complimentary; but the term is one that Homer often applies to Juno, the surpassingly lovely Queen of Heaven.

Had Catullus heard nothing of this voluptuous creature's unsavoury reputation? Had no spiteful tongue told him that she had been suspected of an incestuous relationship with her brother Clodius? Had he not listened at some dinner-party to the malicious story that one of her nicknames was *Quadrantaria* because (so Plutarch explains) "one of her lovers palmed upon her a purse of small brass money instead of silver—the smallest brass coin being called a quadrans"? Whether he knew these things or not, he cannot have greatly cared, for the poems show that he was hopelessly entangled in the thickets of love.

He called her Lesbia. It must have been intended as a compliment, for the island of Lesbos was celebrated for the beauty of its women and it was also the birthplace of the poetess Sappho, whose verses were his inspiration and delight. There is no suggestion that Catullus was aware that Sappho's kind of lovemaking was anything other than the expression of a man's desire for a woman and a woman's for a man. "Lesbianism" had not yet become a literary synonym for homosexuality.

Scholars have subjected the poems to a painstaking examination and have arranged them in such a way as to create a connected story of the love affair, complete with first poem, poems written in the mounting excitement of its development and then in its equally swift decline, and finally a grim, bitter, and thoroughly nasty little piece to wind up. According to the generally adopted reckoning, the first of the series was the one of which a free rendering has been given at the beginning of this chapter. Byron tried his hand at translating it in his *Ad Lesbiam*:

Equal to Jove that youth must be—
Greater than Jove he seems to me—
Who, free from Jealousy's alarms,
Securely views thy matchless charms;
That cheek, which ever dimpling glows,
That mouth, from whence such music flows,
To him, alike, are always known,
Reserved for him, and him alone.
Ah! Lesbia! though 'tis death to me,
I cannot choose but look on thee . . .

and so on. Then come a pair of playful trifles, written about
Lesbia's pet bird, variously called by the translators a sparrow,
starling, song-thrush, and even a canary, which she often
held in her lap and stroked, giving it her finger to nip whenever she, "the glowing lady of my love," felt like a piece of
pretty play. "If only I might play with you as she does," longs
the poet, "and so lighten the heavy load upon my heart!"
Byron tried his hand at translating the second, and made a
solemn mess of it.

My Lesbia's favourite bird is dead,
    Whom dearer than her eyes she loved;
For he was gentle, and so true,
Obedient to her call he flew,
No fear, no wild alarm, he knew,
    But lightly o'er her bosom moved:
And softly fluttering here and there,
He never sought to cleave the air;
But chirrup'd oft, and, free from care,
    Tuned to her ear his grateful strain.
Now having pass'd the gloomy bourne,
From whence he never can return,
His death, and Lesbia's grief, I mourn . . .

Now we have two wild outbursts of amorous passion when
Catullus must surely have become the favoured lover. In one
he refers to his mistress's sleepy question, whether he would

ever get tired of kissing. "You ask how many kissings of you, Lesbia, are enough for me, and more than enough? As many as the grains of the Libyan sands, or as the stars that, in the silent night, look down on the stolen loves of men. If your Catullus, mad Catullus, could kiss you with so many kisses, then this might perhaps be enough . . ."

The other little poem is the *Vivamus, mea Lesbia, atque amemus*, that has been often translated. Here is the young Coleridge's version, written in 1798, the year in which he collaborated with Wordsworth in the *Lyrical Ballads*:

> My Lesbia, let us love and live,
> And to the winds, my Lesbia, give
> Each cold restraint, each boding fear
> Of age and all her saws severe.
> Yon sun now posting to the main
> Will set—but 'tis to rise again;—
> But we, when once our mortal light
> Is set, must sleep in endless night.
> Then come, with whom alone I'll live,
> A thousand kisses take and give!
> Another thousand!—to the store
> Add hundreds—then a thousand more!
> And when they to a million mount,
> Let confusion take the account,—
> That you, the number never knowing,
> May continue still bestowing—
> That I for joys may never pine,
> Which never can again be mine!

Dating from about this time is a poetical letter of thanks to a friend of Catullus's who had lent his house for their love-making. "Thither, up the path that crosses the field, had tripped my lovely goddess—and how her sandals creaked! —to press the threshold with her dainty feet." Another poem records an amusing incident when, following a lovers' tiff, they had made it up and, convulsed with laughter, had

The charm of Roman girlhood is represented in this sculpture
(Museo Nuovo nel Palazzo dei Conservatori, Rome)

A dignified Roman Matron (British Museum)

committed to the flames the verses of the man they agreed was
the very worst of poets. Amusing? So at least Catullus had
thought when they thrust the "filthy wastepaper" of
Volusius's verses into the brazier and watched them curl
and brown and shrivel. Only later did he understand that by
pessimus poeta Lesbia had meant not Volusius but Catullus
himself.

The reconciliation was incomplete. We may imagine the
bickering, the lover's complaints of his mistress's waning
interest and her languid excuses, the harsh words that slipped
out in moments of thwarted passion and were only half-
pardoned by a kiss. The circumstances of the affair had
changed. The pair were now, it seems, in Rome, and whereas
in Verona the attentions of the young poet might be welcome,
now in the great metropolis he was proving himself a bit of a
nuisance. He was always hanging around, and she simply
hadn't the time to listen to his reading his verses when there
were so many other interesting people to meet and interesting
things to do. Why, he even had the cheek to complain that
she was spending too much of her time with her husband!
Really, it was too absurd.

After two years the affair was burning itself out, when in
59 B.C. Clodia's husband died suddenly. The gossips at once
got busy with a story that she had poisoned him, and certainly
she showed herself to be no inconsolable widow. She had
now complete control of her fortune and of her life, and gave
full rein to her inclinations. Just about this time she dropped
Catullus as her preferred lover, and took another in his place.

The poet took it in very bad part. For a time he tried to
delude himself into believing that his expulsion from the
chief place in her affections was only temporary, but at length
he realized the hard truth and resolved to make the best of a
bad job. "What if, in days gone by, the sun shone brightly
when she beckoned you on? You enjoyed them, didn't you"—
so he told himself—"those delightful little games which the

F

woman must have enjoyed too, since she never held herself back? Yes, they were wonderful times, and now they are over. She says 'no' when before she said 'yes'. Well, what of it? You must do the same. Show her you don't care a rap . . . And so farewell, my mistress, Catullus has become as hard as steel. He won't run after you; he won't beg those favours you once accorded him so liberally. But what will happen to you, I wonder? Who will call you his dearest? Whose girl will you say you are? Which man's lips will you be biting? (Well, never mind, Catullus! Keep your pecker up! Never say die!)"

Some time later, when the smart had almost gone and he could look back on the affair with a measure of detachment, he wrote a poem to two good friends of his, asking them to convey a message to "his girl", a message that was short and not sweet. "Bid her farewell for me, bid her love and be happy, she and all the hundreds of lovers whose loins she will drain of their strength with her lusting! And don't let her suppose for a moment that she will ever be able to regain my love. It's gone, gone completely, gone for good, and it was all her fault. She killed it like a flower on the edge of the field is killed when the ploughshare slices it through."

Perhaps he would not have felt it so deeply if his supplanter had not been one of his intimate friends. M. Caelius Rufus the man's name was, and he was several years younger than Catullus. If our dates are anything like correct, he was twenty-three to Clodia's thirty-five. He was the son of a wealthy banker at Puteoli, and was destined to a career in the public service, in preparation for which he had been found a stool in the law chambers of the great Cicero.

Catullus deeply resented what he regarded as his friend's treachery. "I trusted you implicitly, Rufus," he wrote, "as one friend trusts another, and you have robbed me of everything that made life worth living; you have poisoned our friendship." Perhaps it was because of his disgust that Catullus accepted a post on the staff of Gaius Memmius, newly appointed governor of Bithynia, in Asia Minor, or it may have been that he was getting in low water financially. Leaving Rome in 57 B.C. Catullus was abroad for a year or two, and it was while he was away that his former mistress became the centre of a scandal of the most shocking proportions. It arose out of her liaison with Caelius.

That young man had not lasted long as the official lover. He could not stand the pace, and within a year or so the affair was at an end. This time, however, it was the man who broke it off, and the woman raged at the humiliation. She vowed to be revenged on him for the slight, and in 56 B.C. it was announced that she had laid an accusation against him in the courts, alleging that he had robbed her of some gold and had also tried to poison her. Cicero was briefed for the defence.

The trial was held in Rome on the 3rd and 4th April. Cicero spoke on the second day, and his speech, *Pro Caelio*, is considered one of his best efforts.

"In this case, gentlemen," he said in his opening, "we are concerned entirely with Clodia, a woman not only of noble birth but of some notoriety, of whom I will say no more than is necessary to rebut the charges laid against my client." But he wanted it to be clearly understood that it was with her, and her alone, that they had to deal. If she withdrew her charges against Caelius they would of course refrain from attacking her, but as things stood her reputation was a fair target. Cicero professed to be sorry about this, and that he felt somewhat inhibited by the fact that "the woman's husband— I'm sorry, I meant to say her brother: I keep on making that slip!" had been for many years his most bitter enemy. This made the court sit up, for the "slip" was nothing of the kind: it was a calculated indiscretion, referring to the scandal that connected Clodia with her brother Clodius in an incestuous relation.

"As things are," Cicero went on, "I will do my best to act with moderation, and go no farther than my duty to my client requires. For indeed I never thought that I should have to cross swords with women, still less with a lady who up to now has always enjoyed the reputation of being nobody's enemy and everybody's friend." (Another nasty innuendo: the word Cicera uses is *amica*, which usually means "friend" but may also be interpreted as "mistress".) Clodia was at the bottom of the matter, as they would soon find out when they were told of her debauchery and amours, the trips to the seaside at Baiae, her bathing parties, musical parties, boating parties, and all the rest.

Well, now, how would she like him to conduct the case? Would she prefer him to deal with her in a fatherly fashion, or after the modern mode? The first? Well, then, he would call from the Shades the lady's famous ancestor Appius Claudius, the Blind, "for he is least likely to be upset at finding her here, since he won't be able to see her". If he could make his appearance in court, he might remind her of all her ancestors who were Consuls, and of how he himself had constructed the Via Appia (the road from Rome to Capua). "But I didn't build it just so that you could pass up and down it with other women's husbands in tow!" he might exclaim; "nor did I build the aqueduct that bears my name in order that you might use its water to wash off the stains of your degrading amours!" Then the old man might remind her that she was once the wife of a distinguished citizen, a most courageous patriot, and demand how it was that she had got mixed up with Caelius, who wasn't a kinsman, a relative by marriage, or even a friend of her husband's. "And yet he became your intimate! What *was* he then—your lover?"

But enough of this homely and rugged old man, Cicero went on; here was one of the younger generation, Clodia's brother Clodius—"such a perfect man of the world he is, too; a man who loves you most tenderly, and who when he was only a little fellow used to creep into your bed because he was so afraid of the dark!" If he cared to open his mouth, he might say something like this. "Sister, what are you making such a fuss about? Have you lost your senses? One of your neighbours, a good-looking young man, has caught your fancy; you 'fell' for him and wanted to see him as often as you could. Sometimes you went for a walk with him in the park. His father kept him short of cash, and you thought you could use your money to keep him tied to your apron-strings. But he jibs and kicks, doesn't value your gifts, and in a word treats you abominably. What then? Why, try someone else! You have a villa beside the Tiber, and didn't you buy it because it was so conveniently placed, right next to the bathing-station of the young men? Surely you should be able to fix up something with one of them any time you want. And yet you keep on worrying about this fellow who spurns what you have to offer!"

Now Cicero turned to the young man in the dock. He admitted that he was not all that he should be, although he had behaved excellently while he was Cicero's pupil. He had got mixed up in some rather dubious political intrigues, and he had had dealings with courtesans. But what young man hadn't? And really it was not in the least surprising when you consider that he was living next door to such a woman as Clodia, a frisky young widow with plenty of money and no guardian to keep her in order. Her behaviour, her dress, her loose conversation, the way she embraced men in public, the company she kept—all these things proclaimed her to be what she was, a wanton, a hussy, a shameless courtesan! If Baiae could speak! And Baiae does speak; nay more, it cries aloud, about this abandoned female who gives herself to Tom, Dick, and Harry! In broad daylight too!

Was this a true picture of Clodia? If it was, then the worst that could be said of Caelius was that he had got himself entangled with a lady of the most easy virtue. As for the story she told, it wouldn't bear examination. She alleged that she had lent Caelius some gold ornaments—"part of the spoil that this Venus had succeeded in extracting from her lovers" —which *she* said he intended to use to bribe slaves to murder a man who was his enemy, but which *he* said were to be sold to provide funds for a public entertainment. Clodia had handed him the jewels, with no witnesses, and had not asked for them back. If her version of the story was true, then she was ready to become an accessory before the fact of a horrible crime. But *his* version was the true one. As for the charge of trying to poison her, it was too silly for words. Whatever motive had he? And he was supposed to have taken some of her slaves into his confidence! Furthermore, according to the prosecution, the poison was to be handed to one of Caelius's friends—where? At the public baths of all places, where everyone was walking about without his clothes!

So the case went on, and towards the end Cicero made great play with a "most improper story" that was on everybody's lips but which has unfortunately not come down to us. The court knew all about it, however, and we may imagine the smiles on the faces when Cicero urged that, whether it was true or whether it was false, the fact that it could be told without a blush seemed to square nicely with "that lady's" reputation.

By this time there can have been no one in court who did not suspect that the charge was a put up job, and Cicero clinched the matter with an appeal to the jury in the best Old Bailey style. "An only son, gentlemen—a young man of great abilities and promise—you see his poor old father sitting over there?—he's getting near the end of life's road, and death cannot come too soon if you cut off that young man in his prime, just when virtue has taken so firm a root in him—save a son for a father, a father for his much-loved son!" Caelius was acquitted.

Catullus returned from Bithynia in this same year, and he

had not made his fortune. Such pickings as had been had from among the unfortunate provincials had gone into Memmius's purse. It is not known whether the poet met Clodia again, but we may be sure that he read most eagerly the law reports and listened to the tales that were told him at his club. Towards the end of his life, not long afterwards, he published his poems, in which his love affair with Lesbia-Clodia is related from its first raptures to its decline and fall into disgust and hatred.

Clodius perished miserably in a street brawl in 52 B.C. Caelius joined Julius Caesar, but fell out with him and was killed in 48 B.C. Five years later Cicero, too, came to a bloody end, when, having chosen what proved to be the losing side in the civil war that followed Caesar's murder, he was put to death by order of Mark Antony. Only Clodia lived on, and although at the time of the trial she was still under forty we never hear of her again.

V

"Dear Delia"

IF SOMEONE HAD ASKED Albius Tibullus what his idea of bliss was, he might have replied that it was to lie in bed with his girl friend in his country homestead, while the winter winds howled without and the rain slashed at the shuttered windows.

He was a quiet soul, a young man of a gentle and melancholy disposition, who asked little of life but to be let alone to enjoy it in his own quiet way. Unfortunately for him he was born in an age of revolution, and very much against his will he was caught up from time to time in the harsh progress of events. Like most of the Roman poets he came of what is usually referred to as the equestrian or knightly class, although there was no titular distinction attached to it.

The year of his birth is generally given as about 60 B.C., which would make him about a quarter of a century younger than Catullus, but he may have been born as late as 54 B.C. The place also is uncertain, but it was not Rome. His father died when he was a boy, and the small estate that he inherited was very much diminished when in 41 B.C. Mark Antony and Octavian (later the Emperor Augustus), the victors in the latest civil war, rewarded their veterans with estates confiscated from those who had fought against them, or perhaps had only held aloof.

But sufficient was left to enable his mother to give Tibullus a good education, and probably it was family influence that secured him the patronage of Marcus Valerius Messalla Corvinus, one of the most distinguished of the old Roman aristocracy who, although he had been on the losing side in the civil war, had now made his peace with the victors and was the patron of a literary circle that included most of the rising young wits and orators and poets. Tibullus was welcomed into this group, and he may or may not have been pleased when Messalla offered him a post on his staff when he was despatched by Augustus at the end of 30 B.C. to quell a revolt in Aquitania, in south-western Gaul. Tibullus distinguished himself in this campaign and was decorated, but he was not cut out for a soldier and what he saw of war disgusted him. "Who was it that first discovered the horrible sword?" he demands in one of his poems; "what a savage he must have been, made of the same material as his weapon! How I wish I had been born in the olden days, before the first trumpet-call had been sounded. Now I am dragged off to war, and somewhere or other there probably lives the man who is destined to plunge his sword into my side."

When Messalla invited him at a later date to rejoin the Roman eagles, he politely but firmly declined. He had had enough of battles and sieges and wholesale slaughter. "It's all very well for you," he told his patron, "to go campaigning on land and sea, so that you may be able to adorn your house-front with the trophies you have taken from the foe; but that sort of thing doesn't appeal to me any longer. In fact I'm a prisoner already—I'm a captive in the bonds of love, tied fast to a lovely girl! This is the only kind of war I'm good for. In it I'm brave captain and private soldier too. I don't give a fig for trumpets and standards and martial glory. The only thing I care about is love, and I don't mind in the least if people call me sluggard and idler if only I may be left alone with my Delia!"

Dear Delia! This is what he calls her in his poems, but her real name seems to have been Plania. She was a woman in the middle station of life, married (or as good as married), and probably rather older than he was; it appears likely that it was when her husband (or her "protector") was abroad in Cilicia on military service that she and Tibullus came to know one another, or perhaps it was then that their acquaintance matured into friendship, and something more than friendship.

Although he must have been in his middle twenties or even approaching thirty, this was Tibullus's first real love affair, and he pressed his attentions in a way that she may have found embarrassing. As a respectable woman she was bound to have regard to the appearances, but she may have found being a grass widow dull and irksome. No doubt she appreciated the proffered devotion of the handsome young poet, and as soon as the opportunity offered let him have his way with her. It was a distinct advantage that her mother had come to like the young man and furthered the intrigue as much as she could; she used to wait by the door when it was dark and listen for his approaching footfall, and then open it stealthily and usher him in to where his mistress was waiting. "Long may you live, old lady!" he wrote in one of his pieces, "I wish I could add some of my years to yours to enable you to live longer! I will always love you, as I love your daughter."

But Delia had to be careful. There were other people who had their eyes on her—guardians appointed by her husband before he went away, which seems to suggest that he was not without his suspicions, or at least his fears of what a good-looking woman might get up to if temptation came her way.

Tibullus was "warned off" in no uncertain terms, and in one of the earliest of the verses he addressed to Delia he appeals to her to show a little more ingenuity and enterprise in dodging the watch put on her. "Elude thy guardians, Delia," he conjures her (the version is James Cranstoun's, published in 1872):

> Now thou must dare, and Venus aids the brave!
> She smiles when youths have to new thresholds sped,
> Teaches the dear ones to unbar the door—
> To steal unnoticed from the downy bed,
> And tread with noiseless step the tell-tale floor;
> But this love-lore she grants not to the shy,
> Or such as fear the murk of midnight skies . . .

To make matters easier, he had been to a witch, one of those wise old women who made a speciality of preparing love spells and potions, and she had made up for him a charm that would enable Delia to deceive her custodians with the greatest of ease and certainty. "Chant it three times, and then spit three times—and you will see how effective it can be! Why, even if your husband or guardian were to catch us in bed together he wouldn't believe his eyes!" He had every confidence in this particular witch, he assures her; he had "seen her lead the stars adown the gloom . . . woo spirits from the tomb . . . at will her screams the gathering clouds dispel, at will her word in summer brings the snow." So Delia need have no fear: all she had to do was to say the charm three times in a row, and then—spit!

If she would but play her part, he would not hesitate to run the risks of nocturnal encounters with ruffians in the streets (unlighted in those days, and with no policemen on the beat) in order to reach her door; the goddess of Love would look after him, turning aside their weapons and not allowing them even to snatch away his cloak. What if the night were bitterly cold, or it was raining cats and dogs? Still he wouldn't mind in the least, provided he could be sure that the door would be unbarred at his coming and Delia would be there to greet him, not saying anything but just beckoning him with her finger.

Of course this furtive love-making would not content him for long. He let her know that he would not be satisfied until she threw in her lot with him completely and came to live with him in his rural retreat. How happy they would be together, spending all day and all night in one another's company! "In the country I will live," he rhapsodizes, "and my Delia shall be there with me, to keep an eye on the ripening corn and the men and maidens jumping up and down with naked feet in the great vats that hold the grapes from my vines. She will learn to count the sheep in my flocks; she shall have charge of everything on the farm, and everybody shall run to do her bidding. The country children will love to be fondled in her lap. She will come to know all the divinities of the countryside, and at the proper times will visit their shrines and make the appropriate offerings—a cluster of grapes, a sheaf of corn, a flask of home-made wine. And Messalla shall visit us there, and see how happy we have become. Delia will pay him the homage that is his due. She shall pluck the choicest fruit for him from our orchard, and herself act the serving-maid when he sits down to dinner." As for Tibullus himself, he was quite prepared to be a mere nobody, a cipher in his own home. For he had no ambition to excel; he desired nothing more than to live with Delia all his days, and when his last hour came to die in her arms, holding her hand, while kisses mingled with her tears. Then she would follow his corpse to the tomb, and everybody would be weeping for a man who had died before his time. In a mood of delicious melancholy he turned the vision over and over in his mind. How nice she would look in her mourning garb! But she must not carry things too far. Her hair must not be *too* dishevelled, nor must she scratch her face too deeply with her nails.

Such were his dreams and aspirations, but he was soon disillusioned. Delia, it turned out, was not at all keen on burying herself in the country, with no company other than a lovesick young fellow who was quite good at penning pretty verses but not much else. She must have got tired of his constant whining and wheedling, and it is hardly surprising that her door was sometimes shut to him when it was left on the jar for another. He had good reason to believe that she had found a wealthy admirer, and in a fit of temper he flung himself off and vowed he would never see her again. He took to drink and debauchery to solace his smart, but not very successfully.

I've often tried to drown my cares with wine;
  Grief turns the wine to tears: I've often sped
To some fair nymph; when bliss was wellnigh mine,
  The thought of Delia came, and vigour fled.

The lass would swear I was bewitched, and run—
  O shame upon her and her idle tale
Of all the deeds unholy I had done!
  By what dread power could Delia work such bane?
By spells? No, by fair shoulders, queenly charms,
  And golden locks, she lit the witching flame . . .

Perhaps it was about this time that he accepted an invitation
from Messalla to accompany him on another of his campaigns,
but we cannot be sure since the poems are not arranged in
chronological order and have been proved capable of a wide
variety of interpretation. There is one poem which seems to
show that the poet did actually set out to join his patron, but
was taken ill on the way and had to abandon the enterprise.

Lying on his sick-bed his thoughts drifted to the girl he
had left behind him. How he wished he had never left her!
That stumble he had had at the gate when he was saying
good-bye should have warned him that the venture would
come to no good. But what worried him most was the thought
of what Delia was up to at that moment. He recalled how in
days gone by she had gone off to pay her vows, as she put it,
at the temple of Isis—how she had dutifully performed all
the duties demanded of her, the ritual of prayer, the bathing
in clean water, the sleeping alone in the temple precincts. If
they had parted in anger he would have no claim on her now,
but all the same he muttered a prayer to the goddess that Delia
should continue to keep her nightly vigils, and in his mind's
eye he had a soothing picture of her sitting there before the
shrine, dressed in white linen and chanting the praises of the
goddess with her hair falling loosely about her white
shoulders.

Then the poem concludes with a passionate invocation, not
to the goddess but to Delia, who was far more to him than
any mysterious divinity. "Be chaste, my love, and let the old
lady who sits by your side help you to keep your sense of what
is honourable. As she sits there in the soft light of the lamp,
she will tell you stories of the olden days, while all around the
maids are busy at their spinning, until at length sleep steals
upon them and the work drops from their wearied hands. And
then—why then:

> Oh, let me speed, unheralded, to thee,
>   Like an immortal rushing down the sky!
> Then, all undressed, with ruffled locks astream,
>   And feet unsandalled, meet me on my way!

This ardent wish of his is unlikely to have been realized,
since the husband returned from abroad and resumed his old
place in the home. This was bad enough, but Tibullus was
further aggrieved by the discovery that his Delia had taken
another lover.

> The trap is laid: sly Delia's sole delight
>   Is now to clasp another swain by night.
> Oft she denies it, but I can't believe her,
>   For when her husband's jealous of my fever,
> She swears she knows me not—the arch-deceiver!

What upset him most was the realization that she was now
profiting from what he had taught her—how to trick her
guardians, how to make excuses for wanting to sleep alone,
how to open the door so that it did not make a sound, how to
employ the juices and herbs he supplied her with, to remove
the tell-tale signs in her smooth neck of the "tooth of love".
These things so got on his nerves that he took the desperate
resolve of telling the husband all the secrets of their amour.
"Unsuspecting spouse of the faithless wife," he begins, and
then goes on:

> Let her not compliment the young and fair,
>   Nor yet, loose-robed, recline with bosom bare;
> Nor wheedle you with nods, nor dip in wine
>   Her finger-tip, and trace the random line . . .

Many a time he, the poet, had pretended to admire the gems and rings that Delia wore, when his real object was to have the opportunity of clasping her hand in a meaningful squeeze. Many a time he had plied *him* with wine, while he made sure that his own glass was replenished with nothing stronger than water, which had enabled him to keep sober and awake when the husband slipped under the table. "And do you remember that time when your dog kept you awake all night with his barking? He was barking at *me*!"

"Delia goes to attend the rites of the *Bona Dea*, does she? That's bad. No males are admitted into the temple of the Good Goddess, *or so they say*. Why not entrust her to my keeping? I wouldn't let her out of my sight; I would follow her right up to the altar, and not mind in the slightest if the frenzied women tried to scratch my eyes out." Perhaps this was too much to expect, but after all,

> What boots a charming wife you can't retain?
> Surely the locks are on your doors in vain.
> She clasps you, sighs for other youths at once,
> Then feigns a headache . . .
>
> Even now an anxious lover, nor in vain,
> Besets your door, peeps in, sneaks back again,
> Pretends to pass, walks on a few yards more,
> Runs back alone and coughs before your door.

In one way or another the affair came to an end. Delia fades out of the picture, and we may discover nothing of her later years. Nor is there much more known about Tibullus, except that Delia's place seems to have been shortly taken by a heartless charmer named Glycera, who in turn was supplanted by a girl who called herself Nemesis—an obviously fictitious name that suggests a lowly rank in life—and from what he tells us about her seems to have been a professional courtesan of the most rapacious kind. Once he refers to her as a woman "with hollowed palm that ever craves for gold".

Somewhere in the background was a sister of Nemesis's, who died as a little girl—apparently by falling or throwing herself out of a window. Tibullus was very fond of her. "For me," he writes, "she is divine, and to her tomb I will fly and, sitting in the dust beside it, bewail my fate." *His* fate, be it noted, not hers; he was always inclined to self-pity, and we may be right in detecting in his poetry a tubercular strain. Elegant and handsome, he was also physically frail; he must always have a woman to cling to, much as Chopin and de Musset clung to George Sand, and in the end the woman proved too much for him, with her robust inclinations and performance.

"How lucky you are," wrote his friend the poet Horace to him on one occasion. "The gods have given you wealth, good looks, and the capacity to enjoy them. *Your* purse hasn't got any holes in it! But if you take my advice you will go slow with the girls. Avoid emotional entanglements as you would the plague . . ."

In his latter years Tibullus returned to the peaceful country-side at Pedum, not twenty miles from Rome, which he ought surely never to have left, and there he died in 19 B.C.

VI

Horace's Sweethearts

WAS HORACE EVER REALLY in love? The tubby little fellow was fond of feminine company and clearly had a way with the ladies. He wrote charming verses to them and about them (and sometimes verses that were not so charming). He invited attractive girls to spend a week-end or a few days on his Sabine Farm. He was glad of a seat at a dinner-table when he was placed next to a flirtatious little piece who had an easy tongue in conversation and knew how to hold her wine. Sometimes he was elated when a bright pair of eyes looked saucily upon him, or there was a special warmth in a woman's handshake, or she let fall some remark that had a suggestive hint of romance in it.

But in love, really in love? It is hard to imagine him caught up and swept away in such a passion as engulfed Catullus, or sharing in the mournful laments of a Tibullus, or experiencing the fierce desire for possession of a Propertius. It is hard to believe that he ever ran wild through the streets at night, hammered at some reluctant woman's door, risked injury and insult just for the sake of a light o' love. Surely he was much too urbane for that sort of thing, too worldly wise, too well versed in the ways of the world. He would have laughed at such capers. He was frank, brutally frank, about the absurdity of getting into trouble for a woman who was, after all, only one among a whole host of possible charmers. Watch your step, he advised; keep away from women who are married or too closely guarded. Why take such pains to obtain so hard a prize? Why—when there are lots of other girls equally pretty, equally charming and accomplished, and ever so much more accessible—women who will come at your call and give you all you can want without delay or fuss, and without running you into a lot of unnecessary expense?

Quite possibly Horace himself would have resented this valuation of his character. He professes to have had a "mad passion" for one damsel, upbraids another for her fickleness, complains bitterly of being shunned by another. But it is his own fault if we decline to take him seriously. His loves are too numerous, too quickly changed, too lightly dealt with. So much so that more than one of his editors have maintained that his amatory verses are nothing more than graceful poetical exercises and that the ladies they celebrate never existed outside his own brain. True it is, indeed, that as Sir Theodore Martin wrote, "we are absolutely without any information as to these ladies, whose liquid and beautiful names are almost poems in themselves".

About Horace himself we know quite a lot. Most of our information is derived from what he tells us in his writings, but there are also frequent references to him in the other literature of his time, for he made many friends who thought well enough of him to sing his praises. Quintus Horatius Flaccus his full name was, and he lived from 65 B.C. to 8 B.C. He was not a Roman by birth but came from Venusia, in southern Italy, and was the son of a freedman who was a tax-collector in the civil service. From what his son says about him he must have been an excellent fellow, and it is one of Horace's most engaging characteristics that he never shows the least shame in his father's servile origin and lowly way of life but goes out of his way to commend him. Horace was given a first-class education, at Rome and at Athens; and it was while he was in Greece that he joined the army of Brutus and the republican chiefs who had murdered Julius Caesar, and was present at the battle of Philippi in 42 B.C. He fought ingloriously, he admits; he ran away before

Octavian's troops as fast as his legs would carry him, and left his shield behind in the rush.

On returning to Italy he found his small family property had been confiscated, and he went to Rome where his poverty drove him to write verses as the only way open to him of getting a living. By a stroke of exceeding good fortune he was introduced by Virgil (five years his senior) to Maecenas, the immensely rich minister of Octavian, who was already the head of the Roman state and was before long to become the Emperor Augustus. Maecenas took him under his protection, and thus he obtained admittance to the Augustan circle of literary men.

About 33 B.C. the great man gave Horace a small farm near Tibur in the Sabine country, which became the source of so much happiness to him and the inspiration of many of his best verses. Here he built a villa, or enlarged a building already there, and became the master of an establishment of five families of free farmers and eight slaves. The place was in the heart of a wildly beautiful countryside, and yet was only thirty miles from Rome, thus enabling its fortunate owner to visit his friends in the capital whenever he pleased.

Those whom Horace invited to his "happy little Sabine nest" can have had small reason to complain of their reception. Many of them, as already indicated, were women, the kind of gay, accommodating damsels with whom he was most at his ease. "Roll out the barrel!" he writes to a certain Lyde; "fetch down from the loft the wine-cask that has been maturing there since the day Bibulus was elected consul. Bring your harp with you, and, since it will be Neptune's feast-day, sing songs about the green-haired Nereids who inhabit his watery realm. And when night falls we will join in the hymn that Venus loves!" Another of his invitations was extended to the fair Tyndaris, to "come, and whatever I have shall be thine!" And yet another was to Phyllis, a girl who had committed the absurd indiscretion of falling in love with a man far above her in social status. Let her join Horace, and forget:

> I have laid in a cask of Albanian wine,
>   Which nine mellow summers have ripened and more;
> In my garden, dear Phyllis, thy brows to entwine,
>   Grows the brightest of parsley in plentiful store.

This last letter was framed as an ode in honour of his patron Maecenas, and how that richly experienced old aristocrat must have grinned when he read his copy, and learnt that this was Horace's "latest treasure—his final love!"

"My rustic Phidyle" was another of Horace's lady friends: she may have been some farmer's daughter who had felt the appeal of the famous author on holiday from the great city. "I can't put two lines together," he writes again to Maecenas; "I am racked with love for Phryne, a freedwoman, a mistress who isn't content with just one admirer. That's why I haven't been able to finish that poem I promised you".

To another of his friends he complains that he has no longer any heart to write tender verses, not since his "mad passion for Inachia" was brought to a conclusion; "all those highly recommended remedies for thwarted love have done me no good; my shame has gone, and I have given up trying to compete with unworthy rivals, but my heart is still filled with rage".

One of the most charming of his Odes is addressed to a girl named Chloe, and this is Sir Theodore Martin's rendering:

> Nay, hear me, dearest Chloe, pray!
>   You shun me like a timid fawn,
> That seeks its mother all the day
>   By forest brake and upland lawn,
> Of every passing breeze afraid,
>   And leaf that twitters in the glade.

Let but the wind with sudden rush
   The whispers of the wood awake,
Or lizard green disturb the hush,
   Quick-darting through the grassy brake,
The foolish frightened thing will start,
   With trembling knees and beating heart.

But I am neither lion fell
   Nor tiger grim to work you woe;
I love you, sweet one, much too well.
   Then cling not to your mother so,
But to a lover's fonder arms
   Confide your ripe and rosy charms.

Now it is "Glycera's radiance that fires me. She gleams fairer than Parian marble. She's burning me up! Her charming perversity . . . her face, really it is too dazzlingly dangerous to look upon!" Now he is so sorry for girls like Neobule, who are kept at home under the strict eye of a guardian so that they can never get out to play in the game of love. Neaera has broken faith with him: had she forgotten that night beneath the stars, when, clinging to him more tightly than the ivy to the oak, she had sworn to be his as long as the winds should blow? Barine had proved faithless, although she had vowed fidelity on the ashes of her mother; now she was flashing her beauty abroad, attracting the attention of all the bright young fellows of the town. Pyrrha was another girl who had loved and left him, and Horace wrote an ode to her that Milton translated, not too happily:

What slender youth (it begins) bedewed with liquid odours,
Courts thee on roses in some pleasant cave,
   Pyrrha? For whom bind'st thou
   In wreaths thy golden hair,
Plain in thy neatness? . . .

Then there was Lydia, who had thrown him over for a certain Telephus. "When you praise his rosy neck and wax-white arms," he tells her, "my bile rises, the colour fades from my cheeks, the tears begin to flow. Imagine my feelings when I see the bruises on your white shoulders, the marks the lustful brute has left on your lips!"

There is a dialogue between Horace and Lydia that has proved a tempting challenge to the translators; here is Robert Herrick's version, made in 1627:

Horace. While Lydia I was lov'd by thee,
Nor was any preferr'd 'fore me,
To hug thy whitest neck: Than I
The Persian King liv'd not more happily.

Lydia. While thou no other didst affect
Nor Cloe was of more respect;
Then Lydia, far-fam'd Lydia,
I floursh't more than Roman Ilia.

Horace. Now Thracian Chloe governs me,
Skilfull i' th' Harpe, and Melodie:
For whose affection, Lydia, I
(So Fate spares her) am well content to die.

Lydia. My heart now set on fire is
By Ornithes sonne, young Calais;
For whose commutuall flames here I
(To save his life) twice am content to die.

Horace. Say our first loves we sho'd revoke,
And sever'd, joyne in brazen yoke:
Admit I Cloe put away
And love againe love-cast-off Lydia?

Lydia. Though mine be brighter than the Star;
Thou lighter that the Cork by far;
Rough as th' Adriatick sea, yet I
Will live with thee, or else for thee will die!

Was this the same Lydia whom he taunts, in the most ungallant fashion, with approaching old age? "More and more seldom do the saucy young men shake your shutters with their knocks, demanding to be let in. The door which used to move so easily on its well-oiled hinges now stays shut. Your sleep is undisturbed by such laments as 'Lydia, are you sleeping when I, your love, am pining the whole long night through?' In your turn you will become an old woman, and, with a heart still capable of passion and full of feverish desires, will be obliged to seek your lovers in dark and lonely alleyways, and when you are pushed aside and rebuffed will weep with frustration and humiliation."

This is bad, but there is worse to follow, for there is one of Horace's *Epodes* that is so nasty that it is generally omitted from the translations; it is No. 8, "Upon a wanton old woman", and begins, "Can you, grown rank with lengthening years, ask me what has unnerved my vigour?" Then the poet goes on to detail her physical defects: "your teeth are black, your brow withered with wrinkles, your back sinks between your staring hip-bones like an old cow's, your chest is fallen and reminds me of a broken-backed horse, your knees are feeble, your body flabby supported on swollen legs . . ."

This is in the most shocking bad taste, but almost as bad is the Ode in which Horace addresses "Lyce, now growing old"; these lines are from the translation by the eminent Classical scholar John Conington:

> The gods have heard, the gods have heard my prayer;
>   Yes, Lyce! you are growing old, and still
>   You struggle to look fair;
>   You drink, and dance, and trill
> Your songs to youthful love, in accents weak
>   With wine, and age, and passion. Youthful Love!
>   He dwells in Chia's cheek,
>   And hears her harp-strings move,
> Rude boy, he flies like lightning o'er the heath
>   Past withered trees like you; you're wrinkled now;
>   The white has left your teeth,
>   And settled on your brow.

> Your Coan silks, your jewels bright as stars—
>   Ah no! They bring not back the days of old,
>   In public calendars
>   By flying time enrolled.
> Where now that beauty? Where those movements?
>   Where that colour? What of her, of her is left,
>   Who, breathing Love's own air,
>   Me of myself bereft,
> Who reigned in Cinara's stead . . .

Cinara . . . this was the only woman for whom Horace, says Sir Theodore Martin, ever had a feeling which deserved the name of love. She was "his one bit of romance", and his love for her was tinctured with melancholy, for she died young. Once he refers to her as the "rapacious fair one", and in a letter to Maecenas, written years after she was dead, he reminds him of

> The woes blabbed o'er our wine, when Cinara chose
> To tease me, cruel flirt—ah, happy woes!

But "Gentle Cinara" is how he remembered her best and longest.

> But Fate to Cinara gave
> A life of little space;
>   And now she cheats the grave
> Of Lyce, spared to raven's length of days,
>   That youth may see, with laughter and disgust,
>   A firebrand, once ablaze,
>   Now smouldering in grey dust.

Poor Lyce!

VII

Golden Cynthia

GOLDEN CYNTHIA! IN PROPERTIUS's elegies she is preserved for all time, in all the beauty, the ardour and the changefulness, that was hers. According to tradition, her real name was Hostia, and she is thought by some to have been a lady of good family, while others maintain that she was a freed-woman.

Whatever her origin, she was a courtesan of the most superior sort, with her own house in the Suburra quarter of Rome, staffed by a number of slaves. She was strikingly beautiful and accomplished, and she was capable of a measure of disinterestedness rare in a woman of her profession. This is shown most clearly in her relations with Propertius. The first advances seem to have come from her, and the poet was not at all well off.

Sextus Propertius was born in Umbria, probably in Asisium (the modern Asisi) about the middle of the last century B.C. His father had died when he was a child, and most of the family estates had been confiscated in the civil wars. Sent to Rome to study for the bar, he took to writing verses instead. Some of these came to her notice, and she was able to appreciate them as she was a bit of a poetess herself. He joined the circle of her admirers, she encouraged him in his versifying, and was flattered when he made her the subject of some of his most charming lines. She was his senior by several years; he was a young man in the springtime of fancy, and before long he was head over heels in love with her.

Cynthia is the first word of the first poem in the small book of elegies that made his name—and hers. It was published (by which is meant that it was written by hand on sheets of papyrus stuck together to form a long roll, and then sold over the counter by booksellers) in about 26 B.C. Most of the twenty-two poems contained in this first book treat of his affair with Cynthia, and her name appears to a lessening extent in the three succeeding volumes, which may not have been published in the poet's lifetime.

It was Cynthia's eyes that had first ensnared him, he tells us. Dark and glowing they were—such eyes that when you looked into them you found it absolutely impossible not to believe what she said! But the rest of her was all of a match. Her long and tapering hands, her tall and Junoesque figure, her stately walk and her hair of reddish gold—the colour that Roman poets raved over and Venetian painters loved to paint.

When he looked at her he found it hard to believe that such charms should have sprung from mortal womb; Helen of Troy had worn that beauty once, and now it had come down to earth again. And yet it was not her beauty that finally enslaved him—not the loveliness of her complexion that he compared to rose petals dipped in milk, not her glorious hair flowing down the smooth column of her neck, not even the glowing torches of her eyes. Not these, but the accomplishments that made her a woman beyond compare. To quote James Cranstoun's translation:

> Or if, perchance, she strike the speaking lyre with ivory fingers,
>   I marvel how those nimble fingers run the chords along:
> Of if above her slumber-drooping eyes a shadow lingers,
>   My trancèd mind is sure to find a thousand themes of song.
>
> Or if for love's delightful strife repose awhile be broken,
>   Oh! I could write an Iliad of our sallies and alarms;
> If anything at all she's done—if any word she's spoken—
>   From out of nothing rise at once innumerable charms.

When the little book was published, the affair had been

going on for a year or more, and "still there is no end to my madness". At first he had tried to avoid a too close involvement, even after they had become lovers, and she also was not sure of her own mind judging from his complaint that "we have spent no more than a night or two in love, and already you tell me that I am not all that you expect in bed!" Some of his friends also endeavoured to dissuade him from getting entangled with an obviously expensive and demanding courtesan. But before long there was a marked change in their relationship, and even if he had wanted to escape he would have found it impossible. Her magic was far too strong.

If there had been something lacking in their first embraces, this must have been soon remedied under the woman's expert tuition. "Oh, what a happy man I am!" begins one of his poems:

> O bliss! O charming night! O couch thrice dear
> From love delights that all past joys outshone!
> What charming prattle when the lamp burned clear!
> What loving dalliance when the light was gone!
>
> Now with bare breasts she strove, and now delayed
> My eager efforts; then the sweet coquette
> Oped with her lips my sleep-closed eyes and said:
> "Sluggard, is this the way you treat your pet?"

On the morrow of such a night as this he felt "like a god", or as he put it:

> If nights like this she grant me e'er again,
> A single year will be an age to me;
> If many such, I'll be immortal then;
> Even one gives mortal immortality.

But in the very poem that records this night of ecstasy he includes a grumble at his partner because (it seems) she preferred to do her love-making in her chemise and without the light. He thought this most unreasonable.

> Why in the dark the joys of love confound?
> The eyes are aye the pioneers of bliss!

If her figure had been affected by child-bearing he might have understood it, but in fact her breasts were as firm and round as ever. If she insisted in keeping some of her clothes on, he would tear them off her back, and she might in the struggle receive a bruise or two on her arms to show her mother. In the mythological romances, he reminded her, nakedness was ever the rule: "naked was Endymion when he lay with the naked goddess, and Paris himself is said to have been overcome by love when he saw the Spartan, Helen of Troy, rise naked from the couch of her husband Menelaus."

And why was she so silly as to "ape the woad-stained Briton" and add colour to cheeks that surely had no need of it? Far better leave Beauty as Nature made it. Foreign dyes—Belgian rouge and the like—were surely out of place on a Roman woman's face; while as for dyeing her hair . . . words failed him.

Almost one may catch across the gulf of centuries the lady's laugh as she listened to her lover's complainings. But she may well have been really cross when he took it upon himself to remonstrate with her on her behaviour. He objected to her granting her favours to others, did he? The impertinence of it! Why, a husband could hardly be more proprietorial! The poet's verses were very pretty, but they would not help her to pay her butcher's bill, or the baker's, or the dressmaker's. These other lovers of whom he was so jealous paid in hard cash and were well satisfied with value received—they did not whine about trifles and give her a lecture when they had taken their pleasure together. And but for them (she would have him understand) she would not be able to welcome him so often to her board, and her bed.

Of course Propertius could not help himself. Wherever the woman went, she was never far from his thoughts, or safe from his suspicions. When she took a holiday in the country, he congratulated himself that she had gone where there was no risk of her being accosted by young men, there could be no public shows and entertainments to corrupt her morals, nor temples that might afford convenient trysting-places.

But then she decided on a trip to Baiae, the fashionable seaside resort on a small bay to the west of Naples, that had a reputation for naughtiness—the Brighton of the Roman world it has been called sometimes. Here in the season the gay young dogs and the light ladies met and circulated, chattered and flirted and made love with no fear of what people might say or the future had in store. Propertius tormented himself with speculations of her carryings on. How was she passing the time, and with whom? Very likely, at this moment when he was tossing in his companionless bed, she was being escorted by some wealthy admirer to all the gay haunts, or was lying on the beach within arm's reach of some congenial male acquaintance, listening to his silly cooings of affection and more dangerous protestations of love! In a letter to her he protested that he didn't doubt her, but "at Baiae all love's advances give cause for concern. Forgive me if anything I've written seems bitter or suspicious. I can't help myself, for, Cynthia, you are everything to me! So don't stay at Baiae too long. Say good-bye to the gay life there as soon as you can!"

Return she did, and for a time all was well. But their bickering started afresh, and his jealous demands and her occasional rebuffs flamed up into quarrels. Sometimes he resolved to break the chain that bound him, and there is a poem in which he tells how he tried to forget her in the distractions of the town. Then one night—

> Wine-flushed and reeling I had homeward sped,
>   A servant's brandished torch my midnight guide;
> Nor yet had all my wandering senses fled
>   As I with gentlest movement sought her side.
>
> Then Love and Bacchus, gods of iron will,
>   Urged me with double fire to slip my arm
> Beneath her as she lay so calm and still,
>   Kiss her sweet lips, and rifle every charm.
>
> Yet dared I not disturb my darling's sleep,
>   Fearing the bitter taunts I had learned to dread . . .

So he contented himself with gazing into her face, arranged the tresses that had strayed across the pillow, and placed on her head the chaplet of flowers he had brought back with him from the revels. Then bending over her he breathed a prayer that every good gift should be showered upon her, and when she moved in her sleep he started back in apprehension, fearing that she was oppressed by some strange terror or that a phantom lover was possessing her against her will.

Until at length the moon, gliding past the window, cast a beam across her face. She awoke, and, leaning on her elbow, instead of assailing him with the bitter words he had dreaded, gently upbraided him. "So," she said, "you have come home at last, creeping back to my bed when another's scorn has driven you out and shut the door on you! Where have you been in the long hours of the night that you had promised to spend with me? How could you be so cruel? I hope the time will come when *you* have to pass such a night of loneliness as you have made me endure! Last night I kept myself awake as long as I could doing my embroidery, and then turned to my lyre for relief. Ever and anon I moaned softly to myself, thinking of you in another woman's arms, until at last I sank down on my bed and kindly sleep came along. I was still crying when I fell asleep."

Only a little later, however, this tender reconciliation was obliterated by a fresh occasion for jealousy. One of Cynthia's lovers secured almost a monopoly of her affections. He was a praetor or high official in Illyria, on the other side of the Adriatic, and was intending to return there shortly, taking Cynthia with him as his concubine or official mistress. "Have you gone mad?" Propertius protested; "how do you think you are going to stand such a climate, not to mention the perils of the deep in getting there?" The praetor's suit progressed, however, and we find the young poet bitterly complaining that "the tables are laid for feasting, but I am not invited, and Cynthia's door stays open all night, but not for me!" By Jupiter, he reflected, what a shocking thing it was that a man should be able to buy a woman's love in this way! If there were no rich men about, girls would not be tempted to sell themselves for presents, and he would not have to lie awake seven nights in the week, an exile from her bed—that bed in which she was even now clasping a "barbarian" to her breast! "But she's fair—and the fair ones are ever faithless."

This time, however, his worst fears were unrealized. "She hasn't gone!" he writes exultantly. His entreaties and remonstrances must have had their effect, since she had decided to stay at home, and would continue to be his. She said that she loved him, and only him; she had chosen to lie in his arms, even though the couch was poor and cramped, and notwithstanding the tempting offer that had been made to her. "And remember this, it wasn't my money that won her back, for I haven't any. It was just the homage of my verses! After this, no rival will ever be able to steal her away from me. I'm in heaven, walking among the stars. For Cynthia is mine, my very own dearest girl."

Poor deluded young fool! We may suspect that there was a catch somewhere in the praetor's proposals. Very soon we find Propertius railing against his "dearest girl", accusing her of indulging in "nights of shame", making herself the prey of ribald rhymsters, and throwing to the winds all sense of decorum. Once again her door was shut and he would torture himself with imagining her lolling in the arms of another, and he would flounce off and vow that he would put her out of his life and never see her more. But within a few hours he would be hanging about her house trying to have a word with her confidential servant or slave, Lygdamus.

How was she taking their separation, he would enquire of the man anxiously; was she weeping, were the tears raining down her cheeks? Had she done her hair? Was there a mirror near her couch, did her cosmetic-pots look as though they had remained unopened? Had she left off her rings? What was she wearing, nothing showy? And what was the general atmosphere of the place, sad and subdued perhaps, and was she sitting in the atrium surrounded by her maids quietly working at their knitting? We may imagine him firing off his volley of questions, shaking with a nervous irritation, biting his nails, thrusting his fingers through his hair, fearing he knew not what and hardly knowing what he wanted to hear.

Then the tormenting anxieties would be allayed, and their passionate hearts were attuned. One of his happiest poems was penned as a birthday greeting. "My own dearest," it begins, "born under a happy star! May this day pass without a single cloud." Then he maps out a programme for the day, from the time when she gets out of bed and washes the sleep out of her eyes in pure water, does up her shining hair, and puts on the dress she was wearing when he first set eyes on her, until the evening, when they would have dinner together, the wine-cups would be filled again and again, there would be music and dancing and the neighbours would be kept awake by the noise! Then when the last goblet had been drained and her speech had become deliciously wanton, they would celebrate those rites of Venus that the goddess has appointed and approved for the hours of dark.

From what can be made out, the affair lasted for six years or so, although for one whole year they did not see one another. Towards its close it had become a matter of long periods of uneasy truce, interrupted by sprawling battles in which these two self-willed, imperiously demanding spirits struggled for mastery. Often they quarrelled; and not seldom the separation, its cause forgotten, served as a spice for the next savage encounter.

"I'm glad we had that row last night, when, having drunk too much, you shouted insults at me, pushed the table over, and flung a goblet at my head! You can be as angry as you like! Grab at my hair, claw at my face, tear my toga, threaten to burn my eyes out! I like it, I really do! What if my friends at the baths remark next day on the fresh toothmarks on my neck, the bruises on my cheek and arms! A woman must be terribly in love to act like this!"

In the fourth book of the collection Cynthia is mentioned in only two of the eleven poems, but these are among the most important and most unforgettable. One relates a specially squalid and disreputable episode, a night of tumult and outrageous passion.

Cynthia had gone to Lanuvium, a town some sixteen miles from Rome along the Via Appia, where there was a celebrated temple to Juno. She had given as her reason for the trip her desire to perform the rites of the goddess, and it may be that the occasion was the Matronalia, the festival held on the 1st March in each year. This was confined to women, and what is more, to women of good repute; and yet the poet was uneasy. When a lot of women got together, who knows what they might get up to? Cynthia had gone to worship Juno, or so she said; more likely, it was Venus!

Down the road she had driven in her chariot, the wheels whirling madly over the cobbles and she leaning over the pole in a mood of wild excitement. Speeding along beside her had gone a young dandy in a smart equipage, and this had added fuel to the poet's resentment. She had played truant, had she? Well, two might play at that game.

H

Only a few streets away, near the temple of Diana on Mount Aventine, lived Phyllis, a young charmer of his acquaintance who "when she's sober is pretty dull, but when she has had something to drink she's first rate". Then there was Teia, who dwelt near Tarpeia's Grove: "a prettier girl there's none, and when she is warmed with wine she's game for more than one!" He decided to invite the girls over, and very soon they were all three making themselves comfortable on a couch placed in a quiet arbour in his garden. "You want to know how we sat? Well, need you ask: I was in the middle of course."

Time passed very pleasantly. The wine-cups never remained empty for long. A little dwarf from Egypt played on his flute, and Phyllis danced and rattled the castanets while her companions pelted her with roses. But in spite of everything the poet was in no cheerful mood. He could not get out of his head the mistress who had deserted him. The girls sang for him, and he was deaf; they opened their dresses, but he gave their charms hardly a glance.

> I tried the dice for luck with oft-repeated throws,
> By some untoward chance the cursed aces always rose.

Then the lamps flickered, there was the sound of a rasping hinge, a door was opened, and a light footfall was heard approaching. Suddenly Cynthia herself stood there in the doorway, her dress disarranged, her hair in disorder, her face flushed, but how lovely she was in her rage!

Her eyes flash fire, she raves as only woman can.
She thrusts her wrathful nails in Phyllis' face; while wan with fear,
Loud Teia shouts, "From yonder pools bring water quickly here!"
The sleeping Romans ope their eyes in fright, and one and all,
With hurrying feet, dash through the streets to see the midnight brawl.
The quaking pair, with ruffled hair, and tunics flying free,
Rush up the dismal alley to the nearest shop they see.

Now Cynthia revels in the rout; returns, the combat o'er,
And with her vixen hands my face with slaps belabours sore.
She bites my neck—here is the mark—till blood profusely flows;
And still my eyes, that were to blame, receive the heaviest blows.
And when she'd tired her arms, and wreaked her vengeance to the
    dregs . . .
She let me touch her feet at last, and said in words like these:
"If thou wouldst have forgiveness for the wrong that thou hast
    done,
Then list to my conditions as I name them one by one:
Ne'er more in fine attire thou'lt stroll in Pompey's pillar'd shade,
Nor seek the lustful Forum with the combats' sand o'erlaid;
Nor stare round the theatre, neck bent from side to side,
To where the women sit, nor lounge by litter open wide . . .

"Lady, I agree," he said; and she smiled proudly, exulting
in the restoration of her dominion over him. Then,

She smoked each luckless spot whereon my stranger nymphs had
    been,
And then with water from the spring washed all the threshold clean.
The dress and hood I had on she bade me change once more,
And thrice with burning sulphur all my head besprinkled o'er.
The fumigation done, she changed the bedclothes sheet by sheet;
Our quarrel o'er, in bed once more we lay in concord sweet.

Perhaps it was after this deplorable affray that he made a
determined effort to make a final break with the woman
who had captivated him so long. There is a cruel bitterness
in one poem, in which he reminds her that "for five whole
years I have been your faithful and devoted slave, but now I
am leaving you. Don't think to entrap me with your tears:
often they have moved me in the past, but I've seen through
them at last. Not that I shall not shed a few myself . . . But
the memory of what I have been made to suffer at your hands
will stifle my grief at parting". Then he goes on, railing at
the woman who was now not far off middle life: "The day
is coming when you won't be able to hide your real age any
longer! Wrinkles will cover your face and mar its beauty,

and when you look in the mirror you will see any number of grey hairs, far more than you can pull out. When you have turned into an ugly old witch you will be sorry for what you have done . . ."

Did he ever send her this nasty effusion? It is unlikely, for it would seem from the other poem in the fourth book in which Cynthia is mentioned that she had recently died, when they had been living together in her villa beside the little river Anio at Tibur (the modern Tivoli).

That first night after the funeral he could not sleep, and when at last he dropped off he dreamed that Cynthia's sad ghost entered the room where he lay and bent over him where he was tossing and turning in a broken slumber. Her hair and eyes were as he had seen them last, but her dress was charred by the flames of the funeral pyre, and the beryl ring that she habitually wore had been burnt off her finger. The waters of Lethe, the river of Death, had withered her lips; and when she laid her hand on the head of the bed he thought he could hear the bones crackling. And yet, he exultantly realized, *something* had escaped destruction! Death was not the end of everything after all! This pale ghost was the spirit of the woman he had loved and lost, and he thought he heard her voice speaking to him once more.

What was it she was trying to say? She was upbraiding him, as she had so often done in the past, but now there was more sorrow than anger in her complaining. "False heart" she was calling him, and "traitor", and then in the same breath almost was confessing that she had always valued his love and no woman could hope for a lover more true than he had been. But why had he fallen asleep so easily and so soon? Surely he could not have forgotten her already?

> "Faithless," she said, "and faithless still to be,
>   Canst thou already sink in slumber sweet?
> Hast thou forgot our stolen trysts with me,
>   Held nightly in Suburra's wakeful street?

"Hast thou forgot my window worn more wide
    By cunning nightly wiles, and how I'd go
And swing me through it by a rope, and slide
    Hand under hand on to your neck below?

"Oft on the stones we lay in loving guise,
    And sought the lonely nooks to lovers dear;
Alas our secret bond! whose honeyed lies
    Were borne on wandering winds that would not hear!"

Now all that was past and over, and she had been carried
to the grave. Why had he not accompanied her bier? Was
his mourning garb wet with tears? Even if he could not
bring himself to go no further than the door he might at
least have bade the bearers go more slowly down the path.
Surely it was not too much to expect that he should have
flung some fragrant incense into the fire? It would not have
cost so very much to strew a bunch of hyacinths upon the
heap, and break a flask of wine over her ashes!

Then follow some strange remarks that would seem to
indicate that Cynthia's end had been not only sudden but
tragic, and foul play should not be ruled out. When Lygdamus
had handed her that cup of wine, she had felt ill directly, and
suspected that it contained some drug. That cunning slave-
girl, Nomas, knew such a lot about secret poisons! Once
before she had got away with it when subjected to the ordeal
of being given a hot tile to hold; she had been clever enough
to think of spitting on her hands, and her moistened palm
prevented the burns that would have indicated her guilt.
Don't let her escape a second time! As for Lygdamus, see that
his hide is branded with a white-hot iron!

Another woman was already established as mistress of the
household. Only a short while before she had been selling
her nightly favours, but now she dragged behind her a
golden train. Any of the servants or slave-girls who said a
good word about their late mistress were punished. Old

Petale had taken a wreath to lay on her tomb, and had in consequence been made to carry about with her a log of wood, tied to her ankle. And Lalage, Cynthia's maid, "should she dare to ask a favour in Cynthia's name was flogged with whips of hair". And Cynthia's portrait had been thrust out of its golden frame, and the frame had been melted down in order that "that woman" should obtain a dowry from Cynthia's funeral flames!

"But I don't blame you, Propertius, although you well deserve it. Nothing can alter the fact that I reigned supreme for long in your songs. And now I swear most solemnly that I *did* keep faith with you. If I am telling a lie, may the adder hiss as he glides over my tomb and coils in my ashes!"

Then she charged him, if her words still carried some weight with him and he was not completely enslaved by Chloris (his new mistress?) to be kind to those who had served her well. Let her old nurse Parthenie not want for anything in her old age: "after all, Propertius, she was always kind to you, and not all the time cadging a tip!" And "darling Latris", her maid, could some employment be found for her other than having to "hold up the mirror for another mistress"? And there were all those verses that Propertius had written about her and was keeping in his desk. "I beg you, Propertius, to burn them: don't continue to win applause on my account after I am dead." And yet one thing more: "don't think for a moment that the dreams that reach you from Elysium are delusions! When good dreams come, then believe them to be true."

Now there emerged from the woman's clouded brain the superstitious fancies about the Underworld, the mysterious realm of the Dead, from which Propertius himself was not entirely free. When night falls, she tells him, the sullen Gates of Doom fly open, the ghosts flit earthwards, and through the gloom goes prowling the monstrous shape of Cerberus, the Watchdog of Hades. At cockcrow all the vagrant spirits troop back across the river of the Dead, the boatman keeps a strict tally as they reach the bank, and notes them one by one. "For the present," the ghost of Cynthia tells her lover, "let others have you; but the time will come, and come soon, when you will be mine again, all mine. We two shall lie together, and my bones will cling to yours and nothing shall keep us apart."

Finally, here is Cynthia's last behest, as translated by Professor A. F. Paley:

> Clear from my tomb the ivy, which in chains
> Of straggling stems my gentle bones retains.
> Where orchards drip with Anio's misty dew
> And springs preserve the ivory's hue,
> Write a brief verse, that travellers may read,
> As past my tombstone on their way they speed:
> "*In Tibur's earth here Golden Cynthia lies;*
> *Thy banks, O Anio, all the more we prize.*"

So Cynthia vanishes from the scene. She was surely quite the nicest of the loves of the Roman poets. She was a personality, she had an individuality of her own. From what the poet tells us about her it is clear that she was not only beautiful and clever but warm-hearted and generous, capable of forming and maintaining a sincere and faithful attachment, a woman of spirit and sterling character. Furthermore, so Martial asserted, "it was she who made Propertius a poet".

Of Propertius's later years we know nothing. He may have followed her very shortly to the grave (about 16 B.C.), or he may (as one account has it) have lived long enough to marry and have children, for Pliny, a hundred years later, mentions having met a man who counted the poet among his ancestors. Did Propertius ever realize, one wonders, that it was "Golden Cynthia" who had put *him* among the Immortals?

THE LOVE-HATE OF THE SATIRISTS

VIII

What Martial Wrote about Women

FOR THE ROMAN POETS—Catullus and Horace, Tibullus and Propertius and the rest—Woman (with a capital letter) was something lovely and loving and lovable, even though *women* were often mercenary creatures, wayward and delightful, tormenting and at the same time the most worthwhile and satisfying objects of male desire.

Very different was the attitude of the Satirists, among whom Martial and Juvenal take pre-eminence. For them women were indeed a subject of perpetual interest and concern, but they refused to be led astray by a pretty face or accomplishments of the most consummate art. They took a long look at the Face of Beauty, and on the whole they found it not all that good. It is hardly too much to say that for the Satirists, Woman was if not altogether evil—for no less than other men they were appreciative of the pleasures arising out of the sexual relation—at least a mixture in which only too often the unpleasant ingredients were in excess of the good. On the whole, their attitude may be expressed as one of Love-Hate.

Martial was the man who set the satirical tone. His full name was Marcus Valerius Martialis, and he got the unusual cognomen, or surname, from the fact that he was born on 1st March (Latin, *Martius*, the month of the god Mars). That was in about the year A.D. 40, and his place of birth was the small Spanish town of Bilbilis, near the source of the river Tagus. He was of Iberian and Celtic descent, but his parents were Roman citizens and proud of it. After giving him a good education they sent him off to Rome to make his fortune. There were other Spaniards in the great city, and it was hoped that he would be given their patronage. But when Martial arrived in Rome he found they were out of favour. So he was left to his own resources, and for years life was a hard struggle. The only thing he felt himself any good for was writing, and he managed to keep his head above water by writing verses—short, concise, pithy, pointed and frequently barbed—that gave a fresh meaning to the word epigram. His first emergence as an author of any note was in A.D. 80 when he wrote some smart epigrams on the occasion of the opening of the Colosseum by the Emperor Titus. He followed these up with verses intended to accompany gifts sent to friends (*Xenia*) or presents that might be taken home from banquets (*Apophreta*) at the festival of the Saturnalia. The gifts were of the most varied kind, including playthings, articles of dress, furniture, stationery, works of art, pet animals, and even slaves. Often the verses were only a line or two, and they seldom exceeded twenty lines; they might be compared with the mottoes in our Christmas crackers, except that they are far more pungent and sometimes grossly indecent or obscene.

Altogether Martial produced 1,555 epigrams, that are contained in fourteen books, published at intervals of about a year from A.D. 86. Of this number about a hundred and fifty have been usually decided by his editors to be too dirty to be translated out of the Latin.

After a late start, Martial became famous in his special field of literature, and he was rewarded after the fashion of his age. He was given the quaint honour of *jus trium liberorum,* special privileges accorded to the father of three children. This carried with it the advantage that a man so honoured could not be compelled to get married; Martial chose to remain a bachelor. A little later he was raised to the status of a Roman knight, and of the privileges that accrued Martial probably valued most highly the right to claim a front seat in the theatres, just behind the orchestra.

From what may be gathered, his was not a happy life, and it was largely his own fault. Rather than assert a manly independence, he preferred to be a rich man's client or dependant. Very early he seems to have decided that the world owed him a living, and he complained bitterly when it turned out not to be a good one. He was always cadging from his patrons—a new toga or mantle, a seat at the dinner-table, the *sportula* (literally "little basket") or gift of food and more usually of money in lieu made by a rich patron to his followers —or may we say, his hangers-on. He fawned on the great, kow-towed to the powerful, flattered even such a brute as the Emperor Domitian. Yet he made many genuine friends. He was such excellent company when he was in the right mood. He could keep the dinner-table in a roar, and his fund of good stories was inexhaustible. As time passed, his lot became easier. He was able to afford a comfortable apartment in Rome, and a small country place at Nomentum in the Sabine hills that Horace had loved. But when he felt age creeping on, he got tired of Rome and its constant parties and went back to his own country. The last years of his life were spent at Bilbilis, where he found a good friend in the Lady Marcella, who gave him a small estate on which he could live just as he pleased. And there he died, in about A.D. 104.

Now for his writings, the epigrams that have won him a special place in the world of letters. Martial once protested that his pages might be regarded as wanton but his life was honest. The claim may be allowed, for what we know of him is not to his discredit. The worst that can be said about him is that he looked on life with eyes too clear for sympathy, and described what he saw without pity and without shame. He was a realist of the most extreme kind, a man who shrank from nothing, however dull, coarse, or disgusting it might be thought to be. The one thing he was never tired of looking at was Woman, and here are some of the things he said about her: they are not the worst, but they have managed to get past the censor.

To Catulla. Most beautiful of all women that are or have been, but at the same time the most worthless of all women that are or have been! Oh, how I wish, Catulla, that you could become a little less beautiful and a bit more chaste!

This has been rendered by one translator as:

> So very fair, and yet so very common!
> Would you were plainer, or a better woman!

To Matrinia. You ask me whether I can love an old woman? Of course I can, even a very old woman. But Matrinia, you aren't old: you are a corpse!

To Chloe. I could do without your face and your neck, your hands and your limbs and your bosom, and all the other charms that are yours. Indeed, to save myself the trouble of enumerating them all, I could do without you, Chloe, altogether.

There is another one *On Chloe*:

The shameless Chloe placed on the tomb of her *seven* husbands the epitaph, "The work of Chloe". Could she have expressed herself more clearly?

Several have for their theme the *Choice of a Mistress*:

I prefer a lady, but if such is not available then my next choice would be a freedwoman. A slave only in the last resort; but if her beauty makes up for her want of birth, I would prefer her to either of the others.

I have no fancy for a mistress who is so extraordinarily thin that she can make rings make do for bracelets, who scrapes me with her hard hips and pricks me with her knees, whose loins are as rough as a saw or as sharp as a lance. Yet I have no taste for a woman who weighs a thousand pounds. I am a lover of flesh, not of fat.

I prefer one who is free and easy, and who goes about in the loose robe [of the prostitute]; one who has just granted favours to my young slave; one whom a couple of pence will buy. She who demands a good deal of money, and uses grand words, I steer clear of.

And again, this time addressed to his friend Flaccus, and made into verse by some anonymous translator:

> You ask me, were I to change my life,
> What kind of girl I'd take to wife?
> Not one who coy or easy seems,
> I hate alike the two extremes.
> She satiates me who at first complies,
> She starves my love who long denies.
> The maid must not, I'd call my own,
> Say "No" too oft, or "Yes" too soon.

Several of his epigrams have to do with a lady whom he calls Lesbia, which is probably a pseudonym. "Lesbia protests that no one has ever enjoyed her person without paying for it. True enough: when Lesbia wants a lover, *she* does the paying!" And it is Lesbia who always did her love-making with open doors and windows, so that it would seem that she took greater pleasure in being spied upon than in the act itself. "Yet the common courtesan takes care to exclude every Peeping Tom by curtain and by bolt, and few are the chinks in a suburban brothel. Even the monuments of the dead afford hiding-places for harlots. Does my censure seem too harsh? I do not exhort you to be chaste, Lesbia, but only to take precautions not to get caught!"

As a final dip into the ragbag we have what may be called a note on dress. That Roman women sometimes wore brassières is evidenced by some mosaics discovered at Piazza Amerina, in Sicily, which show a number of girls running, using dumb-bells, playing with a large ball and generally enjoying themselves in physical exercise, who are naked but for small bands of cloth wrapped across their breasts and the skimpiest of loincloths. The house in which the mosaics appear was a country villa of a Roman nobleman of about the fourth century A.D., but some hundreds of years earlier we find Martial discharging one of his barbs at a full-figured woman of his own day. "What you are using to keep your breasts in place is far too small. Nothing less than a bull's hide would be big enough for *that*!"

IX

Juvenal's Gallery of Roman Dames

WHAT MADE JUVENAL SO "down" on women? The fact is indisputable. No writer has said nastier things about them, none has shown himself more bitter and biting in his denunciations of the follies and frailties of the female sex. Why did he do it? Had he been soured by some love affair that went wrong? Was he embittered by some woman who had played him false? Or was there something in his temperament that made him peer too closely at the face of Beauty?

There is no answer to such questions, for the very good reason that really we know very little about the man apart from his writings. Nine "lives" of him have come down to us, attached to manuscripts of his satires, but they disagree in almost every detail. And for the same reason we may be sceptical of the interpretations of his character that have been provided by those who have made him their study. He *may* have been an unbending patriot of the good old Roman pattern, a man who was so disgusted by the contemporary depravity that he was impelled to act the part of a moralist, pillorying the vicious in the hope (if in no confident expectation) of getting them to return to the time-honoured ways of their ancestors. This may have been so, but we have only his word for it. Men's motives are usually mixed, and it is at least possible that Juvenal was actuated in his diatribes not so much by a selfless patriotism as by resentment at being pushed around by men of inferior stamp who had managed to get on in the world and left him standing.

Juvenal (his full name was Decimus Junius Juvenalis) began

writing about the time that Martial left off, about the beginning of the second century of our era. His birth may be placed between A.D. 60 and 70, and he died not earlier than A.D. 128 and possibly as late as A.D. 135. His birthplace was probably Aquinum, a town some eighty miles to the southeast of Rome, and he belonged to the lower middle-class. He is said to have practised law and to have held responsible posts in the municipal government of the place, and as a young man to have served under Agricola in the Roman administration of Britain and in later life to have been banished to Egypt in consequence of an offence he had given to the actor Paris, a favourite of the Emperor Domitian. Yet his writings suggest that he spent most of his life at Rome, following the career of a generally needy and sometimes down-at-heels man of letters.

The time came when he was able to afford a villa at Tibur and a house at Rome in which he entertained his friends, but this was at the end of a long and hard road. "It is no easy matter for a man to live anywhere," he tells us, "when his poverty stands in the way of his deserts. But nowhere is it more difficult than in Rome, where you have to pay a high rent for an attic on the third floor, just beneath the tiles, in a house with cracked walls and a leaking roof, and the whole place so ricketty that it may tumble about your ears at any moment."

And the noise! The huge carts rumbling through the streets all night long (they were prohibited during the day), the foul-mouthed shouting of the carters, the cries of lictors clearing the way through the crowds for their master's litter, the constant chatter and chaffer of a great city. The only people who can get any sleep in Rome, he says, are the rich, since they alone can afford to have plenty of space about them and walls thick enough to keep out the din.

Juvenal was not rich, far from it, and we may wonder why he continued to live there. Very likely he had not much choice. There were no publishers in those days, and an author had to attach himself to a patron who would approve his writings and push their sale among the influential and book-buying public.

But how he hated it, the pushing and shoving to reach the patron's door, the hours of waiting in the outer hall, the scheming to get an invitation to dinner, and the humiliations you had to put up with when you had managed to get one! A seat somewhere near the bottom of the table, where you were lucky if you could catch the waiters' attention. For his lordship, away there at the far end of the room, handsome young slave boys are always running up with flagons of the choicest wines, but down here at this end we get only the dregs, served in a cracked cup. For him, a lordly lobster or a fat goose and all the trimmings; but for us, a crust so hard that it will break your teeth to munch, a mess of greens, and perhaps a portion of pike that has fattened on the sewage that drains down from the Suburra, Rome's densest and filthiest quarter.

Not that the master of the house is niggardly or mean: he is just malicious, taking a keen delight in watching your face fall in the disappointment that you cannot manage to conceal. Then when the dinner is over, there is no litter waiting at the door for you, no obsequious slaves handing you your mantle and seeing you comfortably settled on the cushions. You have to make your way home on foot, through streets that are pitch dark and are infested with footpads and young blades who think it funny to stick their swords into a peace-loving citizen just to see how he jumps!

This was the world in which the supreme master of the art of Satire found the victims of his envenomed pen. If we enquire why he embarked on this potentially dangerous form of literature, we have his own assertion, that it was because he found it hard to write anything else. "Am I to be a listener all my days?" he begins. "Am I never to get a word in? Must

I spend all my life listening to interminable bores, spouting their comedies, mouthing their love ditties, declaiming their epics? Shall I never take my revenge on that fellow who has insisted on my hearing his 'tragedy', written on both sides of the roll and even extending into the margins, and still he hasn't finished?"

This is by way of a joke, however; what really turned him to writing satire was the state of the world and the people in it.

When an effeminate eunuch takes a wife; when a mannish woman goes hunting the wild boar in Etruria, spear in hand and with her breasts showing; when a man who not long ago was a slave and even more recently was lathering your chin in the barber's—when you see him hitching a Tyrian cloak about his shoulders and flashing a gold ring in the sun; when informers grow rich on the ruin of their noble patrons, when complaisant husbands are paid to keep their eyes on the ceiling while their wives are rocking in a paramour's arms; when you are shoved aside in the street by men who have taken that royal road to high preferment, the nightly pleasuring between the sheets of elderly women who are rich but not at all stingy—when this sort of thing goes on, it is impossible to keep quiet!

"You don't believe me when I say that such things happen every day? Well, then, let's take our stand at this street corner and see who goes past. Keep your notebook handy: you will soon find plenty to fill it! Now here's a fellow, being carried along on the shoulders of half-a-dozen sturdy retainers: do you know how he got his money? By the skilful use of a scrap of paper and a moistened seal: he forged a signature and got away with it, and now he's a fine and wealthy gentleman! Now here comes a grand lady indeed: *she* poisoned her husband, and now she's wealthy, and is never at a loss for a friend. And this man riding in state was a proconsul who was sent home and put on trial for extortion, but he employed the smartest of lawyers and now he's enjoying his ill-gotten gains.

And who's this youngster, dashing along in his chariot at breakneck speed? He's squandering the family fortunes on horseflesh and doing his best to impress that flashy little feminine piece in a man's greatcoat sitting beside him.

"If you want to be anybody nowadays you must be prepared to run the risk of gaol or exile. Where do you think men get the money to buy their palaces and parks with, their loaded tables and massive silverware? Where, but from the produce of their crimes! Who doesn't lie awake at night thinking of young wives who have been debauched, of daughters-in-law who have been seduced by money, of adulterers who are still teenagers? However much it goes against the grain with me, I just can't keep my mouth shut. I'm boiling over with indignation and rage and disgust, and it is this that has made me a writer of satire!"

Sixteen of Juvenal's satires have come down to us, and they are indeed a mixed bag of critical portraits, grim epigram, moral preachings and a pessimistic recapitulation of the facets and features of the seamier side of Roman life. The longest and most elaborate and brilliantly executed of the series is the Sixth, which had its rise in the report that a friend of Juvenal's was about to get married.

"What's this, I hear, Postumus, that you are thinking of taking a wife? What on earth has come over you? Surely you must have taken leave of your senses! You cannot seriously be contemplating putting your head in the marital noose! And yet I hear that the marriage contract has been drawn up, you have been to the barber's to get your hair trimmed in readiness for the ceremony, and you have even given the girl a ring! Haven't you a piece of rope handy to hang yourself with, or is there no window you could throw yourself out of, or why don't you take a dive off the Aemilian Bridge?"

Surely Postumus couldn't be expecting to find a bride worthy of his vows? He is actually insisting that she is chaste! What a hope! That sort of thing went out ages ago. In the golden days of the world's innocence there *were* chaste wives to be found, when men lived in cattlesheds, dined off acorns, and slept on beds made of leaves and animal skins. The women of those days weren't in the least like the Lesbia whose eyes were dimmed with tears when her pet sparrow died, or the Cynthia of Propertius's elegies; they were buxom dames who suckled their own babies and never gave a thought to their appearance. This happy state of affairs had not lasted long, however; the first sin to creep into the world was adultery, and the Goddess of Chastity took wings to heaven and stayed there.

"What if this girl of yours *is* a country maiden, and has spent all her life on her father's farm. Don't tell me that nothing happens in those out of the way caves and dells on the mountain side! But even supposing she be all that you think she is, remove her to the town and then see what happens. Have you ever watched closely girls in the theatre when Bathyllus is dancing the ballet of Leda the Swan? That maiden over there—she comes from the backwoods of Apulia and has never been in a theatre before in her life. But see how she is bouncing about in her seat with excitement, now that the amorous god is making his approach— just listen to her squeals of delight! She imagines that a man has got his arms round her already. It is in the theatre that rustic girls learn the ways of love and lovers.

"There's something about an actor or circus performer that makes a strong appeal to women. A comedian's favours can fetch quite a good price; some women prefer tragedians, and others stifle a tenor with their kisses. Then there are the gladiators. Do you remember how Eppia, the senator's wife, ran off with one of them—a man who was no longer young, his face was battered, he had a great wen on his nose and a nasty place on his arm, and his eyes were generally running with rheum. What could she see in such a brute? Yet for his sake she, a woman of gentle birth and upbringing and used to every luxury, abandoned her home, her husband, her children, even her country, since she went off with the man to Alexandria. If her *husband* had ordered her to embark she would have been filled with terror, her head would have gone round and round, and she would have been sick all over the place. But it was a gladiator who made her do it, a man with a sword who had been wounded in the arena. For his sake she stepped on board ship without so much as a murmur, took her meals with the crew in the fo'c's'le, roamed about the deck and was always ready to give a hand with the ropes. (Yet if her precious Sergius had been given his discharge and was in 'civvies', she would not have looked at him twice)".

"But there are some good women about surely? There's Censennia, for instance; her husband is always singing her praises, according to him she is the very best of wives."

"Censennia? You make me laugh! Do you know why her husband says she's so wonderful? I'll tell you: it is because she brought a dowry of a million sesterces [say, £10,000]. That was the price she paid him so that he should always proclaim her chaste! It was not love that made him her adorer but the cash. And now she can have as many lovers as she likes, and right under her husband's nose: he won't mind. A woman with money married to a money-loving husband can do pretty well as she pleases."

All this is by way of introduction, and now Juvenal proceeds to display the portraits that he has assembled in what may be styled his Gallery of Roman Dames. Here is the first— the *Perfect Wife*. She is handsome, rich, comes of a good family, and is an excellent mother. No one has ever dared to cast the slightest aspersion on her matronly honour: in fact she is as chaste as chaste can be, she is a prodigy of virtue as rare in the world as a black swan. Yes, she's good—too good, her husband may well think; one must find it hard indeed to live with such a haughty piece! "Speaking for myself, I would rather wed a wench from Venusia than the Mother of the Gracchi herself!"

Some handsome wives are not satisfied with displaying their good looks but strive to make out that they are clever too. So we have the Bluestocking, the *Learned Lady*. Hardly have you sat down to dinner at her table when she will startle the guests with some such question as, Which is the better poet, Homer or Virgil? She is well up in Palamon's "Grammar", and is always quick to correct a mistake ("but surely a husband might be allowed a few slips in grammar!"). She quotes from books that no one has ever heard of, let alone read. She frames definitions, and lays down the law. Scholars keep their mouths shut in her presence, she silences the philosophers, and not even a lawyer or an auctioneer can get in a word edgeways.

A variant of the bluestocking is the woman who knows Greek, who even though she might boast of coming from Ovid's home town of Sulmo prefers to be taken as a Maid of Athens. She jabbers away in it, although surely it would be preferable to speak Latin, even with a mistake or two. Fears and anger, joys and worries of one kind and another—she knows the Greek for them all, and she even comes out in public with such Greek terms of endearment as *Zoe* and *Psyche*. "My Life" and "My Soul"—faugh, such words ought to be kept for between the sheets!

Now we have the *Bossy Woman*, who even when she is sincerely in love with her spouse cannot refrain from ordering him about, for only then can she be sure that she has him well under her thumb. The more subservient he shows himself, the better the poor chap is, the worse he gets treated. He cannot make a present without her permission, he cannot sell or buy anything unless she has said yes. She chooses his friends for him, and she will slam the door in the face of a man who has been his friend and companion since schooldays. And when it comes to making his last will and testament, he may expect to be given a list of legatees in which appear the names of men he has good reason to suspect are rivals in his wife's affections.

The *Nagger* is just as bad. The bed that holds this sort of wife is never free from wrangling; her curtain-lectures are interminable, she never lets her husband get to sleep before she has had her say. She keeps on and on, accusing the poor fellow of this, that, and the other—of having a mistress or being too fond of boys. When her words fail her, she turns on the tears, and he, poor worm, takes them for signs of affection and kisses them away. But if he were to pry into her desk, what a collection of *billets-doux* he might find there! And even if he were to catch her in the arms of another man, whether a slave or a gentleman, the green-eyed deceiver would not be at a loss. "Didn't we agree when we got married," she will declaim, "that you should go your way and I should go mine? Well then!" There's none so brazen as a woman taken in the act.

If your mother-in-law is still alive you may expect no peace or concord, for it is she who eggs on her daughter to make as much as she can out of her husband, who advises her how to reply to her seducer's love-letters and how to dodge or bribe the guard on the door. When a woman is so vicious herself, how can you expect her to bring up her daughter to behave in decent fashion?

Next, the *Gossip*, the tale-bearer, the tittle-tattler, the woman who seeks to know everybody's business. She thinks nothing of pushing her way into meetings intended for men only, and holding forth there with her husband standing by. She knows everything that is going on—who is in love with whom, who is the young man that all the women are running after, who has got that widow with child and even in which month, and what endearments women use when in bed with their lovers. She was the first to spot the new comet in the sky, and she has advance information of what is afoot in the

Balkans or in China. She picks up all the latest rumours, and when these run short sets one or two going herself. (Just look at her now, jabbering away on that street-corner!)

Now here is the *Quarrelsome Woman*, who is never so happy as when she is engaged in some law suit, whether as plaintiff or defendant, and telling counsel how the case should be conducted. The *Musical Woman*: she is always fondling some instrument or other, running her hands over the strings so to show off her rings, and usually with some performer in attendance. The *Flighty Woman*: it's all very well for your friends to tell you to "put a lock on your door and keep her in," but the question arises, *Quis custodiat ipsos custodes*, "Who is to guard the guards themselves?" Such a wife is cunning enough to know that the first thing in starting an intrigue is to make up to the warders, so as to make them accessories before the fact. One husband is not enough for a woman of this type: even while the bridal wreaths are still hanging in the porch she will be back to her old home, where the bed still bears the impression of her form. The list of her husbands grows and grows: "I know of one woman who has had eight husbands in less than five years—a fact that is surely worthy of being recorded on her gravestone!"

And this one, who is wearing the *endromis* [coarse woollen cloak, or sweater of the athlete: the word also means "sportswoman"], is the *Athletic* type. You should see her in the gymnasium, doing "physical jerks" with the men looking on, practising swordplay with a foil, slashing at a dummy, thrusting, stabbing, lunging ("in—out, in—out!"). What a sight she looks with those bandages wrapped round her legs! What modesty can you expect from a woman who puts a helmet on her head and is always showing off her muscles? Yet this same woman will complain that she finds the thinnest of dresses too hot and that even the finest silk chafes her delicate skin! This sort of woman is a regular visitor to the public baths, especially at night; she loves the bustle and sweat, and when she has tired her arms with the dumbbells it is the turn of the masseur to oil her body all over, finishing up with a resounding smack on her bottom. So pleasantly engaged is she that she has forgotten all about her guests who are waiting for their dinner and feeling famished. At last she makes her appearance, red in the face and full of vim, and tosses off a couple of pints from the wine-jar just to give her an appetite—and promptly brings it up again, all over the floor. Her husband looks on, disgusted, and is hardly able to keep from being sick himself.

Now here are some *Religious* types—some sincere, like the lady who on a winter's morning will go down to the river bank and dip herself in the Tiber, and then crawl, naked and shivering, with bleeding knees, across the Campus Martius —all because she believes that this is what the goddess Isis demands of her; and some whose interest in religion is mainly sexual, who seize the opportunities afforded by the mysteries of the Bona Dea, the Good Goddess, to indulge their indiscriminate lusts. And here are the *Superstitious*, the woman who crosses the palm of an Armenian soothsayer and feels herself well rewarded when, after investigating the insides of a dove or a puppy (or perhaps a boy!), comes up with the promise of a youthful lover; the woman who puts her trust in the prognostications of a Chaldaean astrologer and never takes a step without consulting her pocket-calendar; and the woman who is of the opinion that there's no one quite so reliable as that little Jewess down by the hay-market, who boasts that she is thoroughly "up" in all the "laws of Jerusalem".

These women are mostly harmless, but there are also women of an abominable sort, rich dames who prefer abortion to child-bearing—"Who ever saw a woman in a gilded bed going through the perils of having a baby?"— mothers who expose their infants, wives who administer potions to their husbands to make them mad or amenable or just forgetful of the indignities of married life. And now here is Juvenal's portrait of the *Wealthy Wife*, who can indulge her tastes for flashy jewellery and lavish make-up: the translation is William Gifford's (1802).

> A woman stops at nothing, when she wears
> Rich emeralds round her neck, and in her ears
> Pearls of enormous size; these justify
> Her faults, these make all lawful in her eyes.
> Sure, of all ills with which the state is curst,
> A wife who brings you money is the worst.

What a spectacle her face appears, "bloated and foul and plaistere'd to the ears!" Her husband shrinks from applying his lips to the "detested glew", but she doesn't care. She "rots in filth at home, a very pest, and thinks it loss of leisure to be drest". But she makes a very different showing to her lover: "to the adulterer, sweet and clean she goes."

> For him she breathes of nard, for him alone
> She makes the sweets of Araby her own;
> For him, at length, she ventures to uncase
> Her person; scales the rough-cast from her face,
> And (while her maids who know her now begin)
> Washes, with asses' milk, her frowzy skin . . .

> But tell me yet; this thing, thus daub'd and oil'd,
> Thus poultic'd, plaister'd, bak'd by turns and boil'd,
> Thus with pomatums, ointments, lacquer'd o'er,
> Is it a FACE, Ursidius, or a SORE?

Husbands might do well to have a good look at these ladies, noting how they spend their day. Take this one, for instance, who is feeling distinctly aggrieved because last night her husband turned his back on her. She is now in a towering temper as a result.

All, all is lost; the housekeeper is stript,
The tiremaid chidden, and the chairman whipt;
Rods, cords, and thongs avenge the master's sleep,
And force the guiltless house to wake, and weep.
There are, who hire a beadle by the year,
To lash their servants round; who, pleas'd to hear
Th' eternal thong, bid him lay on, while they
At perfect ease, the silk-man's stores survey,
Chat with their female gossips, or replace
The crack'd enamel on their treacherous face.

No respite yet; they leisurely hum o'er
The numerous *items* of the day before,
And bid him still lay on; till, faint with toil,
He drops the scourge; when, with a rancorous smile,
"Begone!" they thunder, in a horrid tone,
"Now your accounts are settled, rogues, begone!"

But worse remains; for, should she wish to dress
With more than common care, and the time press,
(Whether the adulterer for her coming wait
In Isis' fane, to bawdry consecrate,
Or in Lucullus' walks) the house appears
Like Phalaris' court, all bustle, gloom, and tears.
The wretched Psecas, for the whip prepar'd,
Her locks dishevell'd and her shoulders bar'd,
Attempts her hair: fire flashes from her eyes,
And, " Strumpet, why this curl so high?" she cries,
Instant the lash, without remorse, is plied,
And the blood stains her bosom, back, and side.

Whence came all these monstrous women? If our satirist
is to be believed, they were the product of the long peace
brought about by imperial rule, coupled with the ever-increa-
sing wealth that had enabled luxury to grow and flourish. In
the good old days wives were kept chaste by poverty and
toil and short hours for sleep, their hands were roughened
by labour, their homes were modest huts, and the military
virtues were fostered by the threat of Hannibal's invasions.

Now that Rome had been everywhere victorious, the gates had been flung wide open to admit luxuries and the demoralized and demoralizing rabble of the conquered lands of the Orient. Ever since the day that Roman poverty perished, every sort of crime had become a commonplace.

What are we to make of this tirade? How far may we take Juvenal's denunciations as representing a faithful picture of the Roman society of his day and generation? We may grant him his sincerity, but we must also recognize his lack of historical balance, his absurd belief in a state of primitive virtue, his bitter hatred of foreigners, of the wealthy, of the parvenu in particular. His horizon, too, is limited by his prepossessions of class and status. He says nothing of the great mass of the population, but keeps his gaze fixed on the luxury-loving rich, of whom he was not ashamed to be a lifelong hanger-on. He set himself up to be a moralist, the scourge of vice and crime and wrongdoing, but never does he make a single suggestion for the reform of the manners of the institutions of the day.

"IMPERIAL WHORES"

Fantastic Messalina

THE "WOMEN OF THE CAESARS" have had what we should call
a very bad press. If the reports that have come down to us
are anywhere near the truth, they were almost all a thoroughly
bad lot. They were lovers of luxurious living, extravagant
in their tastes, vicious in behaviour, given to indulgence in
the most infamous pleasures. They were schemers and wire-
pullers of the worst kind. They stopped at nothing in pursuit
of their ambitions, for themselves and their partners in guilt.

Were they really as bad as they are painted in the pages of
Tacitus the historian, Juvenal the satirist, and Suetonius the
industrious collector of inspired gossip? At this distance of
time there is no knowing for sure, and in any case some of the
things said about them that the writers of an earlier age found
so shocking have lost for us their titillating essence. Compared
with the goings-on of Hollywood film-stars and West End
tarts the antics of the ladies on the steps of the Imperial
throne no longer appear so very terrible.

But for hundreds of years the stories have made fascinating
reading, and certainly no account of the sexual manners of the
Roman people would be anything like complete without
them. So we proceed to make the acquaintance of some of
these women whose fatality-charged beauty and vicious
inclinations have left an indelible mark on the pages of Roman
history. To begin with, here is the Princess Julia, daughter and
only child of his Imperial Majesty Augustus, first of the
Emperors of Rome, as described by the eighteenth-century
Frenchman Jacques Roergas de Serviez in the book he wrote

K

on "the Women of the first Twelve Caesars", as rendered into English by Bysshe Molesworth in 1752.

Julia, he tells us, "had great beauty, which a noble negligence in her apparel rather set off than otherwise. She was of a cheerful and most agreeable temper, and her conversation had something in it so lively and charming that all who approached her were delighted with it. To the fire and vivacity of a most insinuating and ready wit was joined so large a store of learning that she was able, with a great deal of judgment, to give her opinion of and even criticize books. A graceful person, a smiling countenance, and irresistible charm accompanied her grand and majestic air, which was without affectation or study; on the contrary, her behaviour and all her actions were softened and embellished by that easy and free carriage which is peculiar to such as have been brought up in high life. Her eyes made as many conquests as they cast glances, so dangerous were they to those who would preserve their liberty; and over her whole person was diffused something so bewitching that it was impossible to resist her. In short, one might venture to affirm that Julia was, beyond contradiction, the most charming lady in the Empire."

Yet her fate was most miserable. She was three times married, each time for reasons of state. Her first husband was Marcellus, her first cousin, whom she wed when she was only fifteen; he died after two years, leaving no issue. Next Augustus married her to Agrippa, his chief minister, who was old enough to be her father; this was in 21 B.C., when she was eighteen. She bore him three sons and two daughters, and even so had time for lovers. When one of these expressed surprise that notwithstanding her infidelities all her children seemed to be very like Agrippa, she is said to have made the coarse rejoinder, that she was always careful "never to take a passenger except when the vessel was full". Agrippa died in 12 B.C. and the following year Julia was married to Tiberius, her father's stepson and his eventual successor on the imperial throne. Tiberius was happily married already, but when ordered to put away his wife and marry Julia he had no alternative. The marriage turned out badly, as might have been expected. A son was born and died in infancy. Tiberius was still in love with his ex-wife, and Julia's gay and pleasure-loving disposition matched ill with his gloomy and sullen humour. Before long they had stopped going to bed together, and then Tiberius went abroad, having fallen out of favour with his father-in-law. Julia was left to lead her own life in Rome, and her conduct was soon notorious.

Probably she was experiencing the change of life, and the furious energy she displayed in the pursuit of lovers was a reaction to the inexorable passage of the years. With Tiberius out of the country and her father remote and preoccupied with affairs of state, there was nobody to keep her in check. She had no regard for what people might say, and in fact did say. She took her lovers in troops; senators, knights, consuls, all were welcome. She, says Roergas de Serviez, "was not one of those nice, scrupulous ladies who make a secret of their amours, and conceal them under a grave and demure exterior, so much precaution would have been an insufferable restraint to her. She published her own infamy, and was the first to make a jest of her debaucheries". She ran wild through the streets of Rome at night with her lovers, and afterwards partook of suppers and entertainments they had prepared for her. She "dishonoured every corner of the town with her prostitutions", and even had the impudence to engage in them on the rostrum from which her august father had published his most severe edicts against adultery; and (following the custom of the lawyers, who placed a crown on the base of the statue of Marsyas, one for each successful case) she took it into her head to deposit there as many crowns as she had taken lovers during the night. At least, this is what was reported of her, and what was carried to the ears of her father.

Augustus was slow to credit the stories that were current about her, and even when the evidence had accumulated he would have spared her the punishment that was her due. At length his hand was forced, when he was reminded of the law that he himself had decreed, that in a case of adultery if the husband refused to take action against his erring spouse, or the father against his daughter, then any other person might do so. At first he seems to have contemplated putting Julia to death, but he finally decided to banish her to the lonely island of Pandateria, off the coast of Campania. Several of her lovers were banished and one was put to death. She was still only thirty-seven, and she lived for another sixteen years, until A.D. 14. Many people were sorry for her, and attempts were made to persuade Augustus to grant a reprieve. When he swore that fire and water should sooner agree than that he should allow her to return to Rome, some bright spirits tried to absolve the Emperor of his oath by throwing lighted torches into the Tiber. The old man was adamant, however, and fearing an attempt at rescue he had her removed to Rhegium, in Calabria, where she might be better guarded. And there this brilliant, beautiful, witchlike daughter of the most powerful man in the world ate her heart out in loneliness and despair.

Julia's elder daughter by Agrippa was also named Julia. This Julia the Younger, as she is styled to distinguish her from her mother, was married to L. Aemilius Paulus, by whom she had a son and a daughter. Not much is told about her by the ancient writers, and what little is said is to her discredit. Like her mother, she became the centre of a group of elegant young men, and before long was reported to have broken the same law which had proved so disastrous to Julia the Elder. She was charged with adultery, and in A.D. 9 Augustus banished his erring granddaughter to the island of Tremerus, off the coast of Apulia. She died in A.D. 28.

The year before her banishment, Ovid was banished to

Tomis, on the Black Sea; and although the reason for this remains a mystery, it has been supposed that he had become involved in some way with the Younger Julia's profligacy. The law under which the woman was condemned made accessories to adultery guilty in some degree, and it may be that Ovid had played the part of a go-between, or, as has been also suggested, had actually witnessed an adulterous act of hers. But it has also been surmised that Ovid's disgrace may have been connected with some indiscretion on the part of the Elder Julia, years before.

After Augustus, his stepson Tiberius ruled over the Empire, and he was followed in A.D. 37 by Caligula, who was the grandson of the Elder Julia, Tiberius's wife. To him succeeded four years later Claudius, who was a nephew of Tiberius, and a man of bookish tastes who had reached the age of fifty before he was placed on the throne by the soldiers who had murdered Caligula. He was married four times, and at the time of his accession his wife was No. 3, by name Valeria Messalina, who was descended from Octavia, the sister of Augustus, and related to several of the most noble Roman families. "The name of Messalina has become proverbial for unblushing sensuality," writes Professor J. B. Bury; "the tales that have been preserved of her vices and her orgies bear on them the marks of exaggeration, but there can be no doubt that her conduct was dissolute and that she exercised an evil influence on the women of Rome."

This is the woman whom Juvenal, writing at the safe distance of some fifty years after her death, castigated in his sixth Satire. Here is the passage, rendered into English verse by William Gifford:

> Claudius had scarce his eyes begun to close,
> Ere from his side his Messalina rose;
> (Accustom'd long the bed of state to slight,
> For the rank mattress, and the hood of night;)
> And with one maid, and her dark hair conceal'd

Beneath a yellow tire, a strumpet veil'd!
She slipt into the stews, unseen, unknown,
And hir'd a cell, yet reeking, for her own.

There, flinging off her dress, the imperial whore
Stood, with bare breasts, and gilded, at the door,
And shew'd, Britannicus, to all that came,
The womb that bore thee, in Lycisca's name:
Allur'd the passers by with many a wile,
And ask'd her price, and took it, with a smile;
And when the hour of business was expir'd,
And all the girls dismiss'd, with sighs retir'd;

Yet what she could, she did; slowly she past
And saw her man, and shut her cell the last.
Still raging with the fever of desire,
Her veins all turgid, and her blood all fire,
Exhausted, but unsatisfied, she sought
Her home, and to the Emperor's pillow brought,
Cheeks rank with sweat, limbs drench'd with poisonous dews,
The steam of lamps, and odour of the stews!

(Britannicus was her son by Claudius, and Lycisca the whore whose cell in the brothel she borrowed.)

For some years Messalina had her own way in everything. She is said to have carried on criminal intrigues with several of the Emperor's freedmen, Narcissus his secretary especially, and enabled them to build up huge fortunes out of the sale of honours and privileges. When Claudius complained one day that he seemed always to be short of money, he was told that he would be rich enough if he were to take one of these fellows into partnership. Messalina's position seemed secured when she bore her husband a son—the first case of a son born to a reigning Caesar. Generally Claudius has been accused of indolence, but it may be that he really cared for his brilliant young wife.

There came a time, however, when Messalina carried her

excesses too far. Having become infatuated with a young Roman noble named Silius, she induced him to divorce his wife and promised to marry him after the death of Claudius, whose constitution was so weak that he could hardly be expected to last much longer. But Claudius was slow in dying, and Silius grew impatient and urged on his paramour the desirability of hastening the process. Messalina showed some reluctance, however, possibly fearing that when her lover had achieved his ambition he would spurn her on account of her licentiousness. Yet, declares Tacitus in his *Annals*, she coveted the name of wife, and taking advantage of Claudius's absence at Ostia, celebrated with Silius the full solemnities of marriage!

"It will seem almost beyond belief," writes the great historian, in his account of the happenings of the year A.D. 48, "that in a city like Rome where everything was soon known to everybody, two human beings could have felt so absolutely secure—that on a specified day, with witnesses to seal the marriage contract, a consul designate (as Silius was) and the Emperor's wife should have met for the avowed purpose of effecting a legitimate marriage; that the woman should have listened to the auspices, have assumed the wedding veil, and have sacrificed in the presence of the Gods; that both should have dined with the wedding guests, kissed and embraced one another in their presence, and finally have spent the night in the licence of wedlock. But I have added not a touch of the marvellous to the story; all that I have written about it is what I have obtained by word of mouth or by way of the written evidence of my seniors."

A shudder passed through the imperial household, Tacitus goes on to relate; there could be no doubt what the sequel of such a marriage would be. All those who were not in Messalina's set feared for their offices and their lives, but only Narcissus was man enough to act. By gifts and promises he induced a pair of concubines, "to whose embraces Claudius

was the most habituated", to undertake the dangerous task of
informing him of what was afoot. Calpurnia, one of the girls,
succeeded in obtaining a private audience with her master at
Ostia, and falling on her knees before him, told him that
Messalina had actually married Silius. Cleopatra, the other
girl, who was standing by, confirmed the extraordinary story,
and they then urged that Narcissus should be sent for. The
man was summoned. "Are you aware," he enquired of his
master, "that you have been divorced by your own wife?
that the people, the Senate, the soldiers, have witnessed her
marriage with Silius? Do you understand that unless you
act promptly, the city will be in the hands of 'the husband of
Messalina'?"

Claudius could hardly believe the story, but when it was
confirmed by others of his household he hurried back to
Rome and put himself under the protection of his guards,
while Narcissus was entrusted with his full authority to bring
the criminals to account.

Meanwhile Messalina was celebrating the vintage festival
at Silius's house. "Never had she given voluptuousness a
freer rein," writes Tacitus. Autumn was at the full. The grape-
juice flowed in streams from the wine-presses, and women,
dressed as bacchantes in animal skins, were bounding round
them in wild delirium. Messalina herself was there with
dishevelled tresses and waving the thyrsus (the ivy-wreathed
rod of Bacchus), and at her side, Silius, with a crown of ivy
on his head and wearing the buskins (the high boots worn by
actors in tragedies) was tossing his head as he acted the part
of the young god. Around them "rose the din of a wanton
chorus". The tale runs that one of the party, in some freak of
humour, climbed into a tall tree, and when asked "what did
he spy?" answered, "a frightful storm coming from the direction of Ostia."

The storm soon broke indeed. When news came of the
emperor's return to Rome, the marriage party hurriedly

broke up, but not quick enough for some of them who were picked up by the soldiers despatched by Narcissus. Silius hurried off to the Forum, where he pretended to be busily engaged in public business. Messalina had still not given up all hope: she trusted in her power over her husband, who was besotted by her charms. She despatched the two children she had borne him, the young prince Britannicus and the princess Octavia, to meet their father and silently to plead their mother's cause. Then she begged Vibidia, the senior of the Vestal Virgins, to implore the Pontifex Maximus (who was Claudius himself) for pardon. After this she went to meet her husband, and, so great and sudden had been the decline in her fortunes, she could find no other conveyance than a country cart that was used for taking vegetables to market. Narcissus intercepted the two children before they reached their father, and told Vibidia that though the Emperor would see her, she would do well to attend to her religious duties. Throughout the proceedings, we are told, Claudius maintained a strange silence until Narcissus took him to Silius's house and showed him in the vestibule heirlooms of his family that "had been requisitioned as the price of infamy". Then indeed he spoke a few words of indignant disgust.

After this Claudius proceeded to the camp of the praetorian guards and ascended the tribunal. Silius was brought before him and, having refused to appeal for mercy, was immediately executed. Several others who had enjoyed Messalina's favour were likewise condemned, including a young knight named Traulus Montanus, described as "a modest but remarkably handsome youth, who had within a single night received his unsought invitation and his dismissal from Messalina, who was as capricious in her desires as in her disdains". Claudius might have spared Messalina if she could have got near him. But Narcissus was taking no chances, and when he heard his master after dinner mutter something about sending a message to the "poor woman" he ordered a tribune to take some soldiers and despatch her. They came up with her in the garden of her country house, with her mother (also a woman of infamous reputation) seated beside her. The pair had been long estranged, but in her daughter's extremity the mother had hastened to join her. Now she was advising Messalina that "life is over and done with: there's nothing left to be done but to die with honour". But, says Tacitus, "honour had no place in that lust corrupted soul", and with tears and lamentations the woman resisted her fate. When, however, she saw the soldiers approaching through the trees with their swords drawn she attempted suicide, and she was pointing the steel to her breast when the tribune ran her through.

When word was carried to Claudius that his wife was dead, he asked no questions but called for another cup of wine and continued with the routine of the banquet. He never mentioned the name of the unhappy Messalina again.

XI

Queens of Nero's Court

ONLY A FEW MONTHS after Messalina's dramatic end Claudius married his fourth and last wife. She was Agrippina, the granddaughter of Julia the Elder and the widow of one Gnaeus Domitius Ahenobarbus, by whom she was the mother of a son, now aged twelve. She also happened to be Claudius's niece, but an obsequious Senate agreed to waive the law against incest in the Emperor's favour.

Agrippina lost no time in inducing her husband to adopt *her* boy as his son and heir to the exclusion of the young Prince Britannicus (so-named on account of the conquest of Britain in Claudius's reign) whom he had had by Messalina. So it came about that Lucius Domitius Ahenobarbus changed his name to Nero, and in A.D. 54 on the death of Claudius (brought about, so it was rumoured, by a poisoned mushroom prepared for him at the instigation of Agrippina) he succeeded his adoptive father as emperor.

At the time of his accession Nero was seventeen, and the year before he had been married to Octavia, the eleven-year-old daughter of Claudius and Messalina, and Britannicus's sister. To begin with, Agrippina acted as regent for her son, but she had many enemies at court, including the philosopher Seneca, who had been Nero's tutor and was now his principal minister. Gradually this woman of beauty and wealth and imperial descent, who was also (to continue with Tacitus's list of adjectives describing her) immodest, of bad reputation, and violent in her demeanour, was edged from the seat of power. She was filled with chagrin and resentment, and at length let fall some unguarded expressions to the effect that in her opinion Britannicus was Claudius's rightful heir. Whereupon Nero took alarm, and the young prince's fate was sealed. The same woman who had prepared the fatal dose for Claudius was called upon to prepare a poison for his son. This was administered to him in a cup of warmed wine while the royal family were at dinner, and in a few minutes he was dead. Agrippina strove hard to control her features, says Tacitus, but a spasm of terror passed over her face: "the precedent for matricide had been set". Octavia, notwithstanding her youth and inexperience, was more successful, but terrified none the less. After a short silence the banquet was resumed, while Britannicus's corpse was carried away to the funeral pyre, which had been made ready in anticipation.

To add to the horror of the event, Tacitus reports that contemporary writers asserted that for several days before the murder Nero had been engaged in deliberately corrupting the young prince, so that "lust had done its filthy work before the poison took effect".

Nero professed deep grief at the so sudden passing of his "brother", and the senators believed him, or said they did. Agrippina now posed as the protectress of the Empress Octavia; but her influence over her son, which had been already weakened by his passion for a slavegirl concubine of the name of Acte, was at an end, and she deemed it advisable to retire into obscurity for the time being. Relieved of his mother's restraining hand (for Agrippina had a proper notion of how an emperor should behave at least in public), Nero abandoned himself to buffoonery, hooliganism, and low debaucheries, as well as pleasures such as singing and playing on the lyre and chariot-racing, which, if not blameworthy in themselves, were undignified in the master of the Roman world.

One of the most favoured of his boon companions was Marcus Salvius Otho, whom Plutarch sums up as "a person of fair extraction, but from his childhood one of the most debauched, voluptuous, and luxurious livers in Rome". Suetonius's description bears this out. "From the very prime of his youth," he declares, in the translation of the Elizabethan Philemon Holland, Otho "was riotous, wild, and wanton, insomuch as his father swindged [thrashed] him well and soundly for it; reported also to use night-walking, and as he met anyone either feeble or cup-shotten or overcome with drink, to catch hold of him, lay him upon a soldier's gaberdine, and so to toss and hoist him up into the air. Afterwards, upon his father's death, a certain libertine [freedwoman] woman of the court, a dame very gracious (because he would make the more benefit by following and courting her as his mistress) he pretended love unto, albeit an old trot she was, in manner doting for age. By her means winding himself into the favour of Nero, he easily obtained the chief place among his minions and favourites (such was the congruence of their humours and dispositions) and, as some write, by mutual abusing also of one another's body against kind [i.e. sodomy] . . ."

Being "privy and party to all the counsels of Nero", Otho (about whom it should be said in fairness that he was exceedingly handsome and wealthy, and in later years displayed some excellent qualities) played a principal part in the intrigues that resulted in the elevation to the imperial throne as Nero's consort of the famous, or infamous, Poppaea.

Tacitus has drawn an unforgettable picture of this remarkable woman. She was a woman possessed of every advantage except one, he says—and that a good character. She came of one of the best Roman families. From her mother, a notorious beauty in her prime, she inherited an abundance of good looks, and her wealth matched the distinction of her birth. She was affable and pleasant, and her conversation was often sparkling. She made a great show of modesty, and practised wantonness on the quiet. When she appeared in public, which was not often, she wore a veil that half covered her face, whether she wished to arouse the curiosity of the beholder or simply because it became her. She was never concerned about her reputation, but in her love affairs she was careful not to be carried away by her passionate inclinations to her material disadvantage.

When very young Poppaea had been married to a Roman noble of the name of Rufrius Crispinus, by whom she had a son, and she was still living with Crispinus as his wife when she was "seduced" by Otho, whose youth, good looks, luxurious way of life, and close friendship with Nero made him a most attractive proposition. This is Tacitus's statement, and his account continues on the following lines. Otho married the girl—her husband having agreed to divorce her, or perhaps he had conveniently died—and was so proud of his new acquisition that he sang her praises when he was in the presence of the emperor; or it may have been that this was no amorous indiscretion on his part but a calculated bid to arouse the emperor's interest in his wife, which might turn out to his own advantage. Often he was heard to say, as he rose to leave the table, that he must be returning to his wife, whose rank and beauty were such as all men desired and only the very fortunate were able to enjoy; and Nero (who was in no hurry to join *his* wife, whose juvenile charms had long ceased to please him, if they had ever done so) was stimulated to seek the lady's acquaintance. Poppaea was admitted to the emperor's presence, and soon succeeded in establishing her supremacy. Now she acted the poor, weak woman who was not able to resist her passion for one who was so handsome; and now, when his lovemaking had become more urgent, she turned coy or haughty or assumed the tone of a modest matron. If he demanded that she should spend more than a couple of nights away from home, she reminded him that she had a husband, and insisted that she valued her union with a man who was princely in dress and demeanour—so very different from Nero himself, who had become so accustomed to the embraces of his lowborn concubine Acte that he had caught from her something that was mean and sordid! In this way Poppaea entrapped the monarch, so that before long he had it in mind to make her his consort.

Plutarch's version of the affair is rather different. According to him, Nero became enamoured of Poppaea when she was Crispinus's wife. "But being as yet respectful to his own wife, and standing in awe of his mother, he engaged Otho underhand to solicit her. For Nero lived familiarly with Otho, whose prodigality won his favour . . ." Otho, we may suppose, was nothing loth; he "was beforehand with Nero, first seducing Poppaea himself, and then, with the hope of Nero's favour, he prevailed with her to part with her husband, and brought her to his own house as his wife". But afterwards "he was not content to have a share in her, but grudged to have Nero as a claimant, Poppaea herself, they say, being rather pleased than otherwise with this jealousy. She sometimes excluded Nero, even when Otho was not present, either to prevent his getting tired with her, or, as some say, not liking the prospect of an imperial marriage, though willing enough to have the emperor as her lover. So that Otho ran the risk of his life, and strange it was he escaped".

On turning to Suetonius we have yet another version, which differs from the others in that it represents Nero as doing the "seducing" in the first place. "Dame Poppaea Sabina," we are told, had been "newly taken from her husband" by the emperor and was his paramour, when he committed her to Otho, "upon trust for to keep, under a colour of marriage", until he had succeeded in putting away Octavia. Otho accepted the lady as his wife, but went much further than had been intended, in that "he alienated her heart from Nero and used her body, and loved her so entirely that he could not endure Nero himself to be his co-rival. Certes, it is thought of a truth, that not only the messengers who were sent to fetch her came again without her, but also

that one time he kept Nero himself without doors standing
there and cooling his heels, with threats also and prayers
intermingled, demanding his pawn [pledge or gage] which
he had left with him, but all in vain".

Whatever the origins of the affair, Nero was resolved to
have the exclusive possession of Poppaea; and since the lady
now insisted on marriage, then marriage it would have to be.
Three people stood in the way, and would have to be
removed.

The easiest to dispose of, or rather provide for in his case,
was Otho. He was appointed to the governorship of the
province of Lusitania (Portugal), "on the shores of the
Ocean", i.e. the Atlantic, and lost no time in getting there.
"This course was thought sufficient," explains Suetonius,
"for fear lest his proceeding to any sharper punishment
might have told tales abroad and marred all the play." Did
he regret his Poppaea? We cannot say, but we are told that
Poppaea, when the Emperor seemed somewhat slow in
keeping his promise to her, demanded that she should be
sent back to her husband across the sea. It is to Otho's credit
that as governor of Lusitania he earned a high reputation
that stood him in good stead when, ten years later, after
Nero's death, he himself made a bid for the throne and
indeed reigned as emperor for a few months in the spring
of A.D. 69.

Agrippina, the dowager empress, proved a much more
difficult obstacle. She still retained, or perhaps had regained,
some measure of influence over her son; and one of the nastier
tales told about her is retold by Tacitus, to the effect that so
anxious was she to keep her influence that on several occasions
at midday, when Nero was filled with the warmth of wine
and good cheer, she appeared before him, dressed in the
height of fashion and quite ready to commit incest if it might
serve her ends. Some of the emperor's advisers were so unnerved by her appearance, especially when she covered her

Above, Woman, Wine, and Song. A wall-painting from Pompeii, now in the National Museum at Naples, showing a scene beloved by Roman poets. *Below*, this fresco of a Bacchanalian orgy was found in the Villa Pamphili in Rome in 1787 (Alinari and British Museum)

Left, Fresco showing a woman tempted by Cupid (Alinari and British Museum). *Below*, Compartments in a Pompeian lupanar, or brothel

son with "lascivious kisses and endearments", that they
enlisted the good offices of Acte, the former slave-girl who
was Nero's favourite concubine. Tacitus adds that according
to one account it was Nero who made the incestuous advances,
but the balance of opinion among the authorities he had
consulted led him to believe that it was Agrippina who took
the initiative. After all, she had already committed incest
once when she had married her uncle Claudius, and ever since
she was a girl she had been suspected of amorous intrigues
of one kind or another.

Try as she might, however, Agrippina was soon made
aware that she was fighting a losing battle. All her fair-
weather friends fell away, and she was left alone to face her
son's malice. Still she opposed to the utmost the proposed
marriage of Nero and Poppaea, until the latter's patience was
exhausted. The emperor, driven to fury by his mother's
taunts, resolved to arrange her assassination. The method
proposed was most ingenious: a vessel in which she should
be induced to make a sea trip was fitted with a weighted
canopy that might be let fall and sink the ship.

The dowager empress embarked in the vessel—on a starlit
night and with a calm sea, reports Tacitus—and as had been
arranged the canopy fell and the boat sank. But Agrippina
was not killed as had been anticipated; she escaped over the
side and started to swim vigorously for the shore. One of her
maids who with a view to saving her own life cried out,
when she was struggling in the water, "Help! save me, I am
the empress", was promptly struck on the head with an oar
by one of the men in the plot, and was drowned. Agrippina
got safe to land, and took refuge in a villa, whence she sent a
messenger to inform Nero of her fortunate escape. Nero was
aghast. Without a moment's delay he despatched a trusted
officer—Anicetus, captain of the fleet at Misenum—to
assassinate her. As the man approached she bared her body
and screamed, "strike the womb that bore Nero!" He thrust

L

her through with his sword. Meanwhile Nero had announced
that his mother had become involved in a plot against him,
and that he had been obliged to have her killed in self-
defence. Once again, his extraordinary luck held, and he was
deluged with congratulations from a servile Senate and
people on his narrow escape.

Only Octavia now remained between Poppaea and the
satisfaction of her ambition. Nero had never loved the girl,
and she may well have taken offence, and shown it, at his
rough and rude embracings. He for his part could not forget
that her birth was far superior to his own. Even so, it was
Poppaea who forced his hand. This woman who, as Tacitus
says, had been long his paramour and had dominated him
from the first, now incited one of Octavia's domestics to
accuse her of having had a love affair with a slave—a man
named Eucaerus, a native of Alexandria and a skilled performer on the flute. As was the custom when such a charge
was preferred, her waiting-maids were examined under torture; some of them were forced by their agony into making
groundless admissions, but the rest, and they were the greater
number, persisted in asserting the honour of their mistress.
On such evidence there was no ground for putting Octavia
to death, as Poppaea had wished and intended, but she was
divorced on a pretext of barrenness. Shortly afterwards she
was banished to Campania and put under military guard.

The divorce was very unpopular with the common people;
and when a rumour spread that Octavia was about to be
recalled and reinstated as empress exulting crowds rushed to
the Capitol, flung down the effigies of Poppaea that had been
erected there, and replaced them by garlanded statues of
Octavia. The rumour was false, and Nero had already wedded
Poppaea. But the outbreak played into Poppaea's hands; she
threw herself on her knees before Nero and induced him to
sanction a further attempt at securing Octavia's condemnation
on a capital charge. A plot was concocted, in which the

principal part was to be played by Anicetus, the officer who had murdered Agrippina at his master's behest. He was summoned to the emperor's presence, and was told what was now expected of him. Not murder this time; cold steel was not required, and even force might not be necessary. All he was required to do was to admit an act of adultery with Octavia . . . If he agreed, he would be amply rewarded. And if he refused? Why, then he might expect death, and that speedily.

Anicetus had been so hardened by previous crimes that he at once consented to do all that was required of him; indeed, he "confessed" and invented more than was necessary, in the presence of a special privy council summoned by the emperor. After which he was banished to Sardinia, where, states Tacitus, he endured a not impecunious exile and died a natural death.

Nero then issued a proclamation that it had been discovered that his ex-wife Octavia had seduced the prefect in the hope of securing the aid of his squadron in her escape—that she had procured an abortion (only a short while before Nero had been complaining of the girl's sterility!)—and that these facts had been ascertained by himself. He then ordered that she should be banished to Pandateria (the same island to which Augustus had banished Julia).

After a few days of indignity, she was done to death. The story in Tacitus's sober prose makes horrible reading. She was first tied up with cords, and then a vein was opened in each limb. But the blood, arrested by fright, flowed too slowly, and the girl was then thrust into a vapour-bath and was soon stifled by its fumes. Then as a further piece of atrocious cruelty, her head was cut off and taken to Poppaea in the palace at Rome. In this fashion died Octavia, an emperor's daughter and herself an empress, when she was still little more than twenty.

Poppaea had achieved her ambition. She was empress, and

those who had stood in her way to the imperial throne had been extinguished. Her triumph was rendered even more complete when she gave birth to a child, a daughter, who was named Claudia, and was immediately honoured with the title of Augusta. But very shortly the child died, and joy was turned into mourning. Two years later, in A.D. 65, when she was again with child, she herself met her end. Tacitus says that it was through a chance outburst of anger on Nero's part: he felled her with a kick when she was pregnant. Some people were of the opinion that she had been poisoned, he goes on, but he did not believe this, for Nero was very desirous of having a child and was still passionately in love with his wife. Suetonius for his part asserts that Nero "loved the dame Poppaea entirely", but "even her also he killed with a kick of his heel, for that, being big with child and sickly withal, she had reviled him and given him shrewd [scolding] words for coming home so late one night after his running with chariots". A splendid funeral was accorded her, and after her body had been embalmed it was laid in the mausoleum of the Julian house. Nero delivered a panegyric in which he praised her beauty and accomplishments and other gifts of fortune which (says Tacitus) did duty in her case for virtues.

In history she has her place as the most wicked of beautiful women, the Queen of the Imperial Whores. And yet we know so little of her as a woman. We know she had hair that glowed with an amber tint, for Nero wrote verses on it. She liked looking at herself in her mirror, and liked what she saw, as other people did too. She dressed in the height of fashion, and spent large sums on her clothes. She loved jewellery, and made a great display of it. She spared neither cost nor pains to preserve the beauty with which Nature had endowed her. She employed the most costly washes and perfumes for her skin, and pomades for her hair. She had been told that asses' milk was beyond compare for preserving the skin and keeping it free from wrinkles, and so she maintained a troop of five hundred she-asses that had just had young and were milked every day to make a bath for her. From their milk also she invented, we are told, a kind of ointment to preserve beauty, that was called *poppaeanum* after her. These milk baths of hers have won the admiration of the makers of spectacular films, and to bathe in asses' milk has become almost a synonym for unbounded extravagance and luxury. In our eyes it will not appear so very dreadful. Indeed, if she were living today and went in for this sort of thing she might well become the pin-up girl of the dairying industry.

After Poppaea there were empresses in Rome for nearly three hundred years, and not much that we are told about them is to their credit. Indeed, if we are to believe the chroniclers most of the ladies who were placed on the pinnacle of Roman society were disreputable. There is nothing about most of them to invite closer acquaintance, but perhaps mention should be made of the two Faustinas, mother and daughter, who were the consorts respectively of Antonius Pius (reigned A.D. 138–161) and Marcus Aurelius Antoninus (161–180). Both ladies were of extraordinary beauty and, from what we are told, unprincipled morals; there is also not the least doubt that they were both deeply loved by their husbands, who rank among the most worthy of the Roman emperors.

Of the two women, the younger is the better known, since she has had the misfortune of being made the subject of a paragraph in Gibbon.

"Faustina, the daughter of Pius and the wife of Marcus," he writes, "has been as much celebrated for her gallantries as for her beauty. The grave simplicity of the philosopher was ill calculated to engage her wanton levity, or to fix that unbounded passion for variety which often discovered personal merit in the meanest of mankind. The Cupid of the ancients was, in general, a very sensual deity; and the amours of an empress, as they exact on her side the plainest advances, are seldom susceptible of much sentimental delicacy. Marcus was the only man in the Empire who seemed ignorant or insensible of the irregularities of Faustina . . . and in his *Meditations* he thanks the gods, who had bestowed on him a wife so faithful, so gentle, and of such a wonderful simplicity of manners." To which passage there is appended a typically Gibbonian footnote: "The world has laughed at the credulity of Marcus; but Madame Dacier assures us (and we may credit a lady) that the husband will always be deceived, if the wife condescends to dissemble." It is only right to state that Professor J. B. Bury, Gibbon's modern editor, holds that there is no trustworthy evidence of the truth of the charges that have been brought against her. And one thing stated about her is certainly true, that she bore her husband Marcus Aurelius thirteen children.

Unfortunately included in the number was Commodus, who followed his father on the throne; he turned out to be such a bloodthirsty villain that the story was put about that he was not the son of Marcus Aurelius but of one of the gladiators who were favoured by Faustina.

When every allowance has been made for prejudice and malicious gossip it would seem that there is a good deal of truth in the picture of Roman empresses given over to profligacy. They flourished at a time when women of the upper classes had been emancipated to a degree never seen before and seldom since. The Women of the Caesars were at the top of the social tree, and their conduct was correspondingly unrestrained. There was no place for them, or for any other women, in political life, but they could, and did, exercise great influence in "pillow politics". The Roman was not an hereditary monarchy. Of the first twelve Roman emperors only one succeeded his father, and in the selection of the rest a great part was played by the imperial women who were at the heart of power. In the circumstances it is hardly surprising that they tended to display a capacity for intrigue, a thirst for excitement, and a resolve to obtain through (and for) their menfolk a position of enormous prestige and irresponsible power.

RELIGION AND SEX

XII

The Virgins of Vesta

RIGHT IN THE CENTRE of ancient Rome, where the Via Sacra led into the Forum, stood the Temple of Vesta, goddess of the Blazing Hearth, the spirit of warmth and comfort and all the good things of Home. Within it there was an altar on which burned a Sacred Flame, and for many hundreds of years, in republican times and much later, it was generally believed that the welfare of the City and the State depended on the maintenance of this fire. The solemn responsibility of seeing that it never went out of itself was entrusted to a band of virgin priestesses, whose establishment, known as the *Atrium Vestae* ("Hall of Vesta") or *Domus Virginum Vestalium* ("House of the Vestal Virgins") stood just across the way.

In all the long history of Roman religion no image was ever made of Vesta, whether in marble or ivory or precious metal: as Ovid expressed it, she was "none other than the living flame". And she had no other temple than this, nor did she need one, for every house was her shrine. Each day when the family met round the table at the household meal a pause was made after the main course, and a portion of salted cake that had been baked by the daughters of the house was thrown into the fire that burned on the hearth, as an offering to Vesta and her companion spirits. This was the practice at least among the pious, and here we are using the word to mean what the Romans meant by it, a proper regard for the time-honoured beliefs and ways.

Nothing is known of the origins of the Vesta cult, and it was almost certainly prehistoric, taking its rise in times when the production of fire was a slow and laborious and tricky process. Matches did not come into general use until early in the last century, and in all the ages before that time it was necessary to obtain a spark by friction, by wood on wood or, later, by steel on flint. Thus it became the custom for each village to maintain a fire for the use of the community; and this fire, on the central hearth or *focus*—the Latin word for "hearth"—became the sacred symbol of home and family life. To watch over this fire and see that it never went out would naturally fall to the women, and especially to those women who were not burdened with the cares of motherhood.

The building of the first Temple of Vesta in Rome was popularly attributed to Numa, the successor to Romulus as king of the little city-state. It was round, like the Roman houses of early times, and like them it was built of wood with a roof of thatch. In the course of centuries it was rebuilt again and again on ever grander lines, but the convention of the circular form was retained, as is evidenced by the foundations of the last of the succession of temples that may still be traced. It was King Numa also, if we may credit Plutarch's life of this almost legendary monarch, who decreed that the fire on the hearth in the temple should be tended by a band of virgins, whether because he "fancied the charge of pure and uncorrupted flames would be fitly entrusted to chaste and unpolluted persons, or that fire, which consumes, but produces nothing, bears an analogy to the virgin estate". About the second suggestion, at least, Plutarch seems to have been doubtful, for he goes on to remark that at Delphi and Athens, where there were also "perpetual holy fires", the charge of the flame was committed not to virgins but to widows past the time of marriage. And when he speaks of "chaste and unpolluted persons" Plutarch may well have been influenced by Greek conceptions of the superiority of the virgin state over the married.

The Romans did not think like this. So far from putting

the virgin on a pedestal, they thought that it was the normal and proper thing for a girl to marry and bear children. They insisted that she should come to the marriage-bed as a virgin and that she should remain chaste throughout her marriage, but this was because men looked upon their wives as their personal property and were determined to run no risk of being made to support spurious offspring. They were not in the least inclined to asceticism. Their attitude to sex was very practical, down to earth, frankly realistic. And while insisting upon chastity among their spouses, the Roman males felt no compelling urge to remain chaste themselves.

At the same time there may have been a superstitious element in the stipulation that the priestesses should be virgins and remain such throughout their term of office. Among primitive peoples there has been noted a belief that virgins possess some measure of miraculous power; and that the Romans held some such belief is illustrated by the old story that when in 204 B.C. the ship bearing the sacred stone that was the image of the "Great Mother", the goddess Cybele, from Asia Minor to Rome, got stranded in the Tiber, a noble Roman lady named Claudia Quinta, whose chastity had been questioned, vindicated it by drawing with her virgin hand the ponderous mass that strong men had tried in vain to move.

When Numa instituted the order, there were four vestal virgins, but the number was increased by one of the later kings to six, and later still there is mention of a seventh. Appointments during the early period were made by the king, and then under the Republic and the Empire by the *Pontifex Maximus*, or chief priest, the "Pope" of the Roman state church. A candidate had to be between the ages of six and ten, and thus her virginity was assured to begin with. She was selected from girls of good family; she was to be *patrima* and *matrima,* i.e. having both parents alive, and they were to be freeborn citizens resident in Italy; and she was to be without any physical and mental defects or blemishes of whatever kind.

Vacancies in the order of Vestals must have been rare happenings. When one occurred, a list of twenty possible candidates was drawn up by the Pontifex Maximus, and the final choice was decided by lot. The selected child had her hair cut off, and was solemnly admitted by the Pontifex, who took her by the hand, and, addressing her by the name of *amata* ("beloved"), pronounced over her an ancient formula of initiation. Instruction in what would be required of her as a vestal followed. Although she was not of an age to understand what she was doing, the little girl took a vow to preserve the completest chastity for a period of thirty years, after which time she was free to return to private life in the outside world and might even marry and have a family, although it would seem that this was seldom done; most of the Vestals remained in the House, instructing the novices in their duties and employed in various domestic tasks.

In the earlier days at least the honour of becoming a Vestal was eagerly sought, since the position was one to which much dignity and many privileges were attached. Their dwelling was spacious and splendid, as may be gathered from what is left of it. There were baths, gardens in which fountains played, and courts lined with statues of the noblest members of the order. The women were their own mistresses, completely exempt from any male control save that of the Pontifex Maximus. They lived in a high style, surrounded by every luxury and convenience. They played a part in all the great State and religious ceremonies. They were allotted the best seats at the theatres and public games, except at some of the gymnastic displays in which the men performers were naked. They had the right to drive through the streets of Rome in carriages, and on state occasions were preceded like magistrates by lictors carrying the fasces, the symbol of authority. They had the power of pardoning any criminal whom they happened to meet in the street. They had great influence in the appointment of dignitaries, and, so it was said, "no one durst refuse them anything". They were the custodians of the Emperor's will and of other important State documents. They could own property and bequeath it by will. They received excellent salaries out of Government funds, and were entitled to good pensions on their retirement. To insult a Vestal was a capital offence; Plutarch asserts that anyone who merely pressed against a chair in which a Vestal was being carried along might be put to death.

The statutes of "good king Numa" prescribed that the Vestals in their first ten years of service should learn their duties; in the second ten they should practise them; and in the final decade they should pass on their knowledge to the novices. Their chief duty was tending the Sacred Fire on the altar in the midst of the temple. The fire was kept burning throughout the year until 1st March—New Year's Day in ancient Rome—when it was ceremonially extinguished and lighted again, either by the prehistoric method of rubbing two dry sticks together, or in later times by another ancient and sacred method of bringing the sun's rays to a focus on a concave metal mirror. It was considered a dreadful misfortune if the fire was allowed to go out of its own, and the Vestal responsible for the mishap was severely punished for her negligence: she might be taken into a dark place, stripped of all her clothes, and whipped by the chief priest.

Other duties of the Vestals included fetching water from the sacred spring of Egeria—the nymph who, according to the legend, was King Numa's lover and his guide in affairs of state—to be used in the ceremonial sweeping and sprinkling of the precincts; the offering of a special kind of salt cake and the making of libations on the altar of wine and oil; and the daily offering of prayers for the safety and prosperity of the country and people. The Vestals were also entrusted with a number of sacred objects, of which the most important was

the Palladium, an image of the goddess Pallas Athene that
was said to have been brought from Troy and on which the
safety of the city was believed to depend.

The Vestals wore a special dress, consisting of a long
sleeveless tunic, girdled just below the breasts, over which
when they went out was placed an ample cloak that could be
brought over the head like a hood. When sacrificing in the
temple, the priestesses wore on their heads a sacred garment
called the *suffibulum*, a rectangular piece of cloth, white with a
purple border; this hung down over the shoulders and was
fastened with a fibula or brooch. The hair seems to have been
allowed to grow again after the initiation ceremony, for on
statues of the chief Vestals it is shown long, bound in rope-
like twists of woollen cloth.

June was the Vestals' busiest month; from 7th June to
15th June the *Penus Vestae*, "Vesta's storehouse", was thrown
open to all Roman matrons, who visited the shrine and made
their offerings. On 15th June the doors were shut and the
visitors excluded; the temple was spring-cleaned and the
refuse was thrown into the Tiber.

A high price had to be paid for all the Vestals' honours
and privileges. There is no way of knowing how hardly the
insistence on complete chastity pressed upon the individual
vestal, since none wrote her memoirs—or if she did, no copy
of it has been preserved. We can only guess at the feelings of a
young woman who awoke too late to the real nature of the
vow she had taken as a child, and realized that for the best
years of her life she must put all thoughts of love far from her.
What must have made the restrictions harder to bear was
that the Vestals were not secluded from the world as nuns
are in convents. A nun is not exposed to outside temptations
and no outsider may penetrate the convent walls. But it was
not so with the Vestals in their House. On many public
occasions they went outside and met members of the other
sex, and might be bathed in a pleasurable excitement. Not only

The Nymph Surprised: a painting from a rich man's home in Pompeii

Left, one of the Vestal Virgins (National Museum, Rome). *Below*, Imperial Harlots: *left*, Messalina, wife to Claudius (Uffizi Gallery, Florence); *right*, the Empress Agrippina with her son Nero, at whose hands she was put to death (National Museum, Rome)

might they accept invitations to dinner-parties in the city, but they might return the hospitality during the hours of daylight.

Occasionally the promptings of sex proved too strong, and there was a scandal that shocked society. The Vestal Virgins were commonly looked upon as the guardians, or perhaps we might say the embodiment, of public morality, and any lapse on their part was deemed only too likely to bring dire distress and disaster on the commonwealth. Furthermore, under Roman law unchastity in a Vestal Virgin was regarded as incest, since the Vestals were in theory the daughters of the State and sisters to all citizens. The vows they had taken were of the most solemn and binding description, and to break them was tantamount to insulting the gods, and was punished accordingly. The Vestal who broke the fundamental rule of her order, and got found out, was buried alive.

The punishment is fully described by Plutarch, and there is reason to believe that he wrote as an eye-witness. In Rome, near the Colline Gate, there was (he tells us) a little mound of earth, under which was a small room, reached by steps. Here a bed was prepared, a lamp lighted, and a small quantity of victuals—bread, water, a jug of milk, and some oil—were placed. This was in order that it should not be said that a woman who had been devoted to the most sacred service of religion had been made to perish by famine. The culprit was then "put in a litter, which they cover over, and tie her down with cords on it, so that nothing she utters may be heard. Then they take her to the Forum. All people go silently out of the way as she passes, and such as follow accompany the bier with solemn and speechless sorrow. And indeed, there is not any spectacle more appalling, nor any day observed by the city with greater appearance of gloom and sadness".

Having arrived at the place of execution, "the officers loose the cords; and then the high priest, lifting his hands to heaven,

M

pronounces certain prayers to himself before the act. Then he brings out the prisoner, being still covered, and placing her upon the steps that lead down to the cell, turns away his face with the rest of the priests. The stairs are drawn up after she has gone down, and a quantity of earth is heaped up over the entrance to the cell, so as to prevent it being distinguished from the rest of the mound. This is the punishment of those who break their vow of virginity".

Doubtless there were some cases of unchastity among the Vestals that were hushed up, but those that came to light were estimated at no more than twenty in the course of the thousand years during which the institution subsisted.

One of the earliest of the recorded instances was in 216 B.C. following the battle of Cannae, in which the Roman army had been defeated with great slaughter by Hannibal and his Carthaginian hordes. To the public horror it was disclosed that two of the Vestal Virgins had been proved guilty of unchastity. No wonder the gods were angry! One of the unhappy women took her own life, but the other was promptly executed in the way the law directed.

Another famous instance was in the reign of Domitian, three hundred years later, when the culprit was no less a person than the *Vestalis Maxima*, whose name was Cornelia. This is the case of which Plutarch may well have had personal knowledge, and its details are given in a letter of Pliny the Younger to one of his friends.

Cornelia was accused of having carried on an intrigue with a Roman of middle-class family named Celer. She indignantly denied the charge, but it was unfortunate that only a short time before, in A.D. 83, three of her subordinate Vestals had been charged with unchastity, and condemned; they had been allowed to choose their own manner of death, while their seducers had been banished. Furthermore, Domitian was in a raging fury because of the intense odium that some of his most recent tyrannical acts had brought upon him. Looking round for someone on whom he might vent his malice, he hit on the Chief Vestal and resolved to make an object-lesson of her, apparently thinking that an act of exceptional severity would cast some lustre on his reign. He was resolved to find the woman guilty, and then to have her executed by the ancient punishment, although this had long fallen into disuse.

As emperor, he was Pontifex Maximus, and now, writes Pliny to his correspondent, "using his authority as such, or rather, exercising the cruelty of a tyrant and the wanton caprice of a despot, he summoned the rest of the pontiffs not to the pontifical college where they were wont to meet but to his villa at Alba. There, with a wickedness just as monstrous as the crime which he pretended to be punishing, he pronounced Cornelia guilty without even giving her an opportunity of saying anything in her defence. She was condemned on a charge of incest—and this notwithstanding that he himself had not only committed incest with his brother's daughter but had indirectly brought about her death, for she, while a widow, endeavoured to procure an abortion and died as a result".

Immediately sentence was pronounced, Domitian despatched priests to apprehend Cornelia and to have her put to death. As the unhappy woman was led away she was heard to utter many protestations of innocence and appeals to Vesta and the other divinities for assistance in her desperate hour. Among her other exclamations, frequently repeated, was, "Is it possible that Caesar can really think me polluted, when he has conquered and triumphed when I have been exercising the sacred functions?" by which she probably meant that if she *had* been guilty of unchastity the gods would have spurned the sacrifices she had offered up and would have shown their displeasure in some marked fashion. "Whether she said this in flattery or derision," writes Pliny, "from a consciousness of her innocence or contempt for the Emperor, is not certain, but she continued exclaiming in this manner until she arrived at the place of execution, and whether she were innocent or not, she certainly gave every appearance of being so."

So she was brought to the fatal place, and the stairway opened before her. "As she was lowered into the dreadful pit, her dress got caught up and she turned back to disengage it. The executioner offered her his hand, but she started back with averted face and refused his assistance, as though by a last impulse of chastity she kept her pure and spotless body from being polluted by his loathsome touch. Thus like a truly chaste woman she preserved her modesty to the last, and, as is said of Hecuba in Euripides' play, 'took much care to fall in seemly fashion'."

As for Celer, her alleged paramour, he was scourged to death. "What have I done?" the onlookers heard him say again and again; "what have I done? I have done nothing".

Why did the Romans punish an unchaste Vestal in this awful way? Plutarch did not know, but in his *Roman Questions* he opined that it might be because they would have considered it improper to commit to the flames (as was the usual Roman custom) the body of one who had failed to serve the Sacred Flame in chastity; or it might be that it was because they were reluctant to lay violent hands on a consecrated woman, and they therefore arranged that she should die of herself. But, he adds, this did not rid them of their superstitious fears, since "to this very day the priests go to that place and make offerings to the *manes*, or spirits of the dead".

The Romans certainly had a "superstitious fear" of putting *virgins* to death, for which reason they were deflowered before execution. A famous instance of this was in A.D. 31, following the downfall and disgrace of Sejanus, the late favourite of the Emperor Tiberius. "It was then resolved," writes Tacitus, "that the surviving children of Sejanus should pay the penalty, though by this time the anger of the populace was nearly spent." The children, a boy and a girl, were carried to the dungeon, the boy conscious of the fate in store but the girl so completely ignorant that she kept on asking what she had done wrong and what was the place they were taking her to? She would be a better girl in future, she promised, and was quite prepared to be whipped if she broke her promise. "It is recorded," the historian goes on, "that as it was considered an unheard of thing for capital punishment to be inflicted on a virgin, she was first violated by the executioner, with the halter hanging beside her." They were then strangled, and their bodies were thrown on the *Scalae Gemoniae*, "Staircase of Sighs", down which the bodies of persons executed were dragged with hooks and flung into the Tiber.

XIII

The Worship of Priapus

IN ROMAN GARDENS THERE might often be found a quaint little image of a man, holding a stick or club in his hand, and completely naked and as audaciously rude as the *Manikin pis* in Brussels. If we had asked who or what the image was supposed to represent, the owner of the garden might have said that it was just something to scare away the birds. But if the remark happened to have been overheard by one of the gardeners he would probably have made a propitiatory gesture with finger and thumb. For to the unsophisticated country folk the image was no scarecrow but a god who, though he had come down in the world since he had crossed the sea from Greece, was still supposed to influence in some strange way the reproductive powers of Nature, and of Man in particular.

The name of this divinity was Priapus, and he was said to have been the son of Venus by Mercury or Adonis, or according to the more generally received opinion, by Bacchus. Through the malice of Juno, who happened to preside over the accouchement of her rival goddess, he was born so grotesquely deformed, especially in the magnitude of his male organ, that his mother (ashamed at having given birth to such a monster) ordered him to be exposed on the mountain. But his life was preserved by some kindly shepherds, and he grew up to be a favourite among the people of Lampsacus, his birthplace in Asia Minor. But he took such liberties with their wives that they at length expelled him from their midst. Whereupon he caused them to be afflicted with a disease of the genitals, and in self-protection they called him back, and erected temples for his worship. Festivals were also celebrated in his honour, in which the people gave themselves over to every form of lasciviousness and debauchery. Eventually his cult was introduced into Rome; where, however, he was reverenced chiefly as a god of gardens and orchards.

There are frequent references to Priapus in the Latin authors. Virgil in his *Georgics* has the lines, "the god obscene, who frights away with his lath sword the thieves and birds of prey", and in one of his *Satires* Horace mentions an image of Priapus that had been set up in the garden of his patron Maecenas on the slope of the Esquiline hill. "Once I was the stem of a fig-tree," he makes the image say, "a good-for-nothing log of wood; when the carpenter, wondering whether to make of me a bench or a Priapus, decided to make me a god. So a god am I, the special terror of thieves and birds."

These quotations reflect the educated man's attitude towards the grotesque little images, an attitude of amused condescension and genial recognition of ancient superstition. But as already indicated, to the ordinary folk the image represented a divinity whose help might be sought with advantage in cases of male impotence and female barrenness. His symbol was the phallus (Greek, *phallos*, penis), and phallic amulets were in everyday use in the Roman world, being worn by persons of both sexes, hung round the neck by a cord or chain, the way that people wear "lucky charms" at the present time. These amulets were believed to be protection against the "evil eye", i.e. the power supposed to be possessed by some persons to inflict evil by a look, but they were also considered to be powerful aids to generation. As such they remained in popular use for many hundreds of years, right up to modern times.

A celebrated instance of this was recorded by Sir William Hamilton—the husband of Nelson's Emma—in 1781, when he was British Ambassador at the court of the king of Naples.

In a letter to his friend, the eminent naturalist Sir Joseph Banks, he stated that "in a province of this kingdom and not fifty miles from its capital, a sort of devotion is still paid to Priapus, the obscene divinity of the Ancients". It was very natural to suppose that "amulets representing the phallus alone, so visibly indecent", had long passed out of use in "this civilized capital", but in fact he had learnt that only very recently had the priests put an end to the wearing of such amulets in Calabria and other distant parts of the kingdom. A friend of his had described what he had witnessed only the year before at the ancient city of Isernia, on the occasion of the annual celebration of the feast of Saints Cosmus and Damianus. "In the city, and at the fair, *ex-voti* [offerings made in accordance with a vow; Latin, *votum*, to vow] of wax, representing the male parts of generation, of various dimensions, some even of the length of a palm, are publicly offered for sale. The 'vows' are chiefly presented by the female sex, and the person who was at this fete in 1780 told me that he heard a woman say, at the time she presented a vow [at a table in the church presided over by one of the canons], 'Blessed St. Cosmo, let it be like this,' and another, 'St. Cosmo, I thank you'. The vow is never presented without being accompanied by a piece of money, and is always kissed by the devotee at the moment of presentation."

There is nothing in this letter of Sir William Hamilton's that would have surprised Virgil or Horace in the least, and if either poet had visited Isernia at festival time he might well have found a very similar ceremony in progress, except that Priapus would have been in place of St. Cosmo. The good people of Isernia who bought phallic amulets from their priests were inspired by the same hopes and desires as their pagan forefathers—they believed that by buying the little objects they were securing the interposition on their behalf of the supernatural beings who had control of human generation.

As a consequence of Sir William Hamilton's letter, a wealthy collector of antiquities, Richard Payne Knight, wrote a short book that was published in 1786 under the title *A Discourse on the Worship of Priapus, and its Connexion with the Mystic Theology of the Ancients*, and included therein the letter as a preface. The book caused great offence, partly because of its illustrations of the *ex-voti* that had been on sale at Isernia, and partly on account of the thesis it sustained. This was, in brief, that the phallus, the representation of the male organ of generation, was considered by the ancients to be the symbol of the creative activity of the Deity. This interpretation, Payne Knight allowed, would perhaps surprise "those who have not been accustomed to divest their minds of the prejudices of education and fashion", but he submitted that "in an age when no prejudices of artificial decency existed, what more just and natural image could they find, by which to express the idea of the beneficent power of the great Creator, than that organ which endowed them with the power of procreation and made them partakers, not only of the fertility of the Deity, but of his great characteristic attribute, that of multiplying his own image, communicating his blessings, and extending them to generations yet unborn?"

Generally, he went on, the organ of generation was represented "in that state of tension and rigidity which is necessary to the due performance of its functions", although sometimes it was shown "in that state of tumid languor which immediately succeeds the performance". Many small images of this kind, he reminded his readers, had been found among the ruins of Pompeii and Herculanaum (the two towns destroyed in the eruption of Vesuvius in A.D. 79), attached to the bracelets which the chaste and pious matrons of antiquity wore round their necks and arms . . . in order to show that the devout wearer devoted herself wholly and solely to procreation, the great end for which she was ordained.

In the same way as the male organs of generation were revered as symbols of the generative powers of the Deity, so those of the female were revered as symbols of the generative powers of Nature or Matter. They were usually represented emblematically, by the shell or *Concha Veneris*, which was therefore worn by devout persons of antiquity, as it still continues to be by pilgrims, and many of the common women of Italy.

The union of both symbols was expressed by something that Hamilton also mentioned in his letter to Banks: "a clinched hand, with the point of the thumb thrust between the index and the middle fingers." Hamilton very justly recognized in this a representation of sexual intercourse. Amulets of this form are very widespread, even today, although the women and girls who wear them may be seldom acquainted with their real significance. The *gesture* that takes this form is what is known as the fig, a word ultimately derived from the Latin *ficus*, and applied to it supposedly because of the resemblance of the female sex organs to a half-open fig. In Shakespeare this appears as an insulting gesture, but in antiquity it was a protective device against the "evil eye", as was the image of the phallus. The reason probably lies in the belief that the assistance of the powers of generation was the most potent that could be invoked.

The *Concha Veneris*, "the shell of Venus", it may be remarked, which is usually identified with the cowrie-shell, got its name from its supposed resemblance to the female organ.

Priapus was perhaps the best-known of the sexual divinities of the ancient mythologies, but there were others in great esteem. Liber, for instance, was originally an old Italian god having something to do with general creativeness, but he became identified with Bacchus, the Latin or Roman name for the Greek Dionysus, and was worshipped as the god of the vine. He was celebrated on 17th March at the festival of the Liberalia, when Roman youths generally assumed the *toga virilis* (the plain toga of the citizen) in place of the *toga praetexta* (toga with a purple border worn by freeborn children).

According to St. Augustine (as translated by John Healey in 1610), "Liber's sacrifices were kept with such licence in the highways in Italy, that they adored men's privities in his honour: their beastliness exulting, and scorning any more secrecy. This beastly sight upon his feast days was honourably mounted upon a wagon, and first rode thus through the country, and then was brought into the city in this pomp. But at Lavinium they kept a whole month holy to Liber, using during that space all the beastly words they could devise, until the beastly spectacle had passed through the market-place, and was placed where it used to stand. And then must the most honest matron of the town crown it with a garland. Thus for the seed's success [i.e. to obtain a bountiful harvest] was Liber adored; and to expel witchcraft from the fields, an honest matron must do that in public which a whore should not do upon the stage if the matrons looked on".

On another page of *The City of God*, St. Augustine denounces the foul worship of "Berecynthia, surnamed the celestial virgin, and mother to all the gods". The name by which this goddess is generally known is Cybele, and she was the "Great Mother" who was worshipped in Asia under the guise of a block of stone, itself probably of phallic significance. The stone was fetched from Pergamum to Rome in 204 B.C., when the Romans were in the stress of the war with Hannibal, and (as we have already noted in the chapter on the Vestal Virgins) when the ship that bore it stuck on a sandbank in the Tiber it was towed safely to land by a noble Roman lady who thereby demonstrated her chastity. A temple was built for the goddess's reception on the Palatine hill, but the cult was always looked at with suspicion by the better class of Romans on account of the orgiastic nature of the worship.

The priests of Cybele were the Galli, who emasculated

themselves prior to their entry into her service. Sir James
Frazer, in his great book *The Golden Bough*, says that "these
unsexed beings, in their Oriental costume", used to traverse
the streets of Rome, carrying the image of the goddess and
chanting hymns to the music of cymbals and tambourines,
flutes and horns, while the onlookers, impressed by the fantastic show and moved by the wild strains of the music,
showered alms upon them and buried the image in rose
petals. St. Augustine writes far less tolerantly about them.
"We ourselves (once in our youth) went to view these spectacles, their sacrilegious mockeries; there we saw the
enthusiasts, persons rapt with fury; there we heard the pipers,
and took great delight in the filthy sports that they acted . . .
Their beastly stage players acted such ribaldry, as was a shame
not only for the mother of the gods, but for the mother of
any senator or any honest man, nay, even for the mothers of
the players themselves to give ear to . . . That beastliness of
obscene speeches and actions, which the players acted in
public, before the mother of all the gods, and in sight and
hearing of a huge multitude of both sexes, they would be
ashamed to act at home in private before their mothers."

St. Augustine gives another example of the close connection of religion and sex in the Roman world later in the same
book. This time he is describing the worship of a "virgin
goddess", probably Diana, whom the Romans identified
with the Greek Artemis. "Before the temple gates, where
the idol stood, we beheld an innumerable multitude of people
drawn together, and there saw a large train of strumpets on
one side and a virgin goddess on the other; here humble
adorations unto her, and there, foul and immodest things
acted before her. We could not see one modest mimic, not
one shamefaced actor amongst them all, but all was full of
actions of abominable filthiness. They knew well what that
virgin deity liked, and pronounced it for the nations to learn
by looking on, and to carry home in their minds. Some there

were of the chaster sort, that turned away their eyes from beholding the filthy gestures of the players, and yet though they blushed to look upon this artificial beastliness, they gave scope unto their disposition to learn it. For they durst not behold the impudent gestures of the actors boldly, for being shamed by the men, and less durst they condemn the ceremonies of that deity whom they so adored. But that was presented in the temples, and in public, which none will commit in their private houses but in secret."

That which was "presented in the temples" was almost certainly a ritual in which a priest of the goddess's establishment had sexual relations with a strumpet on a stage in full view of the audience of both sexes and of all ages, the reason for this licentious exhibition being, in the words of Sir James Frazer, that "these feminine deities required to receive from their male ministers, who personated the divine lovers, the means of discharging their beneficent functions: they themselves had to be impregnated by the life-giving energy before they could transmit it to the world". The display, so regarded, was a kind of sympathetic magic: the successful conjugation of the priest and the strumpet, representing or standing in the place of the goddess's lover and the goddess herself, was supposed to encourage a similarly successful act between the members who thronged the temple courts to witness the spectacle.

The temples of these Oriental divinities were reputed, and generally it may be supposed with good reason, to be hot-beds of immorality and general debauchery. This was specially the case with the temples of the goddess Isis, the most important of the divine importations from Egypt, and this notwithstanding that Isis was deeply revered by matrons and other women of excellent character. The temple of Isis in Rome was notorious for the prostitutes that swarmed about its steps and for the number of assignations that were effected in its portico.

Like Cybele and the other Oriental divinities, Isis was served by male priests, and the poet who was on tenterhooks when he learnt that his lady had gone to pay her vows to the Goddess had all too good reason for feeling suspicious. Cases are reported of priests who, whether out of lust or in conformity with an established religious custom, impersonated their divinity and had sexual intercourse with the female worshippers, some of whom were simple-minded enough to believe that when they were in the priest's bed they were actually being enjoyed by the god he served.

The most famous instance of this is given by Josephus, the Jewish historian, in a chapter of his *Antiquities of the Jews* describing events in Tiberius's reign. There was at Rome, he writes (in William Whiston's translation of 1737) "a woman whose name was Paulina: one who, on account of the dignity of her ancestors and by the regular conduct of a virtuous life, had a great reputation; she was also very rich, and although she was of a beautiful countenance and in that flower of her age wherein women are the most gay, yet did she lead a life of great modesty". She was married to a man of excellent character named Saturninus; but Decimus Mundus, a man of wealth and high rank, "was inflamed with love to her, insomuch that he promised to give her 200,000 Attic drachmae for one night's lodging; and when this would not prevail upon her, and he was not able to bear this misfortune in his amours, he thought it the best way to famish himself to death for want of food". Now Mundus had a freedwoman named Ide, who was much grieved at her young master's resolution to kill himself, and she suggested to him a stratagem whereby "he might obtain a night's lodging with Paulina". Knowing that Paulina was very much given to the worship of Isis, the girl went to some of the goddess's priests and "persuaded them by words, but chiefly by the offer of 25,000 drachmae in hand and as much more when the thing had taken effect", to join in beguiling

Paulina. The senior among them went to Paulina and told her that he had been sent by the god Anubis (one of the Egyptian male gods) to tell her that he had fallen in love with her and required her to come to him. "Upon this she took the message very kindly, and valued herself greatly upon this condescension of Anubis; and told her husband that she had a message sent her, and was to sup and lie with Anubis; so he agreed to her acceptance of the offer, as fully satisfied with the chastity of his wife. Accordingly, she went to the temple; and after she had supped there, and it was the hour to go to sleep, the priest shut the doors of the temple; when, in the holy part of it, the lights were also put out. Then did Mundus leap out (for he was hidden therein) and did not fail of enjoying her, who was at his service all the night long, as supposing he was the god; and when he was gone away, which was before those priests who knew nothing of this stratagem were stirring, Paulina came early to her husband, and told him how the god Anubis had appeared to her." She also told her friends, who in the light of her modesty and dignity were almost inclined to believe her. But then Mundus happened to meet Paulina and could not refrain from boasting of the way in which he had enjoyed her and at the same time had managed to save himself 200,000 drachmae. Paulina "began to come to the sense of the grossness of what she had done, and rent her garments, and told her husband of the horrid nature of this wicked contrivance, and prayed him not to neglect to assist her in this case. So he discovered the fact to the emperor; whereupon Tiberius inquired into the matter thoroughly, by examining the priests about it, and ordered them to be crucified, as well as Ide, who had contrived the whole matter. He also demolished the temple of Isis, and gave order that her statue should be thrown into the river Tiber; while he only banished Mundus, because he supposed that what crime he had committed was done out of the passion of love".

Of the "native" Roman goddesses with a sexual aspect perhaps the most popular was Anna Perenna; originally she seems to have been the moon goddess (*perenna* means "ever-circling"), which was supposed to have influence over female periodicity. A carnival was held in her honour on the Ides or 15th March, when the Romans used to flock to the fields beside the Tiber and make merry after the way of a bank-holiday crowd. Ovid has given a charming description of the young men and their girls stretched side by side on the grass, or dancing hand in hand round the wine bowl, while the spectators kept time to the music with their hands. Then at nightfall they made their way home, somewhat unsteadily perhaps, and all who encountered them on the road blessed them and received a blessing in return.

THE BUSINESS OF SEX

XIV

The Roman Prostitute

THERE SEEMS TO HAVE never been a time when prostitution was not a regular feature of Roman life. At the very beginning of the story we read of a woman named Acca Larentia who nursed the twins Romulus and Remus after they were rescued from the Tiber by her husband, the swineherd Faustulus. She was a woman of loose life, a *lupa* or prostitute; and Plutarch suggests that, since in Latin *lupa* also meant a she-wolf, it was from this ambiguity that there arose that part of the old legend which tells of the twins having been suckled by a she-wolf before they were found by Faustulus.

On the same page Plutarch tells of another Larentia, who followed the same profession. The keeper of the temple of Hercules in the city of Alba Longa (he says) was so bored at having very little to do that he proposed to his god that they should play a game of dice together. If the man won, he should be given something of value; but if the god won, then the man would provide him an excellent entertainment and a beautiful woman to lie with that night. The god agreed, and the man threw the dice, first for the god and then for himself. The man lost, and thereupon proceeded to carry out the terms of their bargain. "He prepared a supper, and, engaging for the purpose one Larentia, who was very handsome but as yet little known, he treated her in the temple, where he had provided a bed; and after supper, left her to the enjoyment of the god." At nightfall the god made his appearance and "had some conversation with her, and ordered her to go early in the morning to the market-place, salute the first man she should meet, and make him her friend". This the woman did, and the man she met "took Larentia to his bed, and loved her so well that at his death he left her heir to his whole estate, which was very considerable; and she afterwards bequeathed the greatest part of it by will to the people". Out of gratitude, the Romans honoured her memory at the festival of the Larentalia on 23rd December in each year.

Somewhat similar is the story of Flora, the Roman goddess of flowers and the springtime. She was supposed to have been originally a common prostitute who amassed a huge fortune out of the exercise of her profession, most of which she left to the Roman people. A festival was instituted in her honour in 238 B.C. and this was made annual in 173 B.C. The *Ludi Florales*, "Floralian Games", as the festival was styled, extended over the period from 28th April (which the prostitutes of Rome kept as their feast day) to 3rd May, and were intended as an invocation to the goddess, the protectress of the blossom. Men decked themselves with flowers, and women put on their gayest dresses. General merriment was the rule, and this often degenerated into drunkenness and indecency. A prominent feature of the celebrations was plays or mimes, in which the chief parts were played by drunken prostitutes, who pranced about the stage in complete nakedness. On these occasions even women of respectable character were expected to "let their hair down".

These fanciful stories belong to a period when the prostitute was accepted with an easy-going tolerance. But the time came when it was decided that her activities required the supervision of the public authorities. Prostitution became an institution. So it is true to say that this institution, like so many other modern institutions, began in ancient Rome.

In his *Annals,* Tacitus states that from time immemorial prostitutes had been required to register at the office of the aedile, a public official or magistrate who had the superin-tendence of public and private buildings and was responsible for keeping order at the public spectacles. These were the places and the occasions in or on which prostitutes most usually plied their trade, and we may see in the requirement the beginning of that police regulation of prostitution in the interests of public morals that has been a regular feature in most European countries—and indeed in many others that have inherited Roman ideas—up to the present.

A woman who wished to become a public prostitute, or *meretrix* (from *merere*, "to earn": whence our word "meretri-cious", meaning primarily something characteristic or worthy of a harlot, but by extension, flashy or gaudy) was required to make personal application to the aedile. Standing before his desk she stated her name, place of birth, and age, and also the name under which she proposed to carry on her trade. It was the aedile's duty to try to get her to change her mind, to "go away and think about it" before committing herself to a manner of life which had so many disadvantages and was generally regarded as disreputable. If the woman insisted, however, the aedile was then required to issue her a licence to practise prostitution (*licentia stupri*), ascertain the sum she proposed to charge her clients, and enter her name on the roll of professional prostitutes that was kept at his office.

Sometimes one sees it stated that once a woman's name was on the roll it could never be removed: repentance could never restore her to respectability. But this is disproved by the cases on record of women who had abandoned their profession and returned to respectable life.

Registration at the aedile's office gave the prostitute a legal right to her fee. If a client bilked her she was entitled to make a formal complaint at the office; and the aedile, if he found the complaint proved, was required to compel the man to pay the sum that the woman was entitled to charge.

While her earnings were thus defended by the public

official, the prostitute was required to pay an annual tax equivalent to the amount received in one day from a single client. This tax was paid into the municipal treasury, and the local authority could be relied upon to see that it was demanded by the aedile's officers and duly paid. Women who fell behind in their payments were given a black mark in the aedile's book, and if they fell too much in arrear they might be given a good whipping in public and then chased out of town and warned not to show their face there again.

In his biography of Caligula, Roman emperor from A.D. 37 to 41, Suetonius mentions that he augmented his revenues by imposing a number of fresh taxes and imposts, including, as Philemon Holland puts it in his version, "out of the gets and takings of common strumpets as much as they earned by once lying with a man", and furthermore, "that there should be liable to the tribute not only the parties themselves that by the trade of harlotry got their living, but even they likewise who kept houses of bawdry".

When she had been entered upon the aedile's list the meretrix was required to dress in such a manner as to make clear her profession. She was forbidden, by law, to wear the *stola,* the long dress with slits in the sides for the arms, that was gathered up below the breasts by a girdle; this was considered too modest a dress for a woman of loose morals. Instead she was required to wear a robe that resembled the toga of the men. Certain colours that were considered too loud for respectable females were flaunted by the prostitute, who might be as colourful as she pleased. And instead of attempting to hide her figure in gowns with voluminous folds the meretrix went in for dresses of gossamer fineness and transparency. An appropriate name for such material was "windwoven". While the matron modestly veiled her head when she went out of doors, the prostitute faced the world with a brazenly open face. She might not wear shoes but she was allowed sandals, which very often were gaily coloured and perhaps bejewelled. She was not supposed to wear jewellery, but we may suppose that this ban was not strictly enforced. Among other restrictions she was not allowed to wear purple, as this was the colour of robes of honour, nor to wear her hair in fillets, as these were the marks of maidenly modesty. And while on the subject of hair, it should be mentioned that the meretrix paid great attention to her coiffure. There may even have been a regulation that she should dye her hair a flaming yellow or even a raging red, or she may have preferred to wear a brightly coloured wig instead.

When professionally engaged the prostitute commonly went naked, but if she belonged to the superior sort she might perhaps paint the *papillae* or tips of her breasts with gold leaf—"a species of ornament", explains William Gifford, the eighteenth-century translator of Juvenal, when commenting on the satirist's famous passage describing the amours of the Empress Messalina, "which, however repugnant to our ideas of beauty, is used by many of the dancing-girls and privileged courtesans of the East to this day".

A registered prostitute or meretrix might carry on her profession on her own, taking a room in the suburbs and doing her own soliciting. But more often, it is supposed, she was attached to a "house of bawdry".

The Roman name for a brothel was *lupanar*, and the *lupanaria* were of two main kinds. In one the establishment was owned and managed by a *lupanarius*, the prostitutes were his employees, and all their earnings were his. Generally the fees were collected at the entrance, but anything that the women were given direct was required to be handed over to the manager as soon as the business was concluded. Very often the prostitutes were slaves, actually owned by the brothel proprietor, in which case they were absolutely at his disposal. Even those women who were legally free occupied a position that was only a very little better than slaves, condemned as they were to lead a life of infamy from which there was small hope of their ever being able to make their escape.

In the other sort of lupanar the women's condition may well have been much better. The place was in the nature of an "assignation house", in that it contained a number of rooms which were let by the proprietor to prostitutes on a weekly, monthly, or yearly basis, or it may have been for only a night or even an hour or two at a time. The women made their own financial arrangements with their customers, and after they had paid their rent and their share of the expenses of the necessary staff, heating and lighting, etc., everything that they earned was their own to do what they liked with. Thus notwithstanding their occupation, they were still in considerable measure controllers of their own lives and persons.

Lupanaria differed greatly in size, equipment, cleanliness and general condition, and in their charges. In Rome they seem to have resembled small houses, consisting of a central court or atrium on to which opened a number of small chambers, cells, or cubicles, in which the women operated. In the middle of the court a fountain might be playing, and there was a supply of water laid on. The walls were covered with frescoes of a generally indecent character, including representations of sexual postures and practices that might have an aphrodisiacal effect or perhaps serve as advertisements of the kind of thing that might be indulged in for the appropriate fee. The fitting of the cells were likewise obscene and lust-provoking; thus the lamps might be shaped like a phallus and the chamber utensils figured with suggestive designs.

As for the closets in which the "rites of love" were celebrated, they were dark and gloomy little places, only a few feet square, with one small window high up in the wall or perhaps with no window at all. A curtain was all that separated the cell from the passage, and the only illumination was an oil lamp. The furniture consisted only of a bed or couch. Sometimes this was a wooden frame on which were a mattress and a couple of coverlets, but often it was nothing more than a platform of earth and the pillow a wooden roller. Over the door of each cell was a wooden tablet on which was written the name of its occupant, together with the price of her favours; on its reverse side was the word *occupata,* so that it could be turned round when the woman was going about her business with a customer.

In Petronius's *Satyricon* we are told of a visit to a lupanar. "I observed a company of Beaux reading the Bills o'er the Cells, on which was inscribed the Name of the Whore and her Price; and others of the same Function naked, scuttling it here and there, as if they would not, yet would be, seen." (Translation by William Burnaby, 1694.)

At Pompeii a lupanar has been discovered and restored. It is seen to consist of a ground floor containing a number of cubicles, each just large enough to take a bed, separated by a passage; upstairs a number of discreet little rooms were available for the convenience of clients who preferred some privacy in their "sex". Some of these rooms have balconies over the street. The walls of the passage were covered with indecent pictures; and on the wall of the establishment outside was a large wooden phallus, as a sufficient indication of the kind of activity that was carried on within.

Prostitution in the lupanaria was carried on under the supervision of the aedile, who, in the absence of a proper police force, was responsible for the maintenance of public order. He had a number of men under him to carry out his orders. They patrolled the streets and cleared them of disorderly elements; they had the right of entering a lupanar at all hours, and saw that the places were closed from daybreak until three o'clock in the afternoon; and in the event of brawls, they were empowered to arrest, charge, and punish those reponsible. A lupanar-keeper who failed to keep his list of inmates up to date, or who allowed a woman to work in his establishment who had not been properly registered, was liable to a fine and a public whipping. Another of the aedile's duties was to send unregistered whores packing, but this was not always easy, since they might be under the protection of influential citizens.

The man who ran the establishment was responsible to the aedile for its proper management. He, or it might be she, had control of a staff of employees, large or small as the case might be. In the best houses these included in addition to the domestic staff a cashier (*villiacus*) who sat at a desk near the entrance, arranged the terms with customers, and took the cash; stewards who supplied the guests with wine and light refreshments, boys who carried water to the cubicles, and runners who kept contact with the outside world and brought in fresh clients. Then on the female side there were chambermaids and hairdressers, *ancillae ornatrices* or tire-women, who strove to ensure that their charges always looked their best, and needlewomen and dressmakers whose principal job it was to repair the rents in the flimsy garments that the prostitutes sometimes put on so that their customers might experience the sexual "kick" of ripping them off again. In the downtown establishments there was very likely a "chucker-out", a strong-arm man capable of dealing with any client who made himself a nuisance.

Unless the job was undertaken by the manager, there was also a *leno* or bawd, a man or woman charged with the recruiting of fresh brothel-fodder—a matter of constant concern, since in the harsh and humiliating conditions of work not even the sturdiest woman could be expected to last for long.

In the first sort of lupanaria most, if not all, of the women would be slaves, bought in the open market or through private treaty with a slave-raider, but in those that were akin to assignation-houses the whores would be drawn very largely from the class of freedwomen.

All these women were there because they had to be, no other way of life being open to them. But strange as it must appear, there were also women serving in the establishment of their own free will. The career of a meretrix in a lupanar seems, indeed, to have had an extraordinary fascination for some well born and easy circumstanced ladies. There were no psychoanalysts in ancient Rome, or we might have been provided with some intensely interesting human documents explaining why the performance of the most intimate acts in circumstances which even in the best establishments must have been disgusting and degrading, should have had such an appeal.

The fact seems to be well established. Thus we are told by Tacitus in his *Annals* that in A.D. 19 a Roman lady named Vestilia, married to a man of good position, and herself a member of a highly regarded family, went to the aedile's office and demanded to be registered as a prostitute. This example of female profligacy was too much for the Government, and the Senate promptly passed an ordinance that "no woman should be allowed to trade in her body if her father, grandfather, or husband had been a Roman knight", i.e. belonged to the middle class. Vestilia's husband was also called over the coals. How was it that he had not taken action against his guilty spouse? Even if he had not taken the law into his own hands and slain her as had been the custom in the "good old days", he should have at least shown his resentment at her conduct by repudiating her and obtaining a divorce. The husband made the rather feeble excuse that the law allowed sixty days in which to take action, and that time was not yet expired. It was thereupon decreed that if the husband and relatives of a woman found guilty of unchastity were slow to take action against her, the law might be set in motion by a member of the general public. Vestilia was banished to a rocky islet in the Cyclades, but this does not seem to have had much of a deterring effect, if we may believe Juvenal's story of the Empress Messalina repairing to a brothel to gratify her inordinate lust.

Messalina was an extraordinary exception, but from other sources we may learn that Roman ladies were not over nice in their amours. " 'Tis the wild extravagance of some women to be in love with filth," the lady's maid in Petronius's novel *Satyricon* tells the narrator, when discussing her mistress's strange infatuation for a man who seems little higher than a servant; "nor can they be raised to an appetite but by the charms, forsooth, of some slave or lacquey. Some can be pleased with nothing but the strutting of a prizefighter with a hacked face, or an actor betrayed to prostitute himself on the stage. Of this sort is my Lady, who indeed prefers the paltry lover of the upper gallery, with his dirty face and oaken staff, to all the fine gentlemen of the boxes".

XV

Who's Who of Strumpets

THE STATISTICS OF PROSTITUTION, in whatever age and country, are notoriously unreliable, and it is not possible to gain any certain idea of the number of the registered *meretrices* who worked either on their own or in connection with the lupanaria. Still less is it possible to estimate the number of the unregistered, but there can be no doubt that they far outnumbered those whose names appeared on the aediles' lists.

The *prostibulae,* as these women were called, paid no tax to the municipality, and were outside the protection afforded by the aedile to the prostitutes on his lists. Within their ranks were women of very different types and ways of carrying on their trade.

At the top of the immoral pyramid were the *delicatae,* named from the Latin word meaning soft, tender, dainty. These "dainty ladies" corresponded to the *lorettes* of French novels, and the "kept women" of the demimonde. They were ladies of very easy virtue, but they would have been insulted if they had been looked upon as common prostitutes. To this class belonged most of the loves celebrated by the Roman poets in their verses.

A little lower in the social scale came the *famosae,* from the Latin word that means "much talked of" in a good or colourless sense but also may mean "infamous, notorious". They were women who came from respectable families but took to evil courses through lust or avarice. The Lesbia of Catullus might be included as one of these.

Next we have a strange little class called the *Doris*, who were reported to have such extraordinarily beautiful bodies that they took to going without clothes whenever possible. The *lupae* or "she-wolves", the class to which Acca Larentia belonged, were supposed to haunt woodland groves and commons, and attracted the attention of passers-by by emitting wolf-like howls. The *busturiae* (from Latin, *bustuarius*, "connected with funeral rites") combined the job of professional mourners with prostitution in the macabre surroundings of the graveyard. The *forariae* (Latin, *foras*, "out of doors") were out-door "pick-ups", country girls who lurked in fields and lanes and offered themselves to travellers by the wayside. The *gallinae* (Latin, *gallina*, "a hen") were women who combined robbery with whoredom. *Scorta erratica* were "roving whores", and *ambulatrices noctilucae* were "ramblers by night", i.e. streetwalkers of the most common type. Lower still were the *diabolares* or "devil girls" (Greek, *diabolos*, devil), who had a most unsavoury reputation. But perhaps the worst of the lot were the *quadrantariae*, who offered themselves for less than a farthing (*quadrans*, a fourth part of the *as*, a paltry coin).

The close association of Bacchus and Venus goes back to ages before history began, and it was greatly in evidence in the classical civilizations. In Rome and elsewhere it was generally understood that prostitutes were available at practically every place of refreshment, from the inns of the highest class to the lowest drinking-den. So generally was this understood that *copa*, "hostess of a wine-shop", came to have the secondary meaning of a prostitute.

Among Horace's *Epistles* there is one that he addressed to his personal slave whom he had promoted to be the bailiff of his little estate in the country. After a time the man hankered after city life. "When you were a city drudge," writes his master, "you were always secretly longing for the country, and now you wish that you were back in town!

I know what it is. It's the brothel and the greasy cookshop that stirs your longing; what makes you discontented is that there's no tavern just round the corner where they will supply you with wine and a flute-playing courtesan to whose music you can dance and thump the floor . . ."

One of these taverns has been restored at Pompeii. It seems to have been kept by a woman named Asellina. It was a *thermopolium,* that is, a place in which hot drinks were served, but it was also a brothel, for Asellina herself and her two assistants, Smyrna and Maria, were ready to offer their services to customers in the little rooms on the first floor.

Perhaps it is not surprising that bar-girls should have been expected to do something more than just serve the drinks, but women engaged in less public occupations also had this reputation—those employed in butchers' shops and bakeries, for instance. So far as the latter go, the nature of some of the goods they made and had on sale may have had something to do with it, for a very popular line was little cakes resembling in shape the male and female genitalia. These were primarily intended for sacrifices to Venus and Priapus, to induce their aid in love affairs, but it is said that they appeared on dinner-tables and even at children's tea-parties.

Female dancers were reputed to be especially lax in their moral behaviour. Those from the eastern Mediterranean were much sought after, but those fetching the highest prices in the slave-market were the girls from Spain, Cadiz in particular. The way in which they clacked the castanets and flung their skirts was considered to have a most erotic appeal and significance.

Prostitution was carried on almost anywhere and everywhere. The *bonae mulieres* ("good women"), as the higher grade meretrices were styled, had their quarters to which they conducted their clients, but the *prostibulae* generally had no other place than the pavement: if they had been possessed of a fixed address they would probably have sought admission to the aedile's list. This indiscriminate whoring was one of the features that distinguished Roman prostitution from Greek: it was coarser, more brutal, more unrestrained and much more public.

The porticoes of public buildings and religious temples were a recognized place for prostitutes to meet in and engage with their customers. Even in daylight these were often the scene of open fornication, and there were no police to order the women to "move on". But arches were specially favoured, and there were plenty of these in ancient Rome, what with the great aqueducts crossing the streets and the practice of building the houses of the wealthy on arched foundations. Only the tops of these constructions showed above street level, and they were open at the front. A few feet below the footway there were, therefore, numbers of caverns, dark and dank and filthy, into which it was the easiest thing in the world for a street drab to hurry with her client.

Other arches were even more notorious, those underneath theatres, circuses, and other places of public entertainment. The plays in the Roman theatres were often unabashedly sexual in subject and performance, and the spectacles in the amphitheatre were bloody in the extreme. Sadism and sex often go together, and it is understandable that men whose senses had been inflamed by what they had just witnessed on the stage or in the arena should seek to work off their feelings in conjunction with the women who, as soon as the performance was over, with hair and dress in disorder and uttering wild cries, rushed down the street to meet them.

In Latin the word for an arch, or a series of arches, is *fornix*. So generally associated in the popular mind did these gloomy recesses become with furtive vice that the word came to denote a brothel. From this usage is derived our word "fornication".

Another interesting Latin word with a sexual connotation is *pergula*. Its primary meaning was a projection, whence it was applied to verandas with roofs, loggias, and balconies; the present-day meaning of a structure along a garden path, covered with climbing plants, is a further development. But in the special vocabulary of Roman prostitution we find the word *pergulae*, meaning those "balcony whores" who sought to attract custom by calling from their balconies to the men passing along the street down below. Then there is the word *stabulum*, meaning a standing-place, etc., whence came *stabulae*, yet another name for streetwalkers.

In Rome and other big cities the public baths were a favourite place for assignations. These establishments were often of considerable size, for they contained not only baths and swimming-pools but restaurants, shops for the sale of perfumes and other luxury goods, libraries, picture-galleries, and small rooms that might be hired for the transaction of all sorts of business. The baths were often provided by politicians anxious to cultivate the favour of the populace, and the admission-fees were kept low as a matter of policy. No one who could afford it and was reasonably presentable was refused admittance, and once he was undressed he lost the badge of class and circumstance. In theory there were separate establishments or at least different times of opening for men and women, but in practice the baths seem to have been open to everybody at all hours. Hadrian and Marcus Aurelius issued decrees forbidding mixed bathing, but these seem to have had small effect, and a later emperor legalized what it had been impossible to prevent.

We may imagine the scene in those vast cavernous interiors, dimly lit by lamps and torches. The bathers sitting on the edge of the basins, taking a dip, being scrubbed and massaged and oiled, moving from one bath-chamber to the next; poets trying to collect an audience for a reading of their latest work; philosophers arguing, politicians plotting, business men fixing a profitable deal, women exchanging the latest gossip and showing off their figures. Thieves and pickpockets abounded, and so did procurers on the look out for a likely piece of feminine goods and those men and women in search of amorous adventure.

Much of what we know of Roman prostitution comes from the writings of poets and historians, but writing of a different kind has provided a valuable source of information. This is the *graffiti*, or wall scribblings (the word is Italian, and comes from the Greek *graphein*, to write) scratched on the stucco by a *stilus* (pointed instrument used in writing on wax tablets) or a finger-nail, or written with a piece of charcoal. Several thousand of these have been found at Pompeii, on the walls of the basilica, the covered theatre, the amphi- theatre and other places frequented by the multitude; so many, indeed, that one wit has expressed his wonder that a wall could support such a load of inscriptions. In subject they extend from religious dedications to obscene insults, but a large proportion are amatory.

"You've never seen Venus?" runs one; "there's no need to look far. Take a glance at my little darling: she's really exquisite!" "Good luck to him who loves," runs another; "bad luck to him who doesn't know how to; and the very worst of bad luck to him who stands in the way of my true love!" "A blonde taught me to hate brunettes," is yet another; "I will hate them if I can, but I would find it much easier to love them!"

Some are short and sweet, such as "May you be happy", —Serena, Musa, Poppaea, Lucida, Albana, Chloe, or whatever the girl's name is. "Victoria, may you sneeze sweetly!" (i.e. May you be lucky!). A popular gladiator is hailed as *Sus- pirium puellarum* ("thou for whom maidens sigh"), and another as *Puellarum decus* ("maidens' delight"). In the brothel quarter we read such things as "Here I've had lots of girls", "Felix . . . did it twice here", "Here I had Sabina", and "I had a fine time here", followed by the name of a girl "whom I can thoroughly recommend". Sometimes it is the girl who writes her testimonial: "Vale, Victor, you gave me a splendid time!" "Sollemnis, you are absolutely 'it' as a performer!" "Here Romula slept with Staphylus," reads one, below which someone has added, "And here Staphylus slept with Quincta." The Roman equivalent of a taxi-driver is addressed: "If you were in love with my Venus you would hurry to meet her. So finish your drink, whip up your mules, and let's get going to where my dear love dwells". But some are written in a very different mood. "Here, lovers all," writes one disappointed fellow, "come and watch me caress *my* Venus with a stick and tickle her bottom with a switch!"

XVI

Cicero for the Defence

THE MORALISTS OF THE ancient world had very little to say in condemnation of prostitution. Most of them accepted it as part of the natural order of things, and even when they did not actually approve of it and may have gone so far as to admit that it ought to be controlled, they did not believe that there was any point in trying to suppress it. For if it were suppressed, something much worse might take its place.

The conventional attitude was well expressed by Cicero, in his great speech in defence of Caelius, charged (it will be remembered) with offences against Lesbia, his former mistress. The prosecution had made some play with Caelius's rather wild behaviour as a young man about town. Caelius had become involved with prostitutes—or should we not say, with courtesans? This was admitted, and Cicero was shocked, but not very deeply. It was the sort of thing that might be expected in the circumstances, he argued.

"If there be any one among you," he told the bench, "who thinks that young men should be altogether restrained from the love of courtesans I cannot but think that you are taking up a very exalted view. I am not prepared to say that you are wrong. But this I will say, that you are maintaining something that is not only quite out of tune with our present age but is very different from what our ancestors maintained in generations gone by. When, indeed, was this not done? When was it blamed? When wasn't it permitted? When was that which is lawful now not lawful?"

Intrigues came naturally to men, but the game of man-chases-woman and woman-chases-man had to be played according to the rules. There was one rule in particular that all except the hardened profligate was agreed must be observed. It was stated very clearly by the early Roman playwright Plautus in his comedy *Curculio* ("The Weevil"). There is a highway of love, says one of the characters, on which there are no stop signs, no "trespassers are forbidden" notices, but where (if you've got the money) you can buy any girl who comes along it. "The highway's free—walk where you like—but don't, whatever you do, try to get into any private property with a wall round it! In other words, my boy, keep your hands off wife, widow, and virgin—all the rest are yours, and you can take which you like!"

About the same time Cato the Censor made a remark that has come down to us. One day he was passing along the street when he saw a man of his acquaintance emerging from a *fornix* or low brothel. "There's a good fellow," said the stern old man; "when young men's veins are swollen with sexual passion it is far better that they should come down to such places than that they should tamper with other men's wives."

This story is told by Horace in one of his *Satires* that is sometimes omitted from their editions by editors who are more zealous not to offend the proprieties than to be altogether honest with their author. It is the one in which he warns against running to extremes, and one of the points he makes is that in avoiding one vice fools often run into the opposite. They fail to see that there is a middle course which they might follow to better advantage. Thus there are some men like Cato's acquaintance who repair to a "foul brothel". There are others who go to the opposite extreme and are never so happy as when they are pursuing with their attentions some woman whose ankles are hidden by a long gown—a picturesque way of saying that she is a modest matron. "If any of my readers are contemplating following in these men's footsteps," Horace says in effect, "be warned by their fate.

Most of them have met with disaster; any pleasure they have managed to derive from their experiences has been mixed with a great deal of pain, and has usually been accompanied by cruel perils. One of these adulterers has flung himself from off a roof, another was caught and was flogged to death by the husband's slaves, a third succeeded in getting away from the house but fell in with a savage gang of robbers. Then there was the man who had to pay with his fortune to save his life, and another who was grievously mutilated."

How much wiser they would have shown themselves if they had kept their hands off married women and had trafficked only with freedwomen! "Surely you don't think, Cerinthus," he addresses one of his friends, "that a woman's limbs are any softer and finer for being set off with snowy pearls and green emeralds? Often the strumpet has the advantage; and what is more, what she has for sale she displays openly—unlike some matrons one might mention, who try to arrange their clothes so that you may notice only their fine legs and arms and be blind to such things as narrow hips and a long nose. In a matron you can see only her face; everything else is hidden by her long robe, and if you try to get a closer view you will find all kinds of obstacles put in your way. But with the courtesan, there's no obstacle. Her dress of Coan silk is so transparent that she might easily have got nothing on."

There was the Greek philosopher named Philodemus, Horace continues, who was not above describing the sort of woman he most favoured. She should be fair and tall, but not too fair or too tall, she should not cost too much, nor should she be slow in coming when she was bid. When embracing such a woman, declared the wise man, she was to him an Ilia (the mother of Romulus) or an Egeria (the nymph who was King Numa's friend). When you were with such a woman you never had to worry about what would happen if her husband took it into his head to return from a trip in the country when he was quite unexpected. Imagine the scene in such an event. The dogs barking, the knocking at the gate, the door burst open, the house in turmoil. The woman, white as a sheet, would leap up and away, and the maid would shriek in fright, the one fearing for her limbs and her guilty mistress for her dowry that might be confiscated if she were caught in the act. Then think of the man in the case, running down the road with his clothes half off his back and leaving his shoes behind, and thanking his lucky stars if he succeeds in getting away with only his reputation damaged!

And now Propertius is giving very much the same advice. "Don't waste your time on a mistress who has a husband or a guardian who knows his job," is his counsel; "it really isn't worth while hiding in some hole or corner in order to taste perhaps one night of happiness in a whole year. Perish the love that has to be carried on in utmost secrecy behind closed doors! Far better make a pass at that pert little minx who with her face unveiled, her cloak flung back, goes striding down the Sacra Via in her slippers—and she doesn't mind if they do get a bit muddy. *She* has no guardian to scowl at you when you venture to call at her house. If you accost her, she won't be offended in the slightest. *She* will never put you off, never make demands on you in a nasty little whining voice for presents that she knows you can't afford, since your father keeps you so short of cash. *She* won't say, "I'm so frightened; please hurry up, I implore you, for I've just remembered that this is the day my husband is returning from the country . . ."

This was the attitude of the ordinary Roman male to prostitution. Married ladies were the property of their husbands, and it was considered unfair and undignified to encroach on another man's territory, that he had bought and paid for. But most other women were fair game, and since it was men who made the rules the women may well have been justified in thinking sometimes that the fairness was all on the men's side.

In this moral climate, most men took advantage of the opportunities offered to indulge in amatory adventures, often of the most sordid character. Young men sowing their wild oats (Cicero reminded the court in the Caelius case that many famous Romans had done such things in their youth and got over it as they got older), married men away from home on business trips or who found their wives dull and unresponsive, officials on foreign tours of duty, soldiers and seafarers, men who had lost their partners through death or divorce, and those who just loved variety and change— together they constituted an inexhaustible demand for female flesh.

XVII

The Traffic in "Frail Beauty"

MOST OF THE ROMAN prostitutes were slaves, and most of the women in the courtesan class—the *puellae* of Ovid—were freedwomen, i.e. women who had been born slaves or were the daughters of men who had been slaves and had obtained their manumission.

Slavery has a dreadful sound in modern ears, but the ancients saw nothing particularly shocking in it as an institution. To them it was part of the law of nature. From the beginning there were slaves in Rome, and from the middle of the second century B.C., when Rome set out on the road of world conquest, she was definitely a slave state, in which the slaves may have outnumbered the free population by as many as three to one. The Romans were accused by their enemies of treating their slaves with exceptional harshness, but at least there was nothing among them of the nature of a colour bar. A man was not a slave because he happened to be born with a black skin; few black men were slaves, in fact, and the vast majority of slaves had skins as white as those of their proprietors. It was not race or skin colour that made a slave, but sheer bad luck—misfortune in having been born a slave, or having been taken prisoner in war or made captive by pirates or sold in slavery in discharge of debts. So far from considering it a blot on their civilization, some Roman jurists argued that it was an essentially humane provision, since the alternative might well be slaughter or at least destitution.

In Roman law a slave was not a human being but a *res,*

a thing, a chattel, that could be sold or exchanged or given away in the same way as any other piece of property. As such he had no rights. Under the Republic his master had the power of life and death over him, could punish him with chastisement or imprisonment, and use him for any purpose he pleased. But under the Empire successive steps were taken to improve the slave's status and condition. Furthermore, at all times the slave was not without hope. He might look forward to emancipation, whether by free grant or by purchase out of his own savings, and he was not in the hopeless condition of a Negro slave in the southern states of the U.S.A.

Since he was not a person but a thing, no Roman slave could contract a legal marriage; nor for the same reason could he commit adultery. The union of male and female slaves was countenanced, even encouraged, however, as by Cato the Elder who, we are told by Plutarch, "as he knew that slaves will stick at nothing to gratify their passion for women, allowed them to have the company of his female slaves, upon paying a certain price; but under the strict prohibition of approaching any other women".

This sexual relationship was a mere cohabitation or *contubernium*, to use the Latin term which meant literally "tent companionship", implying that it was the kind of temporary association that men entered into when they were campaigning. The permission might be revoked at any time, without regard for the feelings of the persons most concerned, and any children resulting from the union were the master's, an addition to his "stock" that he might dispose of at will.

The condition of slavery bore most hardly upon the women, for in their case its disabilities were added to those already imposed by their sex. A Roman gentleman could have only one wife, but he might own as many female slaves as his means would allow. They were his chattels, and for them such words as shame, chastity, and self-respect had no meaning. When his wife had ceased to please him or had grown old, he had at his disposal girls who added a spice of novelty to the sexual relationship. His amours might even show a profit, since there is no reason to suppose that the Roman landowner showed any more compunction in sending his natural offspring to the slave-market than did the Southern planter who despatched his mulatto bastards to the slave auctions in New Orleans.

When a slave became a freedman or *libertus* he still remained a member of the household of his former owner, who was now his *patronus*, and was under certain obligations to continue to serve him. In the same way, a slavewoman who became a *liberta* might be required to hold herself in readiness to gratify the sexual demands of her former proprietor. The latter might reserve for himself in the deed of manumission some share in her person, in much the same way as a feudal lord in medieval Europe retained certain rights over his female vassals. The legend of Virginia, told by the Roman historian Livy in ancient times and by Petrarch and Chaucer and many another up to the time when Lord Macaulay made it the subject of one of his famous *Lays*, tells of a young Roman girl who was claimed by a great and powerful nobleman as a slave-girl born in his house. Rather than allow her to pass out of his guardianship her father snatched a knife from a butcher's stall and plunged it into her heart. It may be only a fable, but it describes an incident such as might often occur in a society in which freeborn and slave lived in close proximity and there were no registers of births to determine parentage.

Many attempts have been made to estimate the number of slaves in ancient Rome, but there is no agreement on the figure. Certainly they were exceedingly numerous. Every citizen, however poor and humble, wished to own at least a single slave whom he might order about. For some centuries the chief source of supply was war. The enormous number of prisoners taken in the successive conflicts with Carthage and other Mediterranean powers were conveyed to Italy and put

to work on the fields and in the mines and domestic establishments. After the victory of Aemilius Paulus in Epirus in
168 B.C. some 150,000 Greeks, male and female, were sold
into captivity. Julius Caesar is stated to have put up 63,000
Gaulish prisoners for sale in one go. In the course of the
Jewish wars that Josephus records, 100,000 Jews were sent to
the slave-marts.

Behind these figures is hidden a mass of human misery
impossible to imagine, let alone measure. History is silent
about the fate of these hosts of human unfortunates. Very
likely most of them were dead within a few years, since the
mines and other places to which they were consigned were
places of agonizing squalor, in which human life was, to use
a modern term, expendable. But the demand that had been
fostered continued to exercise, and to ensure a more regular
supply resort was had to piracy. For generations the systematic
hunting of men and women was a profitable activity in Mediterranean waters. The captives were carried usually to the
island of Delos, where as many as 10,000 slaves were put up
for auction in the market-place in a single day. Another chief
centre of the infamous traffic was Capua, on the Italian main-
land. An import duty was levied on each slave brought into
the country, and there was also a "sales tax" when the "goods"
changed hands.

In the nature of things, about half of the captives were
women and girls, and although probably the majority of
these were destined to serve as house servants and in other
domestic capacities, the better educated and most attractive
were picked out for a career in prostitution. The profits in
this department of the trade were great, but there were some
risks attached to it, since if the girl were able to prove before
a magistrate that she was freeborn, the purchaser might be
obliged to release her, in which case he would have to bear
the loss.

Several of the plays of the Roman playwright Plautus

(flourished about 200 B.C.) have a plot turning on a slave-girl heroine who turns out to be a freeborn maiden abducted from her parents when she was a child. Seneca the Elder, who lived in Rome under Augustus, describes how one day he went down to the beach and watched a pirate-ship landing its cargo of captives. Among them was a young girl, who "stood naked on the shore to be criticized by her purchaser. All the parts of her body were inspected and handled. Do you want to hear the rest of the story? Well then, the pirate sold, a pander bought".

Sometimes the pander, or *leno*, obtained a bargain in this kind of "black market". The bawd in Shakespeare's *Pericles* thought he had done well when he agreed to pay the pirates a thousand pieces for Marina. "Has she any qualities, Boult?" he enquires of his minion. "She has a good face, speaks well, and has excellent good clothes," replies Boult. "Boult, take you the marks of her—the colour of her hair, complexion, height, her age, with warrant of her virginity; and cry, 'He that will give most shall have her first'. Such a maidenhead were no cheap thing, if men were as they have been . . ."

Martial has a nasty little piece about a slave-girl who was being "cried" through the Roman streets. "The town-crier was lately offering for sale a young lady of not over good reputation, such as have a seat in the Subura (the quarter where prostitutes were most often encountered). When she had been shown for some time and the bids did not reach the reserve price, the man, wishing to demonstrate what a pure little thing she was, took her in his arms and kissed her. She feigned reluctance, so he kissed her again, and yet again. What do you think was the effect of his kisses? Just this, a man who had been willing to pay six hundred sesterces for the girl hurriedly withdrew his bid."

Scenes such as these were commonplace in the Roman world, in a state of society in which there was always a demand for personable females, especially for those with the blush of maiden innocence on their cheeks. The effect on the people's morals, and their attitude towards the whole female sex, cannot have been anything but bad. Yet for generations there was hardly a voice raised against this white slavery, even in Rome itself, the centre and capital of the world's most advanced civilization.

With the gradual establishment of the *Pax Romana* the supply of slaves drawn from the conquered races began to dry up. Piracy, too, became a thing of the past. The slave-markets continued to do plenty of business, however, as Barbarian chiefs on the fringes of the Empire were ready to trade their surplus retainers, and slaves continued to be bred on the Roman estates and plantations. Roman economists such as Varro in the last century B.C. and Columella in the following century urged on proprietors the economic advantages of producing homebred slaves. Horace has a line in one of his Epodes about "home-bred slaves that gather around the fire-lit household images".

But as the Empire gathered years and prestige the condition of the slave population steadily improved. More and more voices were raised against slavery as an institution, and in course of time the arguments of such Stoic philosophers as Seneca, who wrote that "we are all members of one great body", and Cicero, who maintained the doctrine of universal brotherhood, obtained increasing acceptance. Emancipations were speeded up. Laws were passed that profoundly altered the servile condition, and always for the better. When we are told of Nero's excesses we should in fairness remember that under him it was enacted that no slave should be condemned by his master to fight wild beasts in the arena without a sentence from a judge. Domitian was a terrible tyrant, but it was he who forbade the oriental custom of mutilating slaves to make them eunuchs. Hadrian and his successors, Antoninus Pius and Marcus Aurelius, deprived masters of their right to kill their slaves and treat them with barbarity.

One man of this period should be held in high esteem. It was Dion Chrysostom (Dion "the golden-mouthed"), a philosophical writer who lived in Rome under Domitian and subsequently travelled widely, who, says Sir Samuel Dill in his *Roman Society from Nero to Marcus Aurelius*, "was probably the first of the ancients to raise a voice against the traffic in frail beauty which has gone on pitilessly from age to age. Nothing could exceed the vehemence with which he assails an evil which he regards as not only dishonouring to human nature, but charged with the poison of far-spreading corruption".

The advent of Christianity made little difference at first. The early Christians were living in expectation of the imminent end of the world, and were not inclined to worry themselves about an institution that was so soon to be swept away. St. Paul once sent a runaway slave back to his master with the request that he should be treated kindly. For some two hundred years after the establishment of Christianity in the fourth century progress in legislation affecting slaves was very slight, and there was even retrogression. Thus Constantine, the first Christian emperor, strictly forbade intermarriage between free citizens and slaves, and furthermore decreed that if a free woman had sexual intercourse with one of her male slaves she should be executed and the man burnt alive; by the pagan law, the woman would have been merely condemned to share her paramour's status. Under Justinian (sixth century A.D.) a male slave was permitted to marry a free woman with the permission of his master, and the rape of a slave woman was punished just as if she had been a free woman, i.e. by death.

Slavery continued in Europe for about 800 years after Constantine, but by the twelfth century it was getting rare and by the fourteenth century it had almost disappeared. Its decline and eventual extinction were owing partly to the ideas of brotherhood preached by the philosophers of pagan

Rome and some of the enlightened Churchmen of Christian times, but in the main the greatest influence seems to have been exerted by economic causes and considerations. The growth of capital enabled more men to be profitably employed, and it was found that a free man worked better than a slave. So the slaves became serfs, or villeins, in the country-side, and artisans and guild-members in the rising towns, and out of these classes emerged in due course the populations of today.

Although the matter is shrouded in obscurity, there is reason to believe that the *jus primae noctis*, "right of the first night", i.e. the right of a feudal superior to deflower the bride of one of his serfs, was among the last of the feudal privileges to be given up, and in France some relics of it are said to have survived until the fall of the *ancien régime* at the Revolution.

SEX IN THEORY AND PRACTICE

XVIII

The Roman Kiss

FROM SOMEWHERE VERY NEAR the beginning of the Roman story comes the sound of kissing. The little band of refugees from Troy (fallen to the Greeks at last, after the ten years' siege) had arrived at the western shores of Italy and came to anchor off the mouth of the Tiber. The men (we may suppose) had still plenty of the spirit of adventure in them, but the women had had enough, and more than enough. They were "out of heart and weary of the sea", we read in Plutarch's account, and they demanded of their men-folk, "why go any further?" Not getting any satisfactory answer, and feeling by now pretty desperate, they adopted the proposal "of one of the highest birth and best understanding amongst them whose name was Roma, and burnt the ships".

With which act (so the story proceeds) the men were at first very angry, but afterwards, finding things succeeding "far better than they could hope, in that they found the country very good, and the people courteous, they not only did the Lady Roma other honours but added also this, of calling after her name the city which she had been the occasion of their founding. From this, they say, has come down that custom at Rome for women to salute their husbands with kisses; because these women, after they had burnt the ships, made use of such endearments when entreating and pacifying their husbands".

The ancient Romans distinguished between kisses in a way that has descended to all the peoples of Western civilization. They grouped them in three principal categories, though modern languages do not employ three terms for the three forms. The word "kiss", defined by Dr. Johnson as "a salute given by joining the lips", is not of Latin but of Teutonic derivation. The regular Latin word for a kiss was *osculum*, the primary meaning of which was "a little mouth, a sweet mouth". The osculum was applied to the face or cheeks, and came to be distinguished as the kiss of friendship, although to begin with it may well have been sometimes a salute on the lips such as we may suppose Roma and her companions bestowed on their disgruntled men-folk after the women had burnt the ships.

But in course of time a special word was devised for the kiss on the mouth, *basium*. We are told that the poet Catullus was the first and for some time the only important Roman writer to employ it in preference to *osculum*. Since Catullus came from a part of Italy in which the Celtic element was most pronounced, it has been surmised that *basium* may have been Celtic originally. Perhaps the poet used it in his love passages with Clodia-Lesbia, and she liked the sound of it almost as much as she liked the thing itself. As a consequence he employed it to denote those kisses of which he could never have enough. Coleridge's translation of the famous *Vivamus, mea Lesbia* has been quoted in an earlier chapter, and here is the rendering made by the Jacobean poet Richard Crashaw in 1648:

> Come and let us live, my Deare,
> Let us love and never feare
> What the sourest Fathers say:
> Brightest Sol that dyes today
> Lives againe in bright tomorrow;
> But if we darke sons of sorrow
> Set, O then, how long a Night
> Shuts the eyes of our short light!
> Then let amorous kisses dwell
> On our lips, begin and tell
> A Thousand and a Hundred score,

An Hundred and a Thousand more,
Till another Thousand smother
That, and that wipe off another.
Thus at last when we have numbr'd
Many a Thousand, many a Hundred,
We'll confound the reckoning quite
And lose ourselves in wild delight:
While our joyes so multiply
As shall mocke the envious eye.

From basium come the French *baiser,* the Italian *baciare,* the Spanish *beso* and the Portuguese *beijo.* Some etymologists maintain that it is also the parent of the old English word "buss", meaning a kiss of a rude and playful kind, a smack on the lips.

For the third kind of kiss, that given between the lips with the aid of the tongue, the Romans often used the word *savium,* which meant originally "a mouth, or lips, puckered up to kiss"; a diminutive of this is *saviolum,* "a sweet kiss". From this the transition to the kiss of passion was easy. Although Ovid seems to have preferred *osculum,* there is no better place to look for descriptions of this kind of passionate kiss than his poems. Thus in Marlowe's translation of the *Amores* we read of the girl who "eagerly kissed me with her tongue", and of another who "laughed and kissed so sweetly as might make wrath-kindled Jove away his thunder shake, ... for in my lips lay her whole tongue hid, mine in hers she dips".

Among Martial's verses there is a description of a Roman kiss that is worth quoting in the delightful rendering given in an old MS of the sixteenth century:

Like balsams chaf'd by some exotic Fair,
Or from a saffron field fresh gliding air:
In winter chests like apples ripening,
Or grounds o'erspread with budding trees in spring.
Like silken robes in royal presses, and
Gums suppled by a virgin's soft-white hand;

As broken jars of Falerna wines to smell
Far off: or flowery gardens where bees dwell;
Perfumers' pots, burnt incense tossed on the air,
Chaplets new-fallen from rich perfumed hair.
What more? All's not enough: mix all to express
My dear Girl's morning kisses' sweetnesses;
You'ld know her name? I'll nought but kisses tell;
I doubt, I swear, you'd know her fain too well!

As well as these kisses of affection and love the Romans
had the kiss of homage and of religious veneration. Courtiers
and ministers touched the Emperor's robe with their hand
and then kissed the latter. Similarly the devout in the presence of a religious image or of that of the deified emperor
raised their right hand to the mouth and kissed it, and then
waved it in the direction of the revered object. This "thrown
kiss" was the Roman method of adoration as it was of the
Greeks and other ancient peoples, and it is still met with
today, when we blow a kiss to departing friends or wave our
hand in farewell.

The Romans also employed the "kiss direct" in worship.
Cicero states that the lips and beard of the statue of the old
hero-god Hercules at Agrigentum had been almost worn
away by the kisses of his adorers; and there are frequent
references in Latin literature to the kissing of the phallus of
the statues of Priapus and other divinities most intimately
associated with sex. This practice survived into historic times,
and is not yet quite extinct; in some French villages statues
of holy men have been found with the male member almost
kissed away. At St. Peter's in Rome there is a bronze statue
of the Apostle, said to date from about the fifth century, of
which not only the toe but the greater part of the right foot
have been carried away on the lips of worshippers.

From what has been ascertained, it would seem that the
Romans were among the first European peoples to kiss.
There has always been kissing, of course, of a kind. It is a

specialized form of touch, the "mother of the senses", and is a development of the nuzzling of mammals, the billing of birds, the antennal play of some insects, the interlacing of elephant trunks, etc. From their animal ancestry humans inherited the "olfactory kiss" (Latin, *olfacere,* to smell), described not too accurately by travellers as "rubbing noses". The typical primitive kiss is the application of nose to cheek —the contact of the mucous membrane of the mouth with the skin of the face—followed or accompanied by an inhalation or sniff. This form is found among Chinese, Malays, Eskimos, South Sea Islanders, and many other peoples. But not among the Japanese, who have no word for "kiss" and (except when Western influences have made themselves felt) kissing is not practised save between a mother and her child.

In the essentially European kiss there is no olfactory element, but some anthropologists have detected a trace of a gustatory one (Latin, *gustus,* taste). They would have found support in the experience of the lovers of Poppaea, the beautiful consort of Nero, whose kisses were reported to have the flavour of wild berries. Biting with the teeth is a recognized part of the love-play of passionate lovers, as is evidenced clearly enough in the descriptions of sexual intercourse by the Roman poets.

The earliest home of the nose or sniff kiss seems to have been the India of the Vedic period, round about 2000 B.C., and it was not until the period of the Mahabharata epic (about 500 B.C. ?) that the mouth-to-mouth salutation came into vogue. This was well established when Vatsysyana composed his manual of erotic sex instruction known as the *Kama Sutra* about the beginning of our era. From India the kiss, in one or the other form, spread eastwards to China and west to Persia, Assyria, Syria, Greece, Italy, and so, by way of the channels of Roman influence, throughout Europe. For some reason the mouth kiss seems never to have become properly established among the ancient Egyptians. The Teutonic tribes practised it, but there is no word for it in the Celtic tongues, the Old Irish *pog* and the Welsh *poc* being borrowed from yet another Latin word, *pax,* which from meaning "peace" came to stand for "the kiss of peace".

This term is met with in the early history of Christianity. On the face of it, it seems somewhat strange that the early Christians, who took such a firm stand against pagan ideas and practices, should have adopted into their ceremonial the Roman *osculum.* As soon as a convert had been baptized, he (or she) was formally received into the Church by a kiss of brotherhood, the salutation of peace, and from that time he had the right of saluting all Christians with this sign, irrespective of sex and marital status and class. In the New Testament we find St. Paul enjoining the Christians in Rome to "salute one another with an holy kiss", and likewise the Corinthian and Thessalonian converts, and St. Peter enjoining the recipients of his epistle to "greet one another with a kiss of charity". It is likely that at first this kiss was imparted at every meeting of the faithful, but gradually it became limited to the great sacramental occasions such as baptism and the administration of the Eucharist. "At first, too, and for a considerable time," states Dr. James Donaldson, "the Christian brothers and sisters kissed each other. It is easy to see that such a practice would give rise to scandalous reports, and there is evidence in the ecclesiastical writers that the early Christians did not always make it a holy kiss, as it should have been. Athenagoras [a Christian writer of the second century A.D.] quotes a saying which he attributes to our Lord, and which evidently deals with an abuse of this practice. It is to this effect: 'Whoever kisses a second time, because he has found pleasure in it, commits a sin'."

The "holy kiss" was an essential part of the *agape,* or "love feast" or "feast of charity" which usually accompanied the Eucharist in the primitive Church, and it helped to confirm the pagans in their suspicion that these assemblies, in which the Christians met in secret and generally after nightfall and without distinction of sex or rank, were the occasion of the celebration of the most horrid rites, including the sacrifice of an infant and the drinking of its blood from a cup passed round among the worshippers, and concluded with an orgy in which, all lights having been extinguished, men and women indulged in indiscriminate licentiousness. Notwithstanding the pagan suspicions and the opportunities the function afforded for scandalous behaviour, the agape continued until it was finally suppressed by the Church authorities in the seventh century.

XIX

Corinna's Sin

OVID's *Amores* WAS PROBABLY the first of his works to be written, when he was in his early twenties. As might be expected from the title—the word means "loves"—it is markedly erotic, even more so than the *Ars Amatoria* that followed it some years later, when the author's experience had been enlarged and his poetic gifts more fully developed. Some of the elegies it contains have proved too strong meat for the translators, and in whole or in part have been left in the chaste obscurity of the original Latin. But not in Christopher Marlowe's version. When he sat down to translate the small book he was, it would seem, still an undergraduate at Cambridge, lusty and full-blooded, and without the least inclination to call a spade anything else. The date of the book's publication is uncertain, but *Marlowes Elegres* was ordered to be burnt in 1599 by the Archbishop of Canterbury and the Bishop of London on account of its alleged immoral tendency. By this time Marlowe himself was dead, killed in 1593 in a tavern brawl in Deptford, or we may be sure that he would have been hauled up before the courts and punished for outraging the moral susceptibilities of a far from squeamish age.

A few of the elegies are addressed to a woman who is called Corinna, and much ink has been spilt, not very profitably, on the question whether she was just a lay figure or a real character of flesh and blood. On the whole it seems more reasonable to suppose that Corinna was not a mere creation of the poet's fancy but was a vital and vivid intrusion into his private life. But even so, we are quite in the dark as to her identity.

The name Corinna is obviously a pseudonym, derived from Greek lyric poetry. Some commentators have argued that from what we are told about her she was clearly too unprincipled and vulgar to belong to the class of Roman ladies to which Catullus's Lesbia belonged, Tibullus's Delia and Propertius's Cynthia. She was very likely a *libertina*, or freedwoman, who carried about with her some of the taint of her servile origin. Other students of the elegies have come to the conclusion that Corinna was one of the women who formed the gay circle about the Elder Julia, the only child of the Emperor Augustus. And yet another view, which, strange as it must appear, seems to have been held for hundreds of years, is that she was none other than Julia herself.

From what Ovid tells us, she was married and had a husband at home, lived in comfortable circumstances, was well looked after and closely chaperoned or guarded, and in herself was beautiful and accomplished. In an attempt to piece the story together we may start with a poem in the first book, in which the poet approaches Nape, Corinna's personal maid and confidante, and asks her to carry to her mistress a love-letter.

> I charge thee mark her eyes and front in reading:
> By speechless looks we guess at things succeeding.
> Straight being read, will her to write much back,
> I hate fair paper should writ matter lack.

And yet, after all, what need is there that "she tire her hand to hold the quill? Let this word, *Come*, alone the tablets fill . . ."

The letter was conveyed as he had begged, but the reply was far from encouraging: "This day denial hath my sport adjourned." He might have known that this would happen: had not the girl, when she set off with the letter in her hand,

stumbled when she came to the door? A bad omen indeed:
let her be more careful next time! For of course there was a
next time, and soon we find the poet exultingly proclaiming
that,

> Conquer'd Corinna in my bosom lays,
> She whom her husband, guard, and gate, as foes,
> Lest art should win her, firmly did enclose . . .

> By me Corinna learns, cozening her guard,
> To get the door with little noise unbarr'd;
> And slipp'd from bed, cloth'd in a loose night-gown,
> To move her feet unheard in setting down.

Of course they had to walk warily, for fear of arousing the
husband's suspicions. Often the lover had to "sit gazing as a
bashful guest, While others touch the damsel I love best".
But such an occasion as is celebrated in the elegy entitled
Corinnae concubitus (this latter word meaning "lying or
reclining with, sexual intercourse") more than compensated
for the jealousies, unsatisfied longings, humiliating subter-
fuges, and all the other tormenting accompaniments of an
illicit passion.

> In summer's heat, and mid-time of the day,
> To rest my limbs upon a bed I lay;
> One window shut, the other open stood,
> Which gave such light as twinkles in a wood,
> Like twilight glimpse at setting of the sun,
> Or night being past, and yet not day begun.
> Such light to shamefast maidens must be shown
> Where they may sport, and seem to be unknown.

> Then came Corinna in her long loose gown,
> Her white neck hid with tresses hanging down,
> Resembling fair Semiramis going to bed,
> Or Lais of a thousand wooers sped.
> I snatch'd her gown; being thin, the harm was small;
> Yet striv'd she to be covered therewithal;
> And striving thus as one that would be cast,
> Betray'd herself, and yielded at the last.

Stark naked as she stood before mine eye,
Not one wen in her body could I spy.
What arms and shoulders did I touch and see,
How apt her breasts were to be press'd by me!
How smooth a belly under her waist saw I!
How large a leg, and what a lusty thigh!

To leave the rest, all lik'd me passing well;
I cling'd her naked body, down she fell;
Judge you the rest: being tir'd she bade me kiss;
Jove send me more such afternoons as this.

No doubt the great god was sufficiently obliging, but it was the poet's way to get tired before long of what he had won perhaps too easily. "We scorn things lawful, stolen sweets we affect," he wrote, having discovered that Corinna was what in modern slang would be called "too easy". But "wily Corinna saw this blemish in me, and craftily knows by what means to win me ... she nourish'd my warm fire, and was again most apt to my desire".

Great gods, what kisses, and how many gave she!

How many indeed, and perhaps too many, for at some stage in the intrigue the lover was aghast at the intimation that Corinna was with child, and by him. And worse still was to come, for Corinna was as much taken aback as he was and had resort to desperate measures. She arranged for an abortion, and her life was endangered in consequence.

While rashly her womb's burden she cast out,
Weary Corinna hath her life in doubt ...

The poet was angry, but his wrath was overwhelmed by his fear for the life of the woman who had "conceiv'd of me; or I am sure I oft have done what might as much procure". But his humane instincts were revolted by what he could not but hold to be a sin, a crime.

What helps it women to be free from war,
Nor being arm'd fierce troops to follow far,
If without battle self-wrought wounds annoy them,
And their own privy-weapon'd hands destroy them?
Who unborn infants first to slay invented,
Deserv'd thereby with death to be tormented.
Because thy belly should rough wrinkles lack,
Wilt thou thy womb-enclosed offspring wrack?
Had ancient mothers this vile custom cherish'd,
All human kind by their default had perish'd.

Thou also that wert born fair, had'st decayed,
If such a work thy mother had assayed.
Myself, that better die with loving may,
Had seen, my mother killing me, no day.

Why with hid irons are your bowels torn?
And why dire poison give you babes unborn?

Armenian tigers never did so ill,
Nor dares the lioness her young whelps kill.
But tender damsels do it, though with pain;
Oft dies she that her paunch-wrapt child hath slain;
She dies, and with loose hairs to grave is sent,
And who'er sees her, worthily lament.

Ovid's remonstrances would have been fully understood, even sympathized with, by his fellow writers, but it is clear from his own mentions that abortion was very commonly resorted to in Roman society. There was no law expressly condemning the practice, in the Roman Republic or during the greater part of the Roman Empire; the first Roman jurist to denounce it seems to have been Ulpian, in the early part of the third century A.D. The general opinion seems to have been that the foetus in the womb was a part of the mother's body, and she had as much right to get rid of it if she wanted to as she had to cauterize a tumour on her body. The art of inducing abortion was a recognized and regular part of the doctor's practice, and was apparently well understood. Sometimes, as is clear from the Ovidian quotation given above, instruments were employed, and there was resort also to abortifacient drugs and potions. A long succession of writers represent the practice as avowed and almost universal, and they describe it as resulting not simply from poverty or licentiousness but even from so slight a motive as vanity, which made mothers shrink from the disfigurement of child-bearing. But while writing of voluntary abortion as general and notorious, Ovid was by no means alone in condemning it on humanitarian grounds.

Now the heinousness of the practice had been brought home to him with a dreaful impressiveness, as his wench, as he calls Corinna, lay at death's door. To the gods and goddesses he addressed his prayers, and in particular to Lucina, the name under which Juno was known when presiding over the rites of childbirth.

> On labouring women thou dost pity take,
> Whose bodies with their heavy burdens ache.
> My wench, Lucina, I entreat thee favour,
> Worthy she is, thou should'st in mercy save her.

If the goddess will but answer his prayers and grant his most fervent wish, then he, Ovidius Naso,

> In white, with incense I'll thy altars greet,
> Myself will bring vowed gifts before thy feet,
> Subscribing, "Naso with Corinna sav'd".
> Do but deserve gifts with this title grav'd.

Then he turns to the girl or woman who has brought such trouble and danger on herself: "If in so great fear I may advise thee, To have this skirmish fought, let it suffice thee." In other words, "Let this be a warning to you, my girl, and

don't tempt the gods again: they may not be so forgiving a
second time!"

> Forgive her, gracious gods, this one delict [fault],
> And on the *next* fault punishment inflict.

Corinna's pregnancy was clearly unexpected, and it is not
unreasonable to suppose that the lovers had "taken precautions" that had proved ineffectual. Not even Ovid has
told us anything about Roman contraceptive technique, but
Tacitus refers to the "habit of limiting the number of children", and we are surely entitled to assume that the Romans
practised at least the method that has been adopted from
time immemorial—*coitus interruptus*, what Onan did when, as
is told in *Genesis* 38, he refused to "raise up seed' for his
deceased brother. The Romans were unaware of the existence
of the male spermatozoa and the female ovum or egg, but
they knew enough to recognize the necessary connection
between sexual intercourse and conception. Very likely they
were inclined to underestimate the part played by the female
in the process, but they were cognizant of the generative
power of the male "seed". Ways of preventing this from
reaching the womb may well have presented themselves, and
among these may have been the sponge, and the sheath made
of linen or animal gut, for use by the woman and the man
respectively. Their technique included pessaries, e.g. made of
cyclamen root, and chemically treated suppositories, for
these were recommended by the Arab physicians of the late
Middle Ages, and it is generally agreed that the Arabs
inherited the Roman knowledge of medicine and the allied
arts. Such matters have been considered too immodest for
the historian to inquire into, although he has shown no such
squeamishness in describing the horrors of the torture-
chamber and the battlefield, so there is no pulling back the
curtain that the Corinnas have drawn.

Ovid's condemnation of abortion does him credit, but it

is unlikely to have had much effect. After all (so it was argued), the foetus has no individual existence, it cannot feel anything, it has no claim to a life that has not really begun. It was not until some time after the triumph of Christianity in the Roman world that voluntary abortion was made a crime punishable with extreme rigour. This was because of the Christian belief that the foetus as soon as it acquired animation became an immortal soul, destined to an eternity of bliss in heaven or an eternity of pain in hell—or, as some of the humaner theologians were prepared to allow, to be consigned to a painless and joyless Limbo. What its fate would be depended not on anything that it had done of itself —obviously it could not do anything—but on whether or not it had been baptized. In Christian eyes, therefore, abortion was not only an act of murder but, as the foetus had not been baptized, it deprived an immortal soul of its chances of salvation.

Arising out of this belief was the Christian condemnation of anything of the nature of birth control, or birth prevention.

What would have happened to Corinna's child if it had been born? From what we know of the father, it would probably have been put out to nurse and then brought up to some way of getting a useful livelihood. But in less fortunate surroundings it might have been killed, since the destruction of newborn infants, though forbidden by law, was certainly common. Parents whose sense of pity prevented them from doing away with their infant out of hand might choose the alternative of exposition. In Rome this might mean that it was deposited near a certain pillar in the Velabrum, a valley in the most densely populated and squalid districts of the town. Or it might be left on the edge of one of the dungheaps or cess-trenches which were the only conveniences available to the great mass of the common people. (In the *insulae* or apartment-blocks the only lavatories, i.e. cess-pits, were on the ground floor, but the houses of the well-to-do were provided with individual pits.) Here it might die of neglect, or it might be picked up by some speculator in human flesh and reared to become a slave or a prostitute. If it were very lucky, a childless couple might take pity on it, and bring it up in their home as their own. Juvenal says that Roman wives sometimes presented their unsuspecting husbands with a foundling, rather than face the trouble and risk of child-bearing.

An interesting case of exposure is mentioned by Suetonius in his life of the Emperor Caligula. When the very popular young prince Germanicus died suddenly, the grief and consternation were such that some mothers exposed their newborn infants, declaring that it was not worth while having children when such a brave young man came to an untimely end.

XX

The "Odious Vice"

THE WORD "HOMOSEXUAL" LOOKS as if it ought to be Latin, but in fact the "homo" is not the Latin for "man" but comes from the Greek *homos*, meaning "same". By the term is meant, to quote the dictionary definition, "having, or pertaining to, sexual propensity for persons of one's own sex". The opposite term is heterosexual, and this also is of Greek origin (Greek *heteros,* other).

Homosexuality may be found in women as well as in men, but the special term for this particular form of sexual deviation is Lesbianism, named after the Greek island of Lesbos, whose inhabitants were supposed to be specially addicted to it. Another name for these "unnatural sexual relations between women" is Sapphism, after the Lesbian poetess Sappho (seventh century B.C.), who was believed to be partial to them, although her verses and what we know of her life show that she was by no means indifferent to the love of men.

So far as the history of the word is concerned, the great Oxford English Dictionary traces the first use of "homosexual" to Havelock Ellis's *Studies in the Psychology of Sex* under date 1897, but the pioneer English sexologist disclaimed having invented it and in fact rather disliked it. The thing is, however, of far greater antiquity than the word, whoever coined it and when. The practice of homosexual relations is in fact so old that its origins are lost in the mists of prehistory; it may well be part of mankind's animal inheritance. The Old Testament Hebrews were well acquainted with it, as may be seen from the fate of the city of Sodom and the fierce enactments against it in the Mosaic Code. It seems to have been rife in the peoples of the near east. But it was among the Greeks that *paiderastia,* as they called it (Greek *pais, paidos,* boy, + *erastes,* lover), reached social acceptance, especially among the upper classes and the "intellectuals". So far as our information goes, it was not indulged in to any extent by the poorer classes, and it may be that, as in much more recent times, there was attached to it a measure of social or cultural snobbery. Its prevalence among the Greeks has been attributed in considerable measure to the public games and athletic displays, in which young men engaged in a state of complete nakedness; the spectacle of the male form in all its unclothed beauty is supposed to have given rise to passions which in that society it was regarded as heroic to resist.

Even the popular religion was made to bend to the vice, as when Hebe, the goddess cup-bearer of the gods of Olympus, was replaced by Ganymede, a beautiful youth who (according to the old legend) was snatched away from earth to heaven on the back of an eagle, to satisfy (says Lemprière) "the shameful and unnatural desires of Jupiter". When during Hannibal's invasion, the Roman army was disastrously defeated at Cannae in 216 B.C. there were some superstitious folk who said that this was because there had been recently introduced into Jupiter's temple in Rome an image of Ganymede which had naturally aroused the jealous hostility of Juno, Jupiter's spouse.

It is interesting to note that from the name Ganymede was derived the Latin *catamitus,* whence our word catamite, meaning (as one dictionary puts it) "a sodomite's minion", or (to quote another) "a boy kept for unnatural purposes". Pathic, another word for catamite that is now seldom found, comes from the Greek *pathikos,* "passive". The word most often used by Romans for a homosexual was *cinaedus,* and this may still be made out on walls at Pompeii, attached to two male names, one of them in the possessive case. Another term was *paedicator* or *paedico*. But the most foul-sounding of the words used to describe this vice has reached us by way of the French *bougre* from the Latin *Bulgarus*, "Bulgarian", because in the eleventh century there was a sect of Bulgarian Christians whose beliefs were so heretical that they were believed to be capable of any enormity.

From Greece pederasty passed to Rome, possibly by way of the Etruscans. As already mentioned, it was accorded some sort of religious sanction in the case of Ganymede, and there is reason to believe that it was furthered by the spread of the Oriental religions, the priests of some of which were supposed to be specially partial to it.

In his chapter on Roman jurisprudence, Gibbon declares that "the odious vice, of which modesty rejects the name, and nature abominates the idea", was furthered by the growth of wealth, for "in the mad abuse of prosperity and power, every pleasure that is innocent was deemed insipid". The practice was not discouraged by the severity of public opinion, and "the indelible stain of manhood was confounded with the more venial transgressions of fornication and adultery". In the course of his reading he had come across mention of a certain Scatinian Law directed against it, under which "the rape, perhaps the seduction, of an ingenuous youth was compensated, as for a personal injury, by the poor damages of ten thousand sesterces or fourscore pounds", and he would have been glad to believe that "at Rome, as in Athens, the voluntary and effeminate deserter of his own sex was degraded from the honours and rights of a citizen". But he had to confess that this law was shrouded in obscurity.

Under the early Empire pederasty seems to have been specially rife. "Of the first fifteen emperors of Rome," Gibbon informs us in a characteristic footnote, "Claudius was the only one whose taste in love was entirely correct." As regards most of the others we have a lively account of their

sexual perversions in the pages of Suetonius (flourished about
A.D. 100). Suetonius has been often charged with exaggeration,
but as he was one of the imperial secretaries under the
emperor Trajan, he would have had access to the imperial
archives. Moreover, so far as the later emperors were concerned, he was writing at a time when his statements might
have been challenged by people who had personal knowledge
of the emperors concerned.

There is no doubt that the founder of the Empire, the
great Julius Caesar, was not only a great lover of women but
was a practising homosexual; one of the first things recorded
of him, indeed, is that as a young man serving in the Roman
army in Asia Minor he had homosexual relations with King
Nicomedes of Bithynia. Octavius, his nephew who became
the first emperor of Rome under the title of Augustus, was
rumoured to have been (to quote the English rendering of
Suetonius by Philemon Holland) "deflowered and tasted first
by Caesar". Tiberius in his villa at Capri, for the purpose of
his "secret wanton lusts" had sought out and gathered from
all parts numbers of "young drabs and stale catamites", girls
and young men who were adepts in unnatural practices and
were said to perform before him "monstrous kinds of
libidinous filthiness" to excite his waning appetites. Caligula
was accused of homosexual relations, both active and passive,
with a celebrated actor and numerous other men. Claudius
is said to have been "excessively given to the wanton love of
women" but was "altogether unacquainted with the pre-
posterous abuse of male kind". In the light of Nero's unsavoury reputation it is hardly surprising to be told that in
addition to "keeping other men's wives as his concubines"
and deflowering one of the Vestal Virgins, he was much
given to the "unnatural abusing of boys". The old soldier
Galba was "given overmuch to the unnatural lust of male-
kind", preferring "for his darlings those who were stale
thick-skins and past growth", i.e. fullgrown men of sturdy

physique. Otho (who had been Poppaea's husband before she was appropriated by Nero) shared in that emperor's more infamous pleasures. Vespasian seems to have been satisfied with the attentions of his mistresses, but Titus is said to have kept a troop of catamites and eunuchs. Domitian is merely stated to have been "overmuch given to fleshly lust". He is the last of Suetonius's subjects, and it would be interesting to know the biographer's candid opinion of his master, the Emperor Hadrian, who was so deeply enamoured of Antinous, a Bithynian youth of great beauty and accomplishments, that when he was drowned accidentally in the Nile he pronounced his deification, dedicated a temple to him, and built a city in his honour.

The attitude of the popular writers to homosexuality is somewhat equivocal. While it was accepted as a fit subject for literature, none of the great writers came out definitely in its support, and most of them were inclined to regard pederasts as men whose tastes in love were peculiar to say the least. Virgil and Horace, Catullus, Propertius and Tibullus, all deal on occasion in their verses with the passion of grown men for young boys; the last-named indeed devotes a whole poem to some cynical advice supposed to be given by Priapus on the best ways to win boys to engage in indecent acts. Ovid hardly refers to the subject, but in the *Art of Love* he condemns it on the ground that the partners in a homosexual embrace do not derive equal satisfaction from it. "I hate embraces which do not leave both partners tired out," he declares; "that is why a boy's love appeals to me so little".

Juvenal, who was nothing if not a realist, looked upon pederasty as something that was generally "done", and in his advice to Postumus, it may be recalled, he included the suggestion that he might well find it preferable to take a boy into his bed rather than a wife who might turn out to be a nagger. Very much the same attitude is adopted by Martial, a number of whose epigrams are generally left untranslated because of their homosexual character. It is in the *Satyricon,* the earliest and almost the only example of a Roman novel that has been preserved, that we find the nearest approach to a defence of the "odious vice" that Gibbon stigmatized.

As we have it, the *Satyricon* is only a fragment, or rather a series of fragments. It has been generally assumed that it was written by Petronius Arbiter, one of Nero's intimates who was appointed to be the arbiter (whence the surname) of taste at the imperial court. Tacitus gives an unpleasant picture of the man. He spent his days in sleeping and his nights at work and in the enjoyment of life. The success that most men have to work so hard for he achieved by laziness. Yet he was no spendthrift debauchee but a refined voluptuary, and as governor of Bithynia and later as Consul he showed himself to be a capable and energetic administrator. At length he fell from favour, and was ordered by Nero to take his own life. So he cut his veins and then bound them up again as fancy took him, meanwhile conversing with his friends not seriously or sadly but with an ostentatious courage, and enjoined them to read to him not about the immortality of the soul but out of books of frivolous verse. He dined and dozed, ordered some of his slaves to be rewarded and others to be flogged, and finally, instead of writing fulsome flatteries of his master as other and better men had done in the same circumstances, wrote out a list of the Emperor's debaucheries, in which his male and female partners were all mentioned by name, together with a catalogue of their sexual experiments. This he signed and sealed, and despatched to Nero with his compliments. Then he died, in A.D. 65.

Sometimes it has been supposed that the *Satyricon* is this catalogue of debaucheries, but the identification is far-fetched. The book is a comic novel—at least so it has appeared to those readers who have been able to detect the humour through the grime. The chief of its collection of scabrous incidents is Trimalchio's Banquet, in which a one-time slave is described as wallowing in wealth and luxury and vicious debauchery. But in the remainder of the tale we are made to accompany a pair of male perverts, who carry about with them a boy, whom they maul and fight over and beslobber with their tears. When they find themselves conducted by mistake to a brothel they are deeply affronted and make their escape forthwith; and yet what a "kick" they get out of watching through the keyhole the carefully arranged defloration of a little girl of seven by their minion, who is not so very much older!

Now and again the narrator tells of his engagements with women, but in even the most voluptuous of their embracings he is unable to act the man: only an unnatural passion can sustain his ardour.

From the beginning Christianity set itself most sternly against pederasty. Thus St. Paul in his epistle to the Romans denounces those women who "have exchanged the natural function of sex for what is unnatural", and males who "have abandoned the natural use of women and flamed out in lust for one another, men perpetrating shameless acts with their own sex" (Moffatt translation). As soon as they were in a position to do so, Christian legislators treated pederasty as a horrible crime to be punished with the utmost rigour. Constantine decreed that those guilty of it, whether as active or passive participants, should be executed. Justinian, in the words of Gibbon, "declared himself the implacable enemy of unmanly lust, and the cruelty of his persecution can scarcely be excused by the purity of his motives. In defiance of every principle of justice, he stretched to past as well as future offences the operation of his edicts, with the previous allowance of a short respite for confession and pardon. A painful death was inflicted by the amputation of the sinful instrument, or the insertion of sharp reeds into the pores and tubes of most exquisite sensibility".

XXI

Lucretius Looks at Sex

As a rule philosophers have not very much to say about Love, but the Roman poet Lucretius is an outstanding exception. In the great philosophical poem *De Rerum Natura* in which he sets out to explain the "nature of things" he devoted many a line to that passionate longing for sexual union that is so disturbing an element in the lives of most men and women.

Practically nothing is known of Lucretius himself. All the other great writers of his age tell us something of their own lives, but he maintains an unbroken silence. His contemporaries and successors in the literary scene are equally reticent; many of them had read his poem and were influenced by it, but they do not seem to have thought it worth while to tell us anything about the man whose brain had produced its majestic interpretations of the human situation. His name suggests that he was a member of one of the most distinguished of the great Roman families, but he may have belonged to a junior branch. Probably he was of Roman birth and upbringing, and in this he would be exceptional among the writers of the time. He seems to have lived in easy circumstances, but while he was familiar with the pomp and luxury of city life he greatly preferred the placid joys of a country existence. If he could hold his own in the society of the capital he was more at home in the solitary places of the mountain slopes and green pastures and the dunes of the seashore. Above all, he was a lover of books, and in particular soaked himself in the philosophical writings of the Greek and Roman thinkers.

These things may be gathered from his poem. For the rest we have a brief account of his career from the pen of St. Jerome, written, however, when the poet had been dead for some four hundred years. According to this, Titus Lucretius Carus (to give him his full name) was born in 94 B.C., was poisoned by a love philtre, wrote in the intervals of the madness thus induced some books which Cicero edited, and died by his own hand at the age of forty-four. Of these statements only the last stands up to critical examination. His birth is now generally placed in 99 B.C. and his death in 55 B.C. The love philtre, the madness, and the suicide are put down by most modern scholars to spiteful gossip, but we have to thank the tittle-tattle for one of Tennyson's shorter poems, in which the supposed tragedy of Lucretius' life is related in words of sombre choice and the most moving beauty.

> Lucilia, wedded to Lucretius, found
> Her master cold; for when the morning flush
> Of passion and the first embrace had died
> Between them, tho' he lov'd her none the less,
> Yet often when the woman heard his foot
> Return from pacings in the field, and ran
> To greet him with a kiss, the master took
> Small notice, or austerely, for—his mind
> Half buried in some weightier argument,
> Or fancy-borne perhaps upon the rise
> And long roll of the Hexameter—he past
> To turn and ponder those three hundred scrolls
> Left by the Teacher whom he held divine.
> She brook'd it not; but wrathful, petulant,
> Dreaming some rival, sought and found a witch
> Who brew'd the philtre which had power, they said,
> To lead an errant passion home again.
> And this, at times, she mingled with his drink,
> And this destroy'd him . . .

The "Teacher" referred to is the Athenian philosopher

Epicurus who flourished about 300 B.C. and fathered an intellectual system that has some striking resemblances to modern scientific ideas, and in the sphere of ethics aimed at a perfect harmony of body and mind in the pursuit of virtue. Lucretius in a memorable passage hails him as "the man of Greece who, when humanity was crushed beneath the weight of superstition, dared to stand upright and look out on to the world with eyes filled with the spirit of defiance". This supremely bold thinker had ventured to challenge one of the most firmly held of human beliefs. Without actually denying the existence of the gods, he had taught that they lived in conditions of heavenly bliss that made them not in the least inclined to concern themselves with the affairs of men, and that, therefore, the fear of being punished by the gods in a life beyond the grave for things done or left undone in this present life was something that sensible men would reject out of hand. "The gods are nothing to be afraid of. There's nothing to feel in death. Good can be attained. Evil can be endured." These are the basic principles of the Epicurean scheme of things.

Of great interest, also, is the Epicurean theory of Matter. The Master accepted in the main the atomistic theory of Democritus (fifth century B.C.): the universe is the result of the fortuitous combination of atoms, which are seen as infinitely small bits of matter, so tiny that they are incapable of further division, which are constantly moving about in space. As they float and fly about they throw off *simulacra* (thin outer shells or films) from which all our sense impressions are derived. Another rendering of this really untranslatable term is "images".

The *simulacra* are thrown off by everything that is, not least by human beings, and thus we arrive at the Epicurean explanation of dreams and visions, nocturnal emissions, and of course the mutual attraction of men and women.

Falling in love is the consequence of a number of broken-off fragments of a human body attacking the body of another, and thereby arousing in it the desire for closer and completer union. It is the male who is chiefly affected by this kind of bombardment. When he has reached puberty, his body is charged with seed, which is excited and set in motion by the attacking particles and tends to collect in the generative organs. These organs become swollen, and an irresistible inclination is aroused to eject the seed in the direction of the exciting cause—an effeminate looking youth perhaps, or more usually a woman every part of whose body emanates a feminine attraction. "When a man has been wounded by the weapons of Venus, he inclines towards the quarter whence the blow comes—just as the blood of a man wounded in battle spurts in the direction of the spear-thrust—and yearns to unite himself with it, join body with body, and taste the pleasure that is beyond the power of words to describe."

This is what is called "Venus", and out of it springs the condition that we know as Love. But "when the drip of Venus's honey has trickled over our heart" it is soon succeeded by a chilling heart-ache. Even when the object of our attraction is absent from us we still have her in our mind's eye and her name is always sounding in our ears. What fools we are! If we have any sense we will do our best to put such images far from us. Nothing can be worse than to cherish our passion. We should turn our attention elsewhere: there are plenty of other women about, ready and willing to be wooed and to be won! Unless we do this we are all too likely to lay up for ourselves constant worry and a creeping burden of pain.

When all is said and done, the anticipated pleasure has its mixture of alloy. In the act of love eyes and hands waver and wander, undecided which part of the loved one's body to explore next. Hands go roving here and there over the soft limbs, the whole body is in the grip of desire. At last, when (as H. J. Munro puts it in his translation) "Venus is in the mood to sow the fields of woman", body is interlaced with body, mouth meets mouth, and often teeth bite the lips already bruised with much kissing. By the way the man and woman behave they might seem to be trying to absorb something from the other, or to become so closely united as to be no longer two but one: "so greatly are they held in the chains of Venus, while their limbs melt, overpowered by the might of the pleasure." At length the passion is all spent, and there ensues a pause. But not for long. Soon the frenzy returns, the old madness comes back, and the pair are quite at a loss to know what they are striving so hard to obtain or how to allay the passion that has them in its relentless grasp.

So their strength is wasted in futile labour, their whole life is passed at the beck and call of another. Duties are neglected, their good name slips away, their estate is wasted on such things as Babylonian stuffs and gay slippers from Sicyon, big emeralds glowing with green fire, and garments coloured like the sea that soon will be soaked in the perspiration induced by the activities of Venus. The wealth that the fathers have honourably acquired is converted by the sons into hair-bands and head-dresses, sweeping robes from the Grecian fashion-houses. Feasts are arranged, in which the cuisine is matched by the tableware, perfumes are provided for the guests, and also crowns and garlands of choice flowers. Games and other amusements are laid on. And all for what?

There is a canker in the heart of the rose. From the fountain of delights rises a jet of something bitter, something full of pain. Sometimes there comes in an unguarded moment a feeling of remorse, a conscience-stricken recognition of the fact that the poor lovesick fool is passing his days in sloth and debauchery, ruining himself in the low life of brothels, made miserable because his girl has let slip some barbed remark or because her eyes have rested too fondly and a little too long on a possible rival, and there is sometimes on her face the traces of an ambiguous smile.

Such things as these are only to be expected even when the course of love runs smooth, but they are infinitely worse when the passion is unrequited or comes to grief. Far better, then, to be warned in time, and be on our guard before we become entangled in the nets of Venus. However, there is still a possibility of escape even when you are enmeshed: Take a good look at your charmer, see her as she really is!

Most men are so blinded by their infatuation that they never notice the blemishes of body and mind in the person they court and woo. They may sometimes be heard to say in jest that they fail to understand what a friend "can see in the girl", but they themselves are just as blind where their own girl is concerned. A black-visaged wench is described as a brunette, a slattern displays a "charming disorder"; a green-eyed little cat has eyes like the goddess Athene's, and one who is thin as a rake is said to have a gazelle-like figure; this lump of dough is fit to rival one of the Graces, while that clothes-prop is awe-inspiring and full of dignity! Is the girl tongue-tied, so that she hasn't a word to say for herself? Then she is just bashful. Has she an impediment in her speech? Why, it's a lisp, and a charming one at that. Is she a spitfire, more than a bit of a tease, a born gossip with seldom a good word to say about anyone? She's a girl of spirit, who knows how to stand up for herself. Here's a "slim darling" who in fact carries so much flesh that she can hardly waddle, and this one is merely slender when she is emaciated with TB. Snub-nosed? She's so faun-like! Thick-lipped? How wonderful to kiss! Her breasts are as big and heavy as pudding-basins? Why, she might serve as a model for the goddess Ceres suckling the infant Iacchus!

So we can go on, right through the catalogue. But surely there's no necessity, for even though a woman is the very embodiment of Venus yet there are others. We have lived without her before, and we can live without her in future. And furthermore, we know (who doesn't?) that the loveliest woman is but human, and conducts herself behind the scenes just as does the plainest member of her sex. She uses scent: she *has* to—and how her maids hold their noses and giggle behind her back! Her lover does not know, of course, but (poor silly fool that he is!) when her door is shut in his face, he feels slighted, bursts into tears, strews the threshold with flowers and anoints the doorposts with oil of marjoram, and imprints his kisses on the door. If he only knew! Supposing they did let him in. One whiff, and he wouldn't be able to think up excuses quick enough to take his exit. Of course our Venuses know this as well as anybody, and they take every precaution to make sure that what goes on behind the scenes of life is kept hidden from those whom they wish to retain in the chains of love.

Immediately following upon this depressing picture of the disabilities and disillusionments of love, intended (we may suppose) to scare away the young Roman from the dangerous "paths of Venus", Lucretius suddenly comes down from the pulpit and takes up his stand in the sexological clinic. Having painted in the most unpleasing colours the pains of love, having done his best to persuade his readers that really the business is not worth the trouble and the heartache, he now explains in the plainest fashion how the maximum of sexual pleasure may be obtained.

The lover must not be selfish, he urges; he must not be concerned with only his own satisfaction. He must realize that a woman can take just as much pleasure in the sexual act as her partner, and is fully entitled to expect it. Some men seem to think that when a woman locks her lover's body in her embrace, sucks greedily at his lips and drinks in his kisses, she is "putting it on". As often as not, there is not the slightest make-believe about it. What she does is done from the heart. The pleasure can be, and should be, mutual if the fullest satisfaction is to be derived from it. It is in the ardent hope that it may be so that the woman encourages and incites her lover to pursue the race of love to its climax. "Again and again I repeat, that in the act of sex there is a common pleasure."

Then the philosopher turns to consider something that has puzzled parents from time immemorial: Why does a child "take after" one parent rather than the other? Lucretius knew nothing, of course, of genes as the carriers of heredity: they were not discovered until some two thousand years after his time. But he was ready with an explanation that has survived to our own day. Each parent, he asserts, is endowed with seed of a special kind. In the act of intercourse the woman's seed is mixed with the man's, and if at the moment of consummation she happens to be occupying the dominant position then the resulting child is likely to resemble her rather than its father; if, on the other hand, it is the man who is dominant, then the child will take after him. Children in whom the features are equally blended were conceived at a time when "the mutual ardour of desire" was evenly balanced. Note that it is not the *kind* of seed that is so important, but which kind was supreme at the critical moment. "The female sex springs equally from the father's seed, and males from the mother's."

Supposing a child resembles its grandparents rather than its parents? The explanation is simple. There are always present in human bodies a number of seeds which have been passed on from one generation to another and have not been "used", as it were. Some of these seeds are responsible for hair-colour, the shape of the features, the tone of voice, and so on.

The next subject discussed is barrenness. Why do some people have children and others have none? Lucretius once again is ready with an answer. Don't think that it is owing to the will of the gods: *they* don't worry about such paltry

R

affairs. They don't "debar a man from begetting dear little ones who will call him 'father' ". So it is not the slightest use bombarding the gods with prayers, piling their altars with sacrifices; *that* won't make a wife pregnant. Nor is there any point in putting the blame on an unkind Fate. We must look elsewhere for the cause, and in most cases it is to be found in the quality of the male seed. Sometimes it is too thick and heavy, so that the stroke of the ejaculation is not powerful enough to discharge it on the right spots or to mix it properly with the woman's seed. On the other hand, it may be too thin and light, so that it is unable to obtain a sure hold on the right spots, even when it reaches them, but is carried away and dissipated before it has had any effect.

In the affairs of Venus there is plenty of room for variations in harmony. Some women conceive far more easily than others, no matter who the man is. Some men can impregnate some women, and fail altogether with others. Everyone knows of cases of women who have proved barren after innumerable acts of intercourse, but have soon become big with child when the right man has come along.

The really important thing is to secure just the right mixture of seed; and it has been found that coarse seed mixes well with fine, and fine with coarse and heavy. Here we should have regard to a proper diet, since some foods have the effect of thickening the male seed while others have the reverse effect.

Then the posture taken up in sexual intercourse is also very important. Some authorities think that women conceive more readily when they take up a quadrupedal position in the act of congress, since this enables the seed to reach the right spots more easily and certainly. There is reason to believe that a woman who twists and turns during copulation makes it less likely that she should conceive, "for she thereby drives the furrow out of the straight, and the share is diverted and the seed falls wide of where it ought to go". This sort of

wriggling is often practised by harlots who do not want to
be troubled with child-bearing, but it is surely quite improper
in a respectable married woman.

By way of conclusion, Lucretius offers a word of advice,
of consolation and encouragement, to the plain woman.
What if she does find it difficult to win a husband because
her face and figure leave a good something to be desired?
She has no reason to despair, nor need she waste time offering
prayers to Venus to help her. She has the remedy in her own
hands. Let her cultivate an elegant neatness and niceness of
person, develop an accommodating and attractive manner,
and very soon some man will come along who will be
delighted to make her his companion for life. And even when
there is not much love to begin with, it may well be induced
by the constant living together in one another's company.
And in this way (we may almost hear Lucretius saying)
married life becomes married love.

XXII

The Mysteries of Venus

OVID IN HIS *Art of Love* has a phrase, *Veneris mysteria,* "the
Mysteries of Venus", by which he means a good deal of
what would be included in a modern manual of sex instruction for the newly married, or the just about to be married.
Much of what he says under this head is pretty obvious,
but what *is* novel is his insistence on mutual pleasure in the
sex act (although Lucretius had said it before him). As he
puts it (the quotations in this chapter are from the English
translation of the *Art of Love* made by Francis Wolferston,
"of the Inner Temple, Gent", in 1661):

> I hate the bed which yields not mutual joyes.
> I hate her that gives of necessity . . .
> Pleasure which duty grants I count not so,
> No Maid to me shall such a duty owe.
> I love to hear her wearied voice desire,
> That I would longer stay . . .

In Roman times this was a new idea, and even the Greeks
would have found it strange and unacceptable. For nearly
all the centuries since Ovid's time it has been pushed into the
background. The religious teachers of generation after
generation have insisted that there is something if not
actually degrading at least "not nice" in sexual intercourse,
and whenever possible they have maintained that it should
be engaged in primarily if not always for the purpose of
procreation. Any resulting pleasure, is, as it were, a bonus
on a dutiful act. No respectable woman (according to their

view) should ever allow that she has experienced pleasure in her husband's embrace; a courtesan might do so, but the well-brought-up matron should take pride in her frigid chastity, and every time that her husband takes her she should let him understand that she is submitting to his lustful advances as a matter of wifely duty. This has been the approved attitude right up to our own time, when there has been a revival of the Ovidian contention,

In the light of what follows, it is somewhat surprising that Ovid starts off with a protest against calling a spade a spade. To talk too freely about such things would be a shocking indiscretion, he maintains. In the "Mysteries of Venus" there are no sacred objects hidden in chests in the temple sanctuary as with the "mysteries" of Ceres and other divinities, nor is the summons to perform her ritual sounded by "frenzied blows" on "hollow bronze". Furthermore, the worship is something that almost every man and woman engage in at some time or other; indeed, no rites in all the world are so widely celebrated, or so often. But they are done in secret, removed from prying eyes. A decent reticence is preserved, a proper decorum.

"Venus herself, as often as she lays aside her robes, with a half-stooping gesture covers with her left hand her secret parts." (Latin, *pudenda*, from *pudendum*, to be ashamed of.) The *left* hand, it may be noted; when Ovid wrote this he no doubt had in mind statues of Venus that he had seen or had seen pictured, but the famous Aphrodite of Cnidus, carved by Praxiteles in the fourth century B.C., shows the goddess with her *right* hand extended in this gesture.

Animals will copulate anywhere, Ovid goes on, in the view of everybody, and often one may see a modest young maiden turn away her eyes at the sight. So far as men and women are concerned, we hide the "parts of shame" beneath a garment, and it has always been the practice to perform "Venus's rites" in the privacy of the house behind closed doors, and if not in complete darkness at least not in the full light of day.

Why, even in the days of our remote ancestors, who lived so much in the open that they had no roof to keep out the sun and rain but an oak tree gave them both food and shelter —even in those days men and women enjoyed one another in a forest glade or in the recesses of a cave, so firmly planted in these simple folk was the idea of shame attached to sexual intercourse.

But this is another of the practices of the "good old days" that is going out of fashion, Ovid has to admit. There are some men who make a boast on the morning after of their exploits of the night before. They make a boast of their conquests: "I've had that girl," they say, "and that one too, over there"—indeed, they point a finger at every girl in sight, no matter who! A good deal of what they boast about is made up, but what do they care? Even though they have not been able to possess a girl's body they can defame her repu- tation, however innocent she may be. Her father or her guardian may keep her under lock and key and add a hundred bolts to the door, but what's the good of this when her name is spread abroad? As Marlowe renders a couplet in Ovid's *Amores*:

> What madness is't to tell night's pranks by day,
> And hidden secrets openly to bewray!

The "Mysteries of Venus" were celebrated in no splendid temple with pillared porticoes and frescoed walls and statue- lined galleries, but in the homely surroundings of the Roman bedchamber. It is to be regretted that the poets who write at such length and in such detail about the performance of sexual rites tell us so little about the place. For the great mass of Romans their home was a single room in a huge block or *insula* of many-storeyed apartments, without water supply, without lighting other than candles and torches, without means of refuse disposal, sanitation other than chamber-pots that were emptied out of the window, or indeed any of the other conveniences of civilized living. These people were beneath the gaze of writers, and we have to rely on our imagination for a notion of what life was like in those conditions of overcrowding, poverty, stench, dirt, and general squalor. This book of ours is concerned only with the well-to-do and the wealthy, since these are the people whose existence attracted the attention of their literary hangers-on. And the majority of these people flourished, it may have been noticed, about the turn of the eras, when the Roman Republic was being transformed into the Roman Empire.

Caelius, the discharged lover of Lesbia, had an apartment in an insula, but Lesbia herself had a large and well appointed house, as did Cicero and Cynthia and Horace in his country retreat, and in fact most of the other characters who have walked across our pages. These houses were mostly on one floor, with a hall or *atrium* in the centre, out of which smaller rooms opened on either side, and beyond was a courtyard called the *peristylum* surrounded by columns (that is what the word means), from which again rooms opened out. In the larger houses this courtyard became a garden, planted with shrubs and small trees, and it was in such a pleasance that we may suppose Propertius to have entertained his "nymphs" on the night when Cynthia was away. The domestic apartments, the dining-room, library or study, and the bedrooms were in this peristylum.

There was not much furniture in any of the rooms, and in the bedroom there was little besides the bed. In the mansions of the rich this might be made of fine wood, richly carved and painted, but most people had to make do with beds that were wooden frames on which was placed a mattress stuffed with wool or straw, resting on girths of leather or webbing. The coverings were few and simple, just a blanket or two, and the pillow would be stuffed with wool. Perhaps there might be a chest that served as a dressing-table, on which stood a mirror made of a sheet of polished metal, flanked by my lady's array of cosmetic pots, combs and brushes, tweezers, nail files, and the rest.

Somewhere near may have been a bathroom, containing a bath let into the floor, heated by hot-air pipes underneath and supplied with water from the public main outside. But this was an exceptional luxury, and as late as Nero's time we find Seneca deprecating the modern fashion. "According to those who have handed down the old customs of our city," he writes, "they washed every day their arms and legs which were begrimed with dirt, but it was only once in nine days that they washed all over. How they must have smelt, you say? Of course they did; they smelt of war, labour, heroism. Now we have more baths—and more dirty people." Propertius imagined his Golden Girl washing her face in clean water when she got out of bed, so it would seem that even in the house of this successful courtesan there was no bathroom.

The preliminaries to intercourse cannot have taken long. Undressing was a simple matter, since the Romans, men and women alike, did not wear many clothes. If, paying no heed to Ovid's objections, we take a peep through the key-hole or a half-open door we should see the lady divesting herself, first, of her *palla* or mantle if she has just come in from outdoors; next she unties the girdle about her waist, just below the breasts, and lets fall her *stola*. What has she underneath? No diaphanous underwear, no frilly petticoats, no "foundations", no silk panties—none of these but a chemise, a kind of loincloth not unlike the modern knickers, and, if she be full-bosomed or flabby breasted, a brassière. She has no silk stockings to peel off and hang over the back of a chair: she has no stockings, and very likely no chair either. If she be specially modest, she will keep on her chemise, for there is no pretty nightgown for her to slip on, no filmy négligé, no provocative twin-set. The Romans, male and female, had no special garments to wear in bed, and, we may well suppose, as often as not slept naked.

The woman's partner should require even less time to make ready for the ritual. He has a toga, and underneath this a shirt or tunic and a loincloth, or possibly a garment resembling modern pants. He also has no stockings, but he may be wearing something like a soldier's puttees. He slips off his shoes, and they join the woman's sandals underneath the bed.

No better description of a Roman love-making is to be found than in the Latin romance known as the *Metamorphoses* or *The Golden Ass* written by Lucius Apuleius in the middle of the second century A.D., i.e. in the generation following Juvenal. This passage is quoted from the translation made by William Adlington in 1566, early in the reign of Queen Elizabeth.

The romance takes the form of a personal narrative of his adventures told by one Lucius, a young Greek, and one of the early incidents concerns his affair with a wanton little piece of a slave-girl, a kind of lady's maid in the house where he is a guest. Her name is Fotis, and she is shortly his "dear and sweet love", whose "breath smelled like cinnamon and the liquor of her tongue was like unto sweet nectar". And the evening came when he went to his chamber and found she had made everything ready for the celebration of the rites of Venus. The table was covered with left-overs from the master's supper, the cups were half filled with water to delay and temper the effect of the wine, and the wine flagon was full.

"And when I was entering into the bed, behold my Fotis came in and gave me roses and flowers which she had in her apron, and some she threw about the bed, and kissed me sweetly, and tied a garland about my head, and bespread the chamber with the residue. Which when she had done, she took a cup of wine and delayed it with hot water, and proffered it me to drink; and before I had drunk off all she pulled it from my mouth, and then gave it me again, and in this manner we emptied the pot twice or thrice together. Thus when I had well replenished myself with wine, and was now ready unto Venery not only in mind but also in body, I removed my clothes ... Whereupon she made no long delay, but set aside all the meat and wine, and then she unapparelled herself, and unattired her hair, presenting her amiable body unto me in manner of fair Venus, when she goeth under the waves of the sea. Now (quoth she) is come the hour of jousting, now is come the time of war, wherefore show thyself like unto a man, for I will not retire, I will not fly the field; see then thou be valiant, see thou be courageous, since there is no time appointed when our skirmish shall cease. In saying these words she came to me in bed, and embraced me sweetly, and so we passed all the night in pastime and pleasure, and never slept until it was day: but we would eftsoons refresh our weariness, and provoke our pleasure, and renew our venery by drinking wine."

Ovid, we may be sure, would have read this with the deepest interest, but he would not have approved altogether of the goings-on. He advised his pupils in the art of love to "go easy" with the wine cup. As Francis Wolferston translates a passage,

> Bacchus with Cupid joyn'd no hurt will do;
> Yet do not drink your heads to discompose,
> Nor till your eyes each thing double shows.
> Women will, madifi'd with too much wine,
> In any sordid copulation joyn ...

But after this preliminary warning, the poet proceeds to describe the "Mysteries of Venus" with a particularity all

the more remarkable in the light of his assertion that his
Muse "before the chamber door abides".

> Loe, the concealing bed two Lovers hides.
> There what to say they need not learn, nor will
> Their wanton hands within the bed lie still.
> Their fingers will learn how to act their parts,
> And in what private place love sticks his darts.
>
> Trust me, too soon such pleasure must not be
> Acted, but by degrees and leisurely.
> If you perceive where she would have your hand
> Then let not bashfulness your joys withstand.
> You shall behold her eyes dart radiant beams
> Like the refulgent Sun in liquid streams.
>
> Perhaps she'l shriek, or gentle whispers make,
> Sweetly complain, such yielding language speak.
> What once you do attempt, leave not undone,
> Nor let her in that course before you run.
> Keep both together; pleasure is more sweet,
> In full consent, when both the Sexes meet.
>
> This way observe, when leisure will allow.
> Whenas delay's not safe, then ply the Oar,
> Make use of time, spur a free horse the more.

With this we come to the end of the second book of the
Art of Love, in which his advice has been directed towards
the man. Now in the third book it is the woman's turn to
receive instruction, and here, though the poet makes a great
show of shamefaced reluctance to tell all that he knows,
he winds up with a passage on the various postures that the
woman may assume in the sexual embrace. This is a department of amatory lore in which Ovid has long had the reputation of being a master, but in fact the number of attitudes
he mentions as being seemly and suitable is not at all large.
Each woman must choose which posture will suit her best,

for whatever reason, for "what is right for one will not suit others".

> You that are fair, lie upwards with your face;
> Show you your back, to whom your back's a grace.
> Melanion, Atalanta's legs between
> His shoulders bore; if neat they must be seen.
> Low women ride. She that would have her curious waist espied
> Must sit upon the seat, her neck aside.
> She whose sweet form presents no fault to th' eye,
> Carelessly stretched upon the Couch may lie.
> Shame not to untie
> And 'bout your shoulders let your loose hair fly.
> You on whose breasts Lucina's wrinkles linger,
> Like the swift Parthian, keep your back in sight.
> Love hath a thousand ways performed with ease.
> To lie half Supine on the right side may please . . .

Love is an art, Ovid insists again and again, and it may be some time before it reaches its culmination in "two sharing equal joy".

> Nor pleasing voices, nor sweet tunes refuse,
> And you sometimes must amorous language use.

As for those unfortunate people who are not capable of experiencing the "joys of Venus" to the full they should, in consideration of their partner, at least put up a good showing.

> You to whom Nature Venus' sense denies
> With a mendacious tongue pretend sweet joys.
> Unhappy Maid is she whom sense doth leave,
> Where man and woman equal sweets receive.
> Yet let them not perceive that you do feign,
> And active motions will belief obtain.
> To mention what doth please us (men) forbear,
> Modesty bids, yet secret signs declare . . .

However accurate a rendering it may be, this is poor stuff compared with the exuberant verse of Christopher Marlowe,

so here in conclusion is his translation of lines from one of
the elegies in the *Amores*:

> The bed is for lascivious toyings meet;
> There use all tricks, and tread shame under feet.
> When you are up and dress'd, be sage and grave,
> And in the bed hide all the faults you have.
> Be not asham'd to strip you, being there,
> And mingle thighs, yours ever mine to bear.
> There in your rosy lips my tongue entomb,
> Practise a thousand sports when there you come.
> Forbear no wanton words you there would speak,
> And with your pastime let the bedstead creak.
> But with your robes put on an honest face,
> And blush, and seem as you were full of grace . . .

XXIII

The Legacy of Roman Love

"THE PLEASURE OF THE act of love is gross and brief, and brings loathing after it," is one of the sayings attributed to Petronius. It is the assertion of a tired voluptuary, and might echo the reflections of a Solomon in his seraglio of wives and concubines. It is not a characteristically Roman attitude; and although it was a Roman poet who was responsible for the phrase *Post coitum, omne animal triste est* ("after coition every one is depressed") this was nothing more than a psychological statement of fact. For the Romans as a rule Sex was an activity as honourable as it was pleasant, and there were no notions of guilt associated with it.

That idea came in with the early Christians, although there had been many Romans who deplored the sexual excesses that accompanied some of the Oriental worships that had found their way into Rome. The man chiefly responsible for it seems to have been St. Paul, who came from a part of the Empire where such excesses were specially rife. Tarsus, his native city, was one of the largest and most cultured cities of Asia Minor; but if we may believe the statements of Dion Chrysostom, who knew the place a generation after Paul, its women were, most of them, licentious and corrupt. When they went out, he says, they were wont to appear particularly prim and modest, so muffled up in clothing that they could barely see where they were walking; but this habit was the remnant of a chastity that no longer existed. "They walk," he declares, "with their faces covered but with soul uncovered, and indeed wide open."

From what we may gather from his *Epistles*, the great Apostle had a very poor opinion of women as a sex. They were, by Divine decree, subordinate to men. Wives should submit to their husbands in all things. They should keep quiet in church. They should remain quietly at home, occupied in their household tasks. They should not wear their hair short, and when they went out they should be careful to put on a veil.

These last commandments have a quaint ring about them, but there was doubtless a good reason for them. The absence of a veil would imply that the woman was one of easy virtue; she would be in danger of lewd approaches and possibly assault by the "angels". Paul believed implicitly in these "angels", although he regarded them as demons. He knew well enough what happened to unveiled women, and that many of them were religious prostitutes—there were more than a thousand of these attached to the temple of the goddess of Love in Corinth, a place he knew well. He was not prepared to see Christian women exposed to insult and molestation in a city that was proverbial for its wealth and luxury, and the name of which was a byword for profligacy.

But he carried his dislike of women to an extreme, because he regarded them as the daughters of Eve—the woman who, in the ancient myth, had been created as a companion and helpmeet for Adam and had led him into sin by giving him the forbidden apple to eat in the Garden of Eden. For him, as for most of the early Christian teachers and Fathers of the Church, the "original sin" was the first act of *lustful* sexual intercourse. As St. Augustine explains, before their "Fall" Adam and Eve, the first man and woman, had engaged in sexual relations, but there had been no pleasure in the act. It had been involuntary, as natural as eating and drinking. But when their eyes had been opened, as the Old Testament writer puts it, they lusted after one another; the sexual impulse got out of hand, beyond the control of the human will, and thus became something horrible and degrading.

There is nothing of this attitude to be discerned in the Gospels. In them women occupy a prominent position, and there is no suggestion of a sexual inferiority. Many women followed Jesus and ministered unto him. The Master joined in the joyous celebration of the marriage feast at Cana, conversed with the much-married Woman of Samaria with kindness and sympathy, and rebuked the Pharisee who would have driven away the woman, "which was a sinner", who washed Jesus's feet with her tears, wiped them with her hair, and anointed them with ointment from an alabaster box. Among his dearest and closest friends were Mary and her sister Martha in the house at Bethany. A little band of ever faithful women stood beside the Cross and watched over the Tomb, and the first appearance of the Risen Christ was to a woman. Perhaps if Paul had been a member of that original company he might have taken a very different view of the place of women in the Christian community and the part they might be called upon to play in the infant Church.

To begin with, Paul's attitude had small effect on the development of the Roman world. When he was martyred, as the traditional account has it, under Nero in about A.D. 64, Christianity was only a tiny sect, a Jewish offshoot, looked upon with suspicion by the Government and with intense dislike, verging on hatred, by the populace. But as the years passed, Christianity grew in numbers and importance, until in the reign of Constantine the Great, about A.D. 323, Christianity was established as the official religion of the Roman Empire.

One of the consequences of its rise to power was a gradual deterioration in the position of women. When Christianity dawned on the world women had attained to a position of unparalleled freedom, status, and influence in the Roman Empire. In the early days, indeed, women played a considerable part in the expansion of the new religion, but the theological dogma of the Fall as the result of one woman's sin soon put a stop to the further emancipation of Woman, and she was pushed into a morass of inferiority, subjection, suspicion and dislike, from which it has taken many centuries for her to emerge.

Everything to do with "sex" was also severely treated. St. Paul countenanced marriage, of one man with one woman for life, but he made it clear that he regarded a state of celibacy preferable for both men and women. His successors were far more condemnatory. The ascetic view was preached and won widespread acceptance, that sexual gratification was sin even in marriage; and in place of the model citizen of Roman times—a man upright and active, patriotic and courageous, and a woman who was the companion of her husband and a good mother to her children—there appeared the disgusting spectacle of saints who wallowed in filth and made a glory of their stench.

All this was as yet, when Ovid wrote, a long way in the future, and even in the days of Juvenal the Roman Empire had over four hundred years to run. We should remind ourselves from time to time that "Ancient Rome" covered the period from 753 B.C., the traditional date of the foundation of the city, to A.D. 476 when the Western Empire collapsed at length in ruin. Even then Roman law and culture and traditions continued to flourish in the other Roman Empire that had for its centre the capital that Constantine had founded.

In the West, there succeeded the long night of the Dark Ages, that merged in the half-light of the medieval period, until at length came the glorious daylight of the Renaissance. Then men in Europe rubbed their eyes as men awaking from a long sleep, and looking back across the centuries that separated them from the Rome of the Caesars and of the Republic they were enraptured by what they saw. The

s

Classical civilization was rediscovered and became the inspiration of better civilizations yet to be. And in that picture men glimpsed the figures of the noble Roman matron in all her staunch devotion, the gay courtesans who made a delightful pastime of Love, the poets who sang the grace and beauty of their lady-loves and the satirists who when they railed against the ever-so-naughty women could hardly keep back a smile, the philosophers who made Love a serious study, and the men and women of such varied degree who, whether on the steps of the throne or in a humble cottage, experienced the pleasure and the pain, the glory and the grief, the ecstasy and the sober virtue of ROMAN LOVE.

Table of Dates

Intended to help the Reader to "place" the people mentioned
in these pages in the general framework of Roman History.
c. = *circa*, "about".

B.C.		Personalities
753	Traditional date of Foundation of Rome	
510	Establishment of Roman Republic	
451	Twelve Tables of Roman Law	Plautus *c.* 254–184
		Cato the Censor 234–149
216	Romans defeated by Hannibal at Cannae	
133	Murder of Tiberius Gracchus	Cicero 106–43
		Lucretius *c.* 99–55
		Catullus *c.* 84–*c.* 54
		Virgil 70–19
		Horace 65–8
63	Cicero Consul	Tibullus *c.* 60–19
		Livy 59 B.C.–A.D. 17
58–51	Julius Caesar's conquest of Gaul	Propertius *c.* 50–16
49	Caesar crosses the Rubicon	Ovid 43 B.C.–A.D. 18
44	Assassination of Julius Caesar	
42	Battle of Philippi	
27	Octavian (Augustus), Roman Princeps or Emperor	
4	Traditional date of Birth of Jesus Christ	Seneca the Younger 4 B.C.–A.D. 65

A.D.		
14	Death of Augustus: accession of Tiberius	
37	Accession of Caligula	Martial *c.* 40–104

A.D.		*Personalities*
41	Accession of Claudius	Plutarch *c.* 46–120
54	Accession of Nero	Tacitus *c.* 55–117
59	Murder of Agrippina	Juvenal *c.* 65–135?
		Pliny the Younger 61–113
64	Great fire of Rome	Petronius died 65
68	Death of Nero: accession of Galba	
69	Otho emperor; Vitellius; Vespasian	
70	Capture of Jerusalem by Titus	Suetonius *c.* 70–160
79	Destruction of Pompeii and Herculaneum	
81	Accession of Domitian	
96	Nerva emperor	
98	Accession of Trajan	
117	Accession of Hadrian	
122	Hadrian in Britain: the Roman Wall	
138	Accession of Antoninus Pius	Apuleius flourished 155
161	Accession of Marcus Aurelius	
306	Accession of Constantine the Great	
476	End of the Western Roman Empire	

277

Index

Abortion, Roman attitude to, 238

Acca Larentia, 195

Acte, Nero's concubine, 156, 161

Ad Lesbiam, Catullus's poem, 78

Aedile, Roman law officer, 197, 201

Agape, Christian "love feast", 232

Agrippa, Augustus's minister, 146

Agrippina, empress, 155, 160

Ambulatrices noctilucae, "night-walkers", 206

Amica, Cicero's use of term, 84

Amicetus, captain, 161, 163

Amores, Ovid's poem, 54, 229, 235, 269

Ancilla ornatrices, tire-women, 202

Anna Perenna, goddess, 192

Antinous, Hadrian's favourite, 247

Antoninus Pius, emperor, 165, 222

Aphrodite, goddess, 53; statue of, by Cnidus, 261

Apophreta, species of gifts, 124

Appius Claudius, 84

Apuleius, Lucius, 265

Arches, in ancient Rome, 208

Arria, wife of Paetus, 29

Ars Amatoria (Art of Love), Ovid's poem, 55, 58, 64, 67, 247, 261, 267

Asellina, wineshop keeper at Pompeii, 207

Asses' milk, in Poppaea's bath, 165

Athenagoras, 232

Athens, women in ancient, 22

Athletic women, in Rome, 138

Aufilena, and Catullus, 75

Augustine, St., 48, 50, 187, 188, 271

Augustus, emperor, 27, 31, 57, 99, 146, 148, 246

Bacchus, god, 182, 186

Baiae, seaside resort, 62, 84, 109

"Balcony whores", 209

Banks, Sir Joseph, 184

Banquets, Roman, 61

Barine, and Horace, 101

Barrenness, Lucretius's explanation of, 257

Basium, Roman kiss, 228

Baths, Roman public, 209

Betrothals, in Rome, 41, 52

Bluestockings, Roman literary ladies, 136

Bona Dea, "the good goddess", 95, 138

Bonae mulieres, class of prostitutes, 207

Brassières, Roman use of, 127, 264

Brides, Roman, 42

Britannicus, prince, 150, 155, 156

Brothels, Roman, 199

Brutus, 26

Burnaby, William, translator of *Satyricon*, 201

Bury, Prof. J. B., 149, 166

Busturiae, class of prostitutes, 206

Byron, Lord, translation of Catullus's poem, 78

Cadiz dancing-girls, 207

Caelius Rufus, M., 82, 212

Caesar, Julius, 26, 31, 220, 246

Cakes, in sexual shapes, 207

Caligula, emperor, 149, 198, 246

Calpurnia, Pliny's wife, 34

Cannae, battle of, 178, 244

Capua, slave market at, 220

Catamites, 244

Cato the Censor, 213; the Elder, 21, 218

Catulla, Martial's epigram on, 126

Catullus, Roman poet, 74–87; his Epithalamium, 44; love affairs, 75; passion for Lesbia-Clodia, 76–83; his *Vivamus, mea Lesbia*, 80, 228; use of *basium*, for "kiss", 228

Censennia, in Juvenal, 135

Christianity, and abortion, 241; and marriage, 51; and slave trade, 223; and homosexuality, 249

Cicero, 78, 83, 87, 212, 222, 246

Cinara, Horace's sweetheart, 104

Circus, assignations at, 61

"City of God", St. Augustine's, 48, 187

Claudia Quinta, chaste Roman matron, 173

Claudius, emperor, 149, 154

Clodia (Lesbia), 76–87

Clodius, 83, 84, 87

Coemptio, form of marriage, 36

Coitus interruptus, 240

Coleridge, S. T., 80

Combs, hair, 42

Concha Veneris, 186

Concubines, 18, 219

Confarreatio, form of marriage, 36

Congreve, William, translator of Ovid, 68

Conington, John, translator of Horace, 103

Constantine the Great, 272

Contraception, Roman methods of, 240

Contubernium, cohabitation, 218

Conubium, 39

Copa, wineshop keeper, 206

Corinna, Ovid's mistress, 234

Corinth, 271

Coriolanus, 20, 21

Cornelia, Julius Caesar's wife, 26; Mother of the Gracchi, 25; Vestal Virgin, 178

Cornelius Nepos, 22

Cosmetics, 108

Cosmo, St., and phallic rites, 184

Courtesans, Greek, 23; Roman, 53, 69, 205

Cranstoun, James, translations by, 90, 106

Crashaw, Richard, translation of Catullus, 228

Culta puella, 69

Curculio, Plautus's play, 213

Cutty-stool, in Scotland, 50

Cybele, goddess, 173, 187

Cynthia, Propertius's "Golden Girl", 105-19

Dames, Juvenal's Gallery of Roman, 135

Dancing-girls, 199, 207

Dark, the, in love-making, 46, 108

Days, unlucky for weddings, 41

Delia, and Tibullus, 89-96

Delicatae, "dainty ladies", 205

Delos, slave market at, 220

Democritus, 252

Deverra, god, 51

Diabolares, "devil girls", 206

Dill, Sir Samuel, 223

Dion Chrysostom, 223, 270

Divorce, in Rome, 27, 58

Docta puella, 69

Domiducus, god, 48

Domitian, emperor, 178, 222

Domitius, god, 48

Donaldson, Dr. James, 232

Doris, class of prostitutes, 206

Dowry, 40

Dryden, John, translations of Ovid, 59, 60, 66

Egeria, nymph, and King Numa, 175

Ellis, Havelock, 243

Engagements, *see* Betrothals

Epigrams, Martial's, 124

Epithalamium, Catullan marriage-song, 44

Epodes, Horace's, 103

Epicurus, Greek philosopher, 252

Eppia, senator's wife, in Juvenal, 134

Epponina, heroic wife of Sabinus, 33

Etruscans, 23; ladies of, 24

Eve, 271

Evil Eye, 183

Exposition of unwanted infants, 241

Ex voti, 184

Family, in Rome, 38

Famosae, "notorious women", 205

Faustina, empress, 165, 166

Fig, gesture of, 186

Flame, Sacred, 175

Flamen Dialis, 36

Flammeum, bridal veil, 42

Flora, goddess, 196

Floralian Games, 196

Focus or Hearth, 172

Forariae, out-door "pick-ups", 206

Fornication, origin of word, 208

Fornix, or arch, 213

Fotis, in *The Golden Ass*, 265

Frazer, Sir James G., 188
"Free women", 38
Freedwomen, 57

Gaius, Gaia, terms used in marriage ceremony, 43
Galba, emperor, 246
Galli, priests of Cybele, 187
Gallinae, class of prostitutes, 206
Ganymede, 244
Genius, a man's, 46, 48
Georgics, Virgil's, 183
Germanicus, prince, 242
Gibbon, Edward, 166, 245, 249
Gifford, William, translator of Juvenal, 140, 149, 199
Girdle, woman's, 42, 49
Gladiators, women admirers of, 210
Glycera, and Tibullus, 95
Golden Ass, The, by Apuleius, 265
Gracchi, Tiberius, 25
Graffiti, wall scribblings, at Pompeii, 210
Great Mother Goddess, 173, 187
Greek love terms, 137

Hadrian, emperor, 247
Hair styles, 42
Hamilton, Sir William, 183
Healey, John, 48, 187
Helen of Troy, 108
Hercules, 195, 230
Heroides, Ovid's poem, 54, 70
Herrick, Robert, 102
Hersilia, Romulus's wife, 18

Hetairai, Greek courtesans, 23
Hippomanes, love charm, 65
Hobhouse, L. T., 27
Holland, Philemon, translator of Suetonius, 28, 157, 198
Homosexuality, 243-249
Horace, 97-104; his "Sabine nest", 99; love affairs, 99; critical verses on women, 103; Cinara, his only real love, 104; and Priapus, 183, 206, 213
Hymen, god of Marriage, 45
Hymen, artificial rupture of, 49

Inge, Dean, quoted, 27
Insula, apartment block, 262
Intercidona, god, 51
Ipsithilla, Catullus's "charmer", 75
Isernia, phallic ceremony at, 184
Isis, goddess, 60, 93, 190

Josephus, Jewish historian, 191
Jugatinus, god, 48
Julia, the Elder, 145, 235; the Younger, 148
Julius Caesar, 26
Juno, goddess, 113, 182, 244
Juno, a woman's, 46, 48
Jupiter Farreus, god, 36
Jus primae noctis, 224
Justinian, emperor, 223, 249
Jus trium liberorum, 28, 124
Justum matrimonium, 37
Juvenal, 129-42; account of everyday life in Rome, 132;

criticisms of Roman women, 134; portraits of feminine types, 135–41; description of Messalina, 149; on homosexuality, 247

Kisses, Roman, 227–31; Indian, 231; nose kiss, 231; early Christian, 232
Knight, Richard Payne, on Phallic Worship, 185
"Knot of Hercules", 42

Lalage, Cynthia's maid, 118
Lamb, Hon. George, translator of Catullus, 44
Larentalia, 196
Larentia, prostitute in early Rome, 195
Laudatio Turiae, 30
Lectus genialis, marriage-bed, 46
Lemuria, festival, 41
Leno, Roman bawd, 202, 221
Lepidus, 31
Lesbia, and Catullus, 73–87
Lesbianism, 78, 243
Lethe, river of Death, 116
Letters of Pliny, 29
Liber, god, 48, 186
Libera, goddess, 48
Liberalia, festival, 186
Libertina, freed-woman, 57, 235
Licentia stupri, prostitute's licence, 197
Livy, 219
Lucina, goddess, 239, 268
Lucretia, Rape of, 20
Lucretius, and Sex, 250–9

Lucretius, husband of Turia, 30
Ludi Florales, 196
Lupae, "she-wolves", 195, 206
Lupanar, Roman brothel, 199
Lyce, Horace's Ode to, 103
Lydia, and Horace, 101
Lygdamus, Cynthia's servant, 112, 117

Macaulay, Lord, 219
Maecenas, Horace's patron, 99
Mallonia, and Tiberius, 28
Manturna, goddess, 48
Manus, "hand", in woman's life, 37
Marcus Aurelius, emperor, 165, 222
Marlowe, Christopher, translation of Ovid's *Amores*, 229, 234, 269
Marriage, Roman, 18, 30, 36, 38, 41, 51; of slaves, 219; modern parallels, 52
Martial, epigrammatist, 119, 123–8, 229, 247
Martin, Sir Theodore, translator, 98, 100
Materfamilias, 50, 53
Matronalia, festival, 113
Matrons, Roman, 20, 27, 57
Mauricus, Pliny's friend, 40
Medea and Jason, 65
Medicamine Faciei, Ovid's, 55
Meretrix, Roman prostitute, 54, 197
Messalina, empress, 149–54, 199, 204
Messalla, patron of Tibullus, 88, 92

Milton, John, translation of Horace, 101

Mistress, Ovid's advice on how to win and treat a, 65; Martial's epigram, 126

Modestinus, on Roman marriage, 30

Molesworth, Bysshe, 146

Monogamy, Roman, 18

Mommsen, T., 31

Munro, H. J., translation of Lucretius, 253

Narcissus, Claudius's secretary, 150, 152

Neaera, and Horace, 101

Nemesis, Tibullus's "gold-digger", 96

Neobule, and Horace, 101

Neptune, god, 99

Nero, emperor, 29, 155, 222, 248, 272

Nomas, Cynthia's slave-girl, 117

Numa, king, 172

Octavia, Augustus's sister, 149; Nero's wife, 155, 162, 163

Octavius, see Augustus

"Odious vice", 243

Omens, 42

Oppian Law, and women's dress, 271

Osculum, 228

Otho, emperor, 157, 246

Ovid (Publius Ovidius Naso),

life story and works, 54; description of courtesan class, 57; on management of a love affair, 62; how to retain a mistress, 64; presumed part in the Julia scandal, 149, 171, 192, 229; affair with Corinna, 235; attitude to homosexuality, 247; on the "Mysteries of Venus", 260

Paedicator, Roman term for homosexual, 245

Paul, St., attitude to homosexuality, 249; on position of women, 271

Paetus, 29

Paley, A. F., 119

Palla, woman's garment, 42, 264

Palladium, 176

Papillae, gilded, 199

Parthenie, Cynthia's nurse, 118

Patrima, 173

Paulina, in Josephus's story, 190; Seneca's wife, 29

Pax, kiss of peace, 232

Pax Romana, 56, 222

Pederasty, 244

Penis, 183

Penus Vestae, 176

Pergulae, "balcony whores", 209

Pericles, 221

Pertunda, goddess, 49

Petronius Arbiter, 201, 248, 270

Phallus (penis), 183, 185, 186, 201, 230

Phidyle, Horace's "rustic girl", 100

Philodemus, Greek philosopher, 214

Phryne, and Horace, 100

Phyllis, and Horace, 99; Phyllis, one of Propertius's "nymphs", 114

Pilumnus, god, 51

Plautus, playwright, 213, 221

Plebs, marriage among the, 37

Pledge, in weddings, 43

Pliny the Elder, 65; the Younger, letters of, 29, 34, 40, 179

Plutarch, quoted, 17, 19, 43, 46, 50, 78, 157, 159, 172, 177, 195, 218

Pompeii, 185, 201, 207; *graffiti* in, 210

Pompey's Portico, 60

Pompey the Great, 26

Pontifex Maximus, 36, 153, 173, 174, 179

Poppaea, Nero's empress, 157–64; kisses of, 231

Portia, wife of Brutus, 26

Post coitum . . ., 270

Postumus, 133, 247

Prema, goddess, 49

Priapus, god of gardens and the parts of generation, 49, 182; his symbol, the phallus, 183; in Horace, 183; R. Payne Knight's book on the *Worship of Priapus*, 185; cakes used in worship of, 207; statues kissed by worshippers, 230; Tibullus's reference to, 247

Pro Caelio, Cicero's speech, 83

Pronuba, at Roman weddings, 46

Propertius, Sextus, 105–19; affair with Cynthia, 106; evening with the "nymphs", 115, 263; vision of the dead Cynthia, 116

Prostibulae, Roman prostitutes, 205, 207

Prostitutes, Roman, 195–204; licence to practise, 197; dress of, 198; attached to lupanaria, 199; various classes of, 205–8; haunts of, 208; references to in Pompeian *graffiti*, 210

Prostitution, Roman, early mention of, 195; Government regulation of, 196; taxes on, 198; Roman ladies forbidden to engage in, 203; where practised, 207; Cicero's apology for, 212

Puella, Ovid's term for courtesans, 54, 57, 69; *culta* and *docta puella*, 69

Pyrrha, and Horace, 101

Quadrantariae, prostitutes of the lowest class, 206

Quis custodiat . . .?, 138

Rape of the Sabines, 17

Remedia Amoris, Ovid's poem, 55

Roergas de Serviez, J., 145

Roma, legendary heroine, 227

Roman Questions, Plutarch's, 43, 46, 180

Roman Society from Nero to Marcus Aurelius, 223

Rome, foundation of, 17; taken by Gauls, 20; Juvenal's account of life in, 130; public baths of, 209; houses in, 262

Romeo and Juliet, 75

Romulus, 17

Sabine Farm, Horace's, 99

Sabines, 17, 19, 42

Sabinus, Julius, 33

Sappho, 243

Satires, Juvenal's, 131; Horace's, 213

Satyricon, 201, 204, 248

Savium, kind of kiss, 229

Scalae Gemoniae, in Rome, 181

Scatinian Law, 245

Scorta erratica, "roving whores", 206

Sejanus, execution of children of, 180

Seneca, the Elder, 221; the philosopher-statesman, 29, 155, 222

Seed, human, as described by Lucretius, 257

Sex, Roman attitude to, 47, 56, 173, 196, 212, 271

Sexual intercourse, St. Augustine's description, 49; Ovid and Corinna, 236; Lucretius's explanation, 253; account in *The Golden Ass*, 265; Ovid's advice to lovers, 266

Sidney, Sir Philip, 76

Silius, Messalina's paramour, 151

Simulacra, in Lucretius's sexology, 252

Slavery, Roman, 39, 199, 217, 223

Slave Trade, 220

Snood, Scottish, 50

Society in Rome under the Caesars, 27

Solon, Greek lawgiver, 47

Sperm, 48, 253

Sponsalia, 41

Sportula, 125

Stabulae, street-walkers, 209

Stola, women's robe, 198, 264

Strumpets, classes of, 205–11

Subigus, god, 49

Subura, Roman suburb, 104, 131, 221

Suetonius, his "lives of the Caesars", 28, 159, 164, 198, 246

Suffibolum, in Vestals' dress, 176

S.V.Q. (*sine ulla querela*), 30

Sylvanus, god, 51

Tacitus, his *Annals* quoted, 151, 154, 155, 157, 161–3, 180, 196, 203, 248

Tennyson, poem on Lucretius, 251

Theatres, assignations in, 60

Theopompus, views on Etruscan women, 24

Thermopolium, 207

Tiberius, emperor, 28, 146, 246

Toga, 42, 265

Triclinium, 43

"Trimalchio's Banquet", 249
Turia, wife of Vespillo, 30
Twelve Tables of Roman Law, 51
Tyndaris, and Horace, 99

Ulpian, Roman jurist, and abortion, 238
Underwear, Roman, 264
"Untying the Zone", in marriage, 49
Usus, marriage by prescription, 37

Veil, bridal, 42
Venus, goddess of Love, 47, 48, 49, 53, 207; in Lucretius, 253; Mysteries of, 261
Vespasian, emperor, 34, 247
Vespillo, Q. Lucius, 30
Vesta, goddess of the Hearth, 171
Vestal Virgins, 171–181
Vestalis Maxima, 178
Vestilia, 203
Via Appia, 84, 113

Vibidia, chief Vestal, 153
Villanovans, 23
Villiacus, cashier in lupanar, 202
Virgil, 99, 183
Virgenensis, goddess, 49
Virginia, legend of, 219
Virginity, Roman attitude to, 172, 180
Virgo, Roman maiden, 57
Vivamus, mea Lesbia, 80, 228
Volusius, 81
Vows, wax offerings, 184

Weddings, Roman, 41–50
Wives, Roman, in law, 20, 27
Wolferston, Francis, translation of Art of Love, 260, 266
Women, Roman, compared with Greek, 22
Women's emancipation, in Rome, 22, 27
Wreath, bridal, 42

Xenia, species of gifts, 124

Zone, woman's belt, 42, 49